SOME PEOPLE CHANGE YOUR LIFE FOREVER

KB015867

CAROL

CAROL

캐롤
패트리샤 하이스미스의 『소금의 값』 원작

감독	토드 헤인즈 Todd Haynes	밀드레드 피어스 (TV) 아임 낫 데어 파 프롬 헤븐 벨벳 골드마인
출연	케이트 블란쳇 Cate Blanchett 캐롤 역	블루 재스민 호빗 벤자민 버튼의 시간은 거꾸로 간다 엘리자베스
	루니 마라 Rooney Mara 테레즈 역	에인트 뎀 바디스 세인츠 사이드 이펙트 밀레니엄: 여자를 증오한 남자들 소셜 네트워크
각본	필리스 나지 Phyllis Nagy	해리스 부인
제작	스티븐 울리 Stephen Woolley	위대한 유산 메이드 인 다겐함 뱀파이어와의 인터뷰 크라잉 게임
	엘리자베스 칼슨 Elizabeth Karlsen	위대한 유산 메이드 인 다겐함 라벤더의 연인들 작은 목소리

캐롤

필리스 나지
패트리샤 하이스미스의 『캐롤』(초판 발행 원제: 소금의 값 The Price of Salt) 원작

작가 소개

필리스 나지는 뉴욕에서 나고 자란 영화감독이자, 각본가이며 극작가이다.
1990년대 초 런던으로 이주한 그녀는 스티븐 달드리의 예술지도 하에
유서 깊은 로열 코트 극장에서 상임 작가로 활동하면서 네 편의 희곡을
무대에 올렸고 이후 당대의 가장 명망 있고 중요한 극작가로 성장했다.

그녀가 각본과 연출을 맡은 장편 영화 데뷔작 〈해리스 부인〉은
토론토 국제영화제와 HBO에서 처음으로 상영되었다.
이 영화로 그녀는 에미상, 미국배우조합상, 골든글로브상에 작가와
연출가 모두의 자격으로 다수 노미네이트 되었다.

국제적 성공을 거둔 영화 〈캐롤〉(2015)을 통해 그녀는 2016년 아카데미
시상식 최우수 각색상 부문을 비롯하여 미국작가조합상, 영국아카데미상,
스피릿어워즈 외 수많은 비평가협회상에 노미네이트 되었다.
뉴욕영화비평가협회는 그해 최우수 각본상에 〈캐롤〉을 선정했다.

필리스 나지는 현재 넘버나인필름스와 CJ엔터테인먼트가 각각 제작하는
두 편의 장편영화 『SO MUCH LOVE』 『NO WHERE』의 각본 작업 중에
있으며, 두 작품 모두 그녀가 연출까지 맡을 예정이다.

---

* 뉴욕영화비평가협회는 2015년 시상식에서 〈캐롤〉에게 최우수 각본상 외에도
　최우수 작품상, 최우수 감독상, 최우수 촬영상까지 4개 부문 수상을 안겼다. (편집자 주)

Biography

Phyllis Nagy is a filmmaker, screenwriter and playwright who was born and raised in New York City. She moved to London in the early 1990s, where she became Writer in Residence at the Royal Court Theatre under the artistic direction of Stephen Daldry, and where four of her plays premiered, and where she became one of the most renowned and important playwrights of her generation.

MRS. HARRIS, her feature film debut as writer and director, premiered at the Toronto International Film Festival and premiered on HBO. The film garnered multiple Emmy, Screen Actors Guild and Golden Globe nominations, including nods for Nagy as both writer and director.

She was nominated for an Academy Award for Best Adapted Screenplay for her work on CAROL, along with nominations from the Writers Guild of America, BAFTA, Spirit Awards, and numerous critics awards, including the New York Film Critics Circle, from whom she received their Best Screenplay award.

Nagy is currently at work on two films, SO MUCH LOVE and NO WHERE, for Number 9 Films and CJ Entertainment respectively, both of which she will also direct.

영화 〈캐롤〉은 2015년 칸 영화제 경쟁부문 진출을 통해 처음으로 상영되었다.
루니 마라는 칸 영화제 최우수 여자 연기상을 수상했다.
이후 2015년 11월 20일에 미국에서,
2015년 11월 27일에 영국에서 정식 극장 개봉되었다.

CAROL first screened at the Cannes Film Festival in 2015
where Rooney Mara received the Best Actress Award.
The film was released theatrically in the USA on 20th November 2015
and in the UK on 27 November 2015.

목차

ANIMATED LOGOS: CHECKERBOARD FORMAT, LEFT TO RIGHT

Logo 1   Local Distributor's animated logo

Logo 2   Film4

OPENING CREDITS

1   Film4 presents

2   In association with STUDIOCANAL, Hanway Films,
                           Goldcrest, Dirty Films, InFilm

3   A Karlsen / Woolley / Number 9 Films / Killer Films Production

4   in association with Larkhark Films Limited

5   A Film by Todd Haynes

MAIN TITLE CAST CARDS

1   Cate Blanchett

2   Rooney Mara

3   # CAROL

4   Sarah Paulson

5   Jake Lacy

6   John Magaro

7   Cory Michael Smith

8   Carrie Brownstein   Kevin Crowley   Nik Pajic

9   and Kyle Chandler

10   Casting by
                            Laura Rosenthal

11	Costume Designer Sandy Powell
12	Music Supervisor Randall Poster
13	Music by Carter Burwell
14	Film Editor Affonso Goncalves
15	Production Designer Judy Becker
16	Director of Photography Ed Lachman, ASC
17	Co-produced by Gwen Bialic
18	Executive Producers Tessa Ross Dorothy Berwin Thorsten Schumacher
19	Executive Producers Bob Weinstein Harvey Weinstein Danny Perkins,
20	Executive Producers Cate Blanchett Andrew Upton Robert Jolliffe
21	Produced by Elizabeth Karlsen Stephen Woolley Christine Vachon
22	Based on the novel THE PRICE OF SALT by PATRICIA HIGHSMITH
23	Screenplay by Phyllis Nagy
24	Directed by Todd Haynes

작가의 말

〈캐롤〉을 만든 사람 중 누구도 이 영화가 이토록 많은 사람의 가슴에
가 닿을 줄 몰랐다.

그때 우리가 알고 있었던 건 토드 헤인즈를 필두로 뛰어난 예술가들이 모여,
서로의 재능에 믿음을 갖고 협업하여 진실한 영화를 만들고 있다는 것뿐
이었다.

개봉한 지 거진 4년이 지난 지금까지도 끊이지 않는 〈캐롤〉에 대한 여러분의
마음에 놀랍고 감사할 뿐이다. 전 세계에서 편지와 메시지가 날아들고,
10대부터 90대를 망라하는 관객들이 각자의 이야기를 들려주며 자신의
경험에 말 걸어준 이 작품에 감사를 표하고 있다. 그 수많은 이야기를 읽으며
눈물을 흘리고 웃음을 터뜨렸다. 하지만 소중하고 공감할 수 있는 경험으로
만들어준 한 사람 한 사람에게 감사해야 할 사람은 바로 나다.
이들 덕에 영화를 개봉하기까지 겪었던 고난과 어려움 모두 가치 있는
순간이 됐다.

여기 출판된 각본은 내가 제작 단계 직전까지 작업했던 버전으로,
편집 과정에서 삭제된 장면들까지 포함되어 있다. 테레즈가 자신의 미래가
될까 두려워하던, 흡사 크리스마스의 유령 같은 백화점 직원 루비 로비첵이
나오는 장면, 캐롤과 테레즈가 여행을 떠나기 직전 애비와 두 사람이 함께
등장하는 장면, 그리고 테레즈가 캐롤의 장갑을 부쳐주는 운명적 순간 직전에
있던 리처드와 테레즈의 장면 등이다.

이 책을 통해 각색의 과정을 즐겁게 들여다보길 바란다. 각본이 제작과
후반 작업에서 어떻게 바뀔 수 있는지, 혹은 바뀌어야 하는지 이해하게
되기를 바란다. 이 영화는 내 각본과 패트리샤 하이스미스의 원작 소설을
가능한 최선의 방식으로 존중하고 있다. 몇 번이고 영화를 다시 봐도,
나조차 매번 새로운 점을 발견한다.

2019. 11.
필리스 나지

Preface

None of us involved with the making of CAROL knew or expected that it would touch so many lives.

We knew only that we were making a film of great integrity with Todd Haynes at the helm, and that the extraordinary artists who assembled to create and collaborate did so out of a shared belief in the talents of the team.

The response to CAROL, nearly four years after its release, amazes and humbles me. I continue to receive letters and messages from around the world, from teens and nonagenarians alike, who share their stories and express their thanks for a piece of work that speaks to their personal experiences. I've been moved to tears by many of these stories, to joyous laughter by others. But it's I who should thank each and every person whose engagement transforms CAROL into a cherished shared experience. It makes the challenging road to its release worth every moment of struggle or setback.

The version of the screenplay published here represents the work I did just prior to entering production including scenes that were shot but subsequently cut in the editing room. These include the scenes with Ruby Robichek, a Frankenberg employee who truly is Therese's ghost-of-Christmas-future; a sequence of scenes among Carol, Abby and Therese just prior to Carol and Therese leaving for their road trip, and an early scene between Richard and Therese, just prior to Therese fatefully mailing those gloves back to Carol.

I hope the script provides an enjoyable and illuminating glimpse into the adaptation process and how scripts may be—and should be—transformed in production and post-production. I believe the film honors both the script and Patricia Highsmith's novel in the best possible ways. No matter how many times I watch the film, even I discover something new.

NOV. 2019
PHYLLIS NAGY

제작자의 말

우리는 필리스의 런던 에이전트 소개로 처음 만났다.
우리가 어떤 감수성을 공유하고 있다고 생각한 그의 직감은 정확했다.
이 첫 만남은 필리스가 각본과 연출을 맡고 아네트 베닝이 출연한 영화
〈해리스 부인〉으로 이어졌다. 그 영화를 만들던 중 패트리샤 하이스미스의
『소금의 값』을 원작으로 한 〈캐롤〉에 대한 이야기를 나누었다. 나는 20대
초반에 하이스미스의 『리플리』 시리즈를 즐겁게 읽긴 했지만, 〈캐롤〉에
대해서는 알지 못했다.

하이스미스로서는 굉장히 의외의 작품이라는 점에 놀랐다. 부드럽고,
감성적이고, 정신을 고양시키는 작품이었고, 매우 보기 드물게도 두 여자,
그것도 사랑에 빠진 두 여자에 대한 이야기였다. 하이스미스에게 몹시
개인적인 작품이라고 느껴졌지만, 동시에 이 작품을 스크린으로
옮겨오는 것이 말할 수 없이 중요하다고 생각했다. 필리스는 아름답게
세공되고, 겉으로는 교묘하게 단순해 보이는 각색을 해냈다. 필리스는
하이스미스의 소설을 110페이지 길이의 각본으로 영리하게 탈바꿈하며
극 중의 시간을 신중하게 압축하고, 자신만의 목소리를 더하면서도
하이스미스의 시선을 절대 잃지 않았다. '병리학'적 사랑에 대한 탐구는
『리플리』 시리즈에 뿌리를 두고 있지만, 하이스미스는 이 작품에서 당대
미국의 젠더와 섹슈얼리티의 정치학을 계몽적 시선 없이, 말 없는 인류애와
함께 과감히 살핀다. 필리스는 현대의 관객들을 위해 이 작품을 손질했고,
영화에 쏟아진 압도적 찬사는 테레즈와 캐롤의 사랑 이야기가 오늘날에
얼마나 유의미한지 깨닫게 해주었다.

취리히에 있는 하이스미스 유산 관리처는 너무 오랜 기간 허공을 떠돈
이 프로젝트의 판권을 다시 한번 독립제작자에게 내놓기를 꺼렸기에
그들을 설득하는 것이 큰 과제였다. 다행히도 필름4와 내 파트너 스티븐
울리가 보여준 지지와 우리의 끈기가 그들을 움직여 소설의 판권을
따낼 수 있었다.

우리가 불러모을 수 있었던 재능들이 곧 이 각본의 힘을 말해주었다. 케이트 블란쳇이 이 프로젝트에 보여준 헌신은 우리의 오랜 협업자인 킬러 필름스와의 파트너십을 이끌어냈고, 토드 헤인즈와 루니 마라까지 차례로 합류하게 만들었다.

필리스는 토드의 의견을 살피고 현장 상황을 감안하여 리허설과 촬영 내내 각본을 다듬었다. 토드가 연출한 필리스의 각본은 카메라 앞뒤로 가장 재능 있는 예술가들을 끌어들였다. 〈캐롤〉은 내게 지나치다 싶을 정도로 자랑스러운 작품이며, 이 경이를 만들어 내기 위해 일한 모든 이들에게 빚을 진 기분이다. 이 작품이 세계 곳곳에서 누구도 예상하지 못했던 수의 관객들을 얼마나 깊이 감동시켰는지를 끊임없이 상기하게 된다.

2019. 11.
엘리자베스 칼슨

* **엘리자베스 칼슨(Elizabeth Karlsen)**: 영화 〈캐롤〉을 제작한 엘리자베스 칼슨은 영국의 명망 있는 영화 제작자다. 동료이자 남편인 스티브 울리와 함께 2002년 설립한 넘버나인필름스(Number 9 Films)를 통해 〈해리스 부인〉〈메이드 인 다겐함〉〈위대한 유산〉〈캐롤〉〈유스〉〈체실 비치에서〉〈콜레트〉 등 비평과 흥행 양면에서 영국뿐만 아니라 국제적으로도 높은 성취를 거둔 20여편의 영화를 제작했고, 50개가 넘는 BAFTA(영국 영화 텔레비전 예술 아카데미) 노미네이션을 기록했다. 영국 영화의 비평적, 산업적 지평을 넓힌 성과를 인정받아 2019년 제72회 BAFTA 시상식에서 스티브 울리와 함께 공로상(Outstanding Contribution to British Cinema)을 수상했다. (편집자 주)

Foreword

Phyllis and I were introduced by her London agent, who thought we had a shared
sensibility. Her instinct was right – our first meeting led to *Mrs. Harris*, starring
Annette Bening, which Phyllis wrote and directed. During that production
we spoke about "Carol" an adaptation of Patricia Highsmith's *The Price of Salt*.
I had read with relish during my early-twenties Highsmith's *Ripley* series,
but was not aware of this novel.

I was struck by how much of a departure it was for Highsmith.
The story was so tender, emotional and uplifting and, so unusually,
about two women - two women in love. It felt deeply personal to Highsmith,
yet extraordinarily important to bring to the screen. Phyllis's adaptation was
beautifully crafted and deceptive in its simplicity - she intelligently transposed
Highsmith's novel into a 110-page screenplay, judiciously compressing the time frame,
adding her own particular voice whilst never losing sight of Highsmith.
The exploration of the 'pathology' of love has its roots in Ripley, but Highsmith
boldly examines the politics of gender and sexuality of that time in America without
didacticism and with untold humanity. Phyllis rendered this exploration for a modern
audience and we have realised, through the overwhelming reception of the film,
just how relevant Therese and Carol's love-story is today.

It was challenging to secure the rights to the novel which The Highsmith Estate,
based in Zurich, were loath to assign once again, to an independent producer,
after the project had floundered for so many years. Fortunately, tenacity and the
support of Film 4 and my partner, Stephen Woolley, convinced them to grant us
an option on the book.

The calibre of talent we were able to engage is testament to the screenplay's power.
Cate Blanchett's commitment led to a partnering with our long-time collaborators,
Killer Films, to director Todd Haynes coming on board, then Rooney Mara.

Phyllis honed the script through rehearsals and shooting, taking notes from Todd and allowing for the exigencies of production. Her script, under Todd's remarkable direction, attracted the most talented artists in front of and behind the camera. It is a film I am inordinately proud of and indebted to all of those who worked to make it the marvel it is. I am constantly reminded of how deeply it has touched, beyond any expectation, so many people around the globe.

NOV. 2019
ELIZABETH KARLSEN

Elizabeth Karlsen is one of the most prolific film producers in the UK. She co-founded Number 9 Films with her collaborator and husband Stephen Woolley in 2002 and produced *Mrs. Harris*, *Made In Dagenham*, *Great Expectations*, *Carol*, *Youth*, *On Chesil Beach*, *Colette*, and many others. Over 20 successful films were produced to critical acclaim all over the world; Number 9 Films received over 50 BAFTA(The British Academy of Film and Television Arts) nominations. Elizabeth Karlsen and Stephen Woolley were presented with the Outstanding Contribution to British Cinema Award at the 72nd EE British Academy Film Awards in 2019 for their contribution to the UK film industry.

Synopsis

1952년 뉴욕.

캐롤은 우아하고, 세련되고, 부유한 유부녀다.

테레즈는 이제 막 인생을 시작한 나이로 무엇이 되고 싶은지 확신하지 못하고 있다.

맨해튼의 한 백화점에서 우연히 마주친 두 여성 사이에 특별한 우정이 피어난다. 이혼 절차를 밟고 있는 캐롤은 딸의 양육권을 놓고 치열한 싸움을 벌이는 와중에 이 신비롭고 조용한 미녀에게 마음을 사로잡힌다.

크리스마스를 혼자 보내게 된 캐롤은 테레즈를 초대해 미국의 중심부로 즉흥적인 로드트립을 떠난다. 마법 같은 여정에서 둘은 서로에게 속수무책으로, 절박하리만치 사랑에 빠진다.

하지만 1952년의 보수적인 사회 분위기로, 캐롤은 이 관계로 인해 모든 것을 잃을 위험에 처한다.

『열차 안의 낯선 자들』과 『리플리』의 저자 패트리샤 하이스미스의 베스트셀러 소설을 원작으로 한 〈캐롤〉은 금지된 사랑의 긴장과 위험, 그리고 흥분으로 달아오른 강렬한 로맨스다.

캐롤 각본

✳

작가 필리스 나지가 승인/제공한
출판 버전을 위한 최종고

1. EXT.
뉴욕 지하철역. 1953년 4월. 밤.

어둠 속에서 도착하는 열차의 끼익거리는 신음이 들린다. 어두운 몸뚱이 한 무리가 렉싱턴 59번가역으로 빠져나온다. 우리는 군중을 덮쳐 코트 차림에 모자를 쓴 20대 후반의 젊은 남자, 잭 태프트를 찾아낸다. 그는 설핏 구름이 낀 하늘 아래 우산을 펴는 몇몇 통근자들을 이리저리 피해 빠져나온다. 잭은 가판대에서 석간신문을 산 뒤 59번가를 건넌다.

2. EXT. / INT.
리츠 타워 호텔. 밤.

잭이 호텔로 들어서고 우리는 로비를 가로질러 바로 향하는 그를 따른다. 잭은 어렵지 않게 빈자리를 찾아 바텐더에게 묵례를 하고 신문을 건넨다. 바텐더가 드워스 병을 가리키자 잭이 엄지를 내민다. 잭은 바와 가까운 쪽의 칵테일 라운지를 둘러본다. 역시 특별한 일은 없어 보인다. 술에 취해가는 회사원 몇 테이블, 나이 든 커플 한 쌍, 눈에 띄지 않는 구석 테이블에 앉은 두 여자. 잭은 손목시계를 확인하고 바텐더는 그의 술을 내놓는다.

잭
금요일 치곤 한산하네요.
바텐더
시간이 이르니까.

잭은 스카치를 비우고 빈 잔을 바텐더에게 민 뒤 바의 가장자리를 박자 맞춰 두드린다.

잭
칼, 더블로 주실래요?
그리고 제가 한 잔 사죠. 전화하고 올게요.

잭이 일어선다.

3. INT.
리츠 타워 호텔. 바/라운지. 밤.

잭은 라운지를 가로질러 전화 부스로 걸어간다. 그는 대화에 깊이
몰입한 구석 자리의 여자 둘을 다시 한번 쳐다보고는, 그중 하나
를 아는 것 같다고 생각한다. 그는 여자들에게 다가간다.

잭
테레즈? 너야?

둘 중 젊은 쪽 여자, 테레즈가 잭을 향해 돌아본다.

잭 (CONT'D)
이게 누구야? (그가 걸어오기 시작한다)
어쩐지 아는 사람 같더라니!

그녀가 일어나 가벼운 포옹으로 잭과 인사하기까지, 반응하는 데
잠깐의 시간이 걸린 것 같다.

테레즈
잭.
잭
이렇게 반가울 데가! 본 지 몇 달 됐지?

테레즈
응.

테이블에 앉아있던 다른 여자가 담배에 불을 붙인다. 테레즈는 여자를 힐끗 바라보고, 테레즈가 예의라는 것을 기억해내기까지 짧고 강렬한 시선이 오간다.

테레즈 (CONT'D)
잭, 이쪽은 캐롤 에어드 씨.

잭이 손을 내민다. 캐롤이 맞잡고 악수한다.

잭
반갑습니다.
캐롤
저도요.

캐롤은 담배를 피우며 다시 생각에 빠져든다.

잭
저기, 테드 그레이가 오기로 했어.
필이 파티 열어서 가기로 했거든. 너도 가지?
테레즈
응, 난 그냥 좀 있다 가려고...
(캐롤을 바라보며)
캐롤
둘이 가요.
잭
같이 가실래요?

                                    캐롤
                        아뇨, 아뇨. (테레즈에게)
                   어차피 저녁 식사 전에 연락할 데가 있어서.
                           나도 일어나야 해요.

                                    테레즈
                             정말 괜찮아요?

                                    캐롤
                               그럼요.

                                    테레즈
                                (잭에게)
                        그럼 가는 길에 나도 태워줘.

캐롤은 테레즈를 향해 한 걸음 내딛지만, 더는 나아가지 않는다.

                                    캐롤
                   둘이 즐거운 밤 보내요. 반가웠어요, 잭.

                                     잭
                             반가웠습니다.

그리고 캐롤은 간다. 테레즈는 움직이지 않는다. 뒤돌아 캐롤이
떠나는 것을 쳐다보지 않는다.

                                 잭 (CONT'D)
                    그럼 이 녀석들 오는 중인지 확인하고 올게.
                               금방 올게.

잭이 떠난다. 테레즈는 잠깐 그대로 있다가 뒤돌아 바 너머를 둘
러보며 캐롤을 찾지만 그녀는 이미 갔다.

4. INT.
리츠 타워 호텔. 바/라운지. 잠시 후

전화 부스 문의 유리 너머로 보이는 잭이 통화를 마치고 있다. 부스를 빠져나온 그는 나가는 길에 바를 지난다. 그를 발견한 바텐더가 신문을 들어 보인다.

잭
가지세요!

잭은 테레즈를 두고 온 곳으로 가지만 그녀가 보이지 않자 주변을 둘러본다. 웨이터에게 물어보려는 찰나, 여자 화장실에서 나오는 테레즈를 발견한다. 그녀는 창백해 보인다.

잭 (CONT'D)
여기 있었네! 날 따돌린 줄 알았지. 괜찮아?
앞에서 테드 만나기로 했어.

5. INT./EXT.
뉴욕의 택시. 밤.

테레즈는 택시 뒷자리 차창에 기대어 앉아있다. 택시를 가득 메운 20대 남녀들은 우리가 들을 수 없는 활발한 대화를 나눈다. 택시가 신호에 걸려 멈추고 테레즈는 길모퉁이에서 팔짱을 끼고 있다가 신호에 맞추어 길을 건너는 우아한 커플을 발견한다. 거센 바람이 불어와 녹색 실크 스카프를 머리에 두르려는 여자를 방해한다. 그들이 반대편 인도에 도착하자마자 여자는 잠시 대로 쪽을 돌아봤다가 도로 고개를 돌린다. 그들은 소용돌이치는 빛과 기억

속으로 사라진다.
CUT TO:

6. 회상: 1952년 12월
짧은 쇼트들 (INT. 프랑켄베르크 백화점 - 장난감 코너)

장난감 기차가 백화점에 진열된 미니어처 행인들의 얼굴들을 스쳐 지나간다. 멀리서 보이는 겨울 코트 차림의 캐롤 에어드가 서서 그것을 보고 있다. 그녀는 머리에 녹색 실크 스카프를 느슨하게 두르고 있다.

그녀가 뒤돌아, 미소 짓는다.

7. INT.
테레즈의 아파트. 이스트 50번가. 1952년 12월 아침.

이불 속에 웅크린 테레즈 벨리벳의 잠자는 얼굴 위로 알람이 요란하게 울린다. 알람이 이어지지만 테레즈는 꿈쩍도 하지 않는다. 마침내 테레즈가 능숙한 한 번의 동작으로 침대에서 일어난다. 담요는 여전히 둘러쓴 채. 그녀는 알람 시계를 찾아 꺼버린다. 시계를 본다. 아침 일곱 시다.

테레즈는 자신의 아침 의식을 이어간다. 블라인드를 걷고, 조그만 스토브로 옮겨가 성냥으로 불을 붙여 냉기를 가시게 한다. 한쪽 구석에 설치된 싱크대는 부분적으로 자가 암실을 겸하고 있다. 현상액과 정착액 쟁반들이 싱크대 한쪽에 쌓여있고 그 위 선반에는 1930년대 후반 모델인 아거스 C3 카메라가 붉은 등, 인화지와 함께 놓여있다.

가구는 듬성듬성하고, 벽의 대부분은 테레즈가 찍은 흑백사진으로 덮여있다. 대개가 뉴욕의 길거리와 도시의 풍경을 담은 사진들이다. 테레즈가 이를 닦고 있을 때 벨이 울린다. 한 번. 두 번. 세 번. 그녀는 담요를 여미고 창가로 가, 창을 열고, 몸을 내민다.

8. EXT.
테레즈의 아파트 건물. 계속.

테레즈의 남자친구, 리처드 셈코가 자전거에 앉아 길에서 그녀를 올려다본다. 스카프와 모자로 잘 여민 모습이다.

테레즈
낙서 예쁜데?

리처드는 아이들의 분필 낙서로 가득한 길을 둘러본다.

리처드
응, 그리느라 좀 바빴어. (그녀를 향해 웃으며)
어떻게 눈뜨자마자 그렇게 예쁜지 모르겠네.
테레즈
금방 내려갈게.

9. EXT.
센트럴 파크. 뉴욕. 아침.

리처드는 공원을 지나 테레즈를 직장으로 태워다 준다. 리처드가 일어서서 페달을 밟는 동안 그녀는 그의 허리에 팔을 두르고 앉아있다.

리처드
배편 일정표 우편으로 받았어. 듣고 있어?

테레즈
듣고 있어! 일정표 받았다며.

리처드
프랑스행은 6월에 두 번, 7월에 한 번 있어.

테레즈
와.

리처드
어떻게 생각해?

테레즈
음... 너무 추워서 생각을 못 하겠어.

리처드
그래? 그럼 땀 좀 내자.

리처드가 속도를 높인다. 테레즈가 웃으며 더 꼭 끌어안는다. 리처드가 노래를 시작한다. "난 여름날의 파리를 사랑해!" 그들은 속도를 높여 멀어진다.

10. EXT.
프랑켄베르크 백화점. 아침.

직원 출입구 앞, 리처드와 테레즈는 대체로 젊은 직원들로 이루어진 긴 줄에 서 있다. 모두가 몹시 추위에 떨며, 얼마간 소련 공장 노동자 같은 우울함을 띤 채 똑같은 모습을 하고 있다.

리처드
어쨌든 너한테 해주고 싶어 하시니까, 일단 생각한 이상 싸워도 소용없어. 에스더 말곤 집안에 여자가 없어서...

경비가 문을 열어 줄이 움직이기 시작한다.

직원들은 들어가며 산타 모자를 하나씩 받는다. 의무적으로 착용해야 한다. 리처드가 문 앞에서 모자를 받고 말없이 쓴 뒤 안으로 들어간다. 테레즈의 모자도 하나 받는다.

경비
경영진의 선물입니다.

테레즈는 모자를 받아 쓰지 않고 안으로 들어간다.

리처드
매장 열러 가볼게.

11. INT.
프랑켄베르크 백화점. 직원 식당. 아침.

구석 테이블에 앉은 테레즈가 커피를 홀짝이며, 산타 모자를 쓰고 유니폼을 입은 채 말없이 아침 식사 줄에 서서 끈적이는 계란과 커피 몇 잔을 받아드는 직원들의 바다를 바라본다. 테레즈는 프랑켄베르크 직원 지침서를 내려다본다. 우리는 정보 일부를 힐끗 읽을 수 있다. "...5년 근속 시 2주 휴가, 15년 근속 시 4주 휴가... 연금 보장, 복지..." 그녀가 페이지를 넘긴다. "당신은 프랑켄베르크에 맞는 인재입니까?"

받아들이기엔 너무 우울하다. 테레즈는 지침서를 가방에 다시 밀어 넣고 제임스 조이스의 「젊은 예술가의 초상」을 꺼낸다. 하지만 그녀가 자리를 잡자마자, 빛나는 빨간색 할리퀸 안경을 쓰고 거들

먹거리는 책임자 로버타 윌스가 테레즈를 덮쳐 그녀의 머리에 산타 모자를 단단히 씌운다.

로버타 윌스
벨리벳 양, 매장으로 올라와요. 빨리.

12. INT.
프랑켄베르크 백화점. 인형 창고. 아침.

똑같이 생긴 크리스마스 인형들에 둘러싸인 테레즈가 재고를 확인한다. 테레즈는 일고여덟 개의 커다란 상자를 들고 헐떡이며 창고 층을 힘겹게 가로지르는 중년의 직원, 루비 로비첵을 바라본다. 루비가 시야를 가린 상자 너머로 고개를 내밀어 앞을 보려다 상자를 우르르 바닥에 떨어트린다. 테레즈는 도와줄 사람이 자기밖에 없다는 걸 금세 알아차리고, 상자를 줍기 위해 무릎을 꿇으려 진을 빼고 있는 루비를 도와준다.

테레즈
(무릎 꿇고 루비를 도우며)
제가 도와드릴게요.

루비는 무릎을 꿇지 않아도 된다는 사실에 기뻐하곤, 테레즈가 건네주는 상자들을 진열대에 쌓는다.

루비 로비첵
너무 고마워요. 연휴 땐 창고 직원 더 필요하다고 위에다
그렇게 얘길 했는데, 18년이 되도록 듣질 않아.

테레즈
여기 18년이나 계셨어요?

루비 로비첵

오, 물론이지. 자기도 이 정도로 오래 일하고 나면
상자 나르는데 창의력이 생길 거야.

테레즈

저는 연휴 동안만 임시로 일하는 거예요.

루비 로비첵

(어깨를 으쓱하며)
나도 그렇게 말했었지.

13. INT.
프랑켄베르크 백화점. 장난감 코너. 아침.

개장 직전, 초현실적인 차분함과 정적이 맴돈다. 산타 모자를 쓰
고 임시 붕대를 두른 테레즈가 정교한 장난감 기차 세트 옆에 서
있다. 그녀가 전원을 켜자 기차 세트가 생명을 얻는다. 조그만 전
구들, 기차가 선로를 따라 칙칙폭폭 달리면 엔진에서 새어 나오
는 조그만 휙 소리. 요란한 버저가 울린다. 테레즈의 뒤로, 우리
는 아날로그식 엘리베이터 표시등이 움직이기 시작하는 것을 본
다. 5층, 4층, 3층... 엘리베이터가 그날의 첫 번째 손님들을 맞이
하러 내려가고 장내 방송이 우렁찬 소리를 낸다.

매장 아나운서 (V.O.)

메리 크리스마스!
프랑켄베르크 백화점입니다.
2층 침구 매장에서 연말 세일을 진행 중이오니
많은 이용 부탁드립니다. 그리고 1층에 있는
전자제품 코너에서도 특별 기획전을 마련하여
신제품 TV와 오디오를 저렴하게 판매 중입니다.

테레즈의 뒤에서 엘리베이터 문이 열리고, 일순간 테레즈는 매니저와 직원, 손님들의 홍수 속으로 삼켜진다.

14. INT.
프랑켄베르크 백화점. 인형 코너. 잠시 후.

테레즈는 인형으로 가득 찬 진열장 뒤에 앉아있다. 몰래 책을 읽으며 눈에 띄지 않으려 애쓰는 중이다. 인형 코너는 아이들에게 선물을 사주려는 엄마들로 가득하다. 날카로운 비명이 들리고, 테레즈가 독서를 멈춘다. 그녀는 고개를 들어 짜증을 부리는 아기와 상황을 통제하려 노력하는 당황한 엄마를 본다. 바로 그때 로버타 윌스가 황급히 코너를 가로질러 와 테레즈의 머리를 가리킨다. 산타 모자 어딨어? 로버타 윌스는 말하지 않고도 말하는 것 같다. 테레즈는 황급히 책을 핸드백에 던져넣고 모자를 꺼낸다. 로버타 윌스는 테레즈를 향해 고개를 끄덕이고는 지나간다.

테레즈는 다시 자리에 앉아 지루해한다. 한 손님이 뭔가 기대하듯 테레즈를 바라보지만 그녀는 손님을 못 본 체하고 다시 책을 꺼내기 위해 핸드백으로 몸을 숙인다. 손님이 갔는지 확인하기 위해 진열대 위를 올려다본 테레즈의 시선에 다른 여자가 힐끗 들어온다. 녹색 실크 스카프를 머리와 목에 느슨하게 두른 여자가 테레즈의 시선을 끈다. 이 여자는 거기 유일하게 존재하는 단 한 명의 손님처럼 보인다. 캐롤 에어드다. 캐롤은 기차 세트를 살피기 위해 몸을 굽히고 무심코 전원을 껐다 켰다 한다. 기차가 멈춘다. 캐롤이 일어나, 인형 코너를 향해 돌아선다. 마치 도움을 청하듯, 미소를 지으며.

테레즈는 묘한 찰나의 순간 동안 캐롤과 눈이 마주친다. 당황한 엄마와 소리를 질러대는 아기가 다른 무엇도 보이지 않게 테레즈의 시야를 가로막기 전까지.

당황한 엄마
화장실이 어디죠, 아가씨?

테레즈
남성화 코너 지나 왼쪽으로 가셔서,
넥타이 코너에서 오른쪽으로 꺾으세요.

당황한 엄마가 감사의 묵례를 하고 아기를 들어 올려 사라진다. 테레즈는 캐롤을 찾지만 그녀는 더 이상 거기에 없다. 기차 세트는 다시 돌아가고 있고, 몇몇 아빠와 아들들이 경탄하며 그것을 지켜본다.

15. INT.
프랑켄베르크 백화점. 인형 코너. 잠시 후.

진열대 뒤에 앉은 테레즈는 몰래 책을 읽을지 고민하다 그만둔다. 언뜻 고개를 들었다가 검은 가죽 장갑 한 켤레가 진열대 위에 놓이는 것을 본다. 테레즈가 고개를 들어 자기 앞에 선 캐롤을 본다.

캐롤
인형을 하나 사려고 해요.
키는 (몸짓을 해 보인다) 이만하고 몸통은...
(다시 생각하고는) 다시 할까요?

캐롤은 한 걸음 물러서 가방을 뒤지고, 테레즈는 그녀의 잘 재단된 수트와 금발 머리, 녹색 실크 스카프로부터 눈을 뗄 수 없다. 캐롤은 구겨진 종잇조각을 꺼내더니, 진열대로 다시 다가와 테레즈에게 그것을 건네며 활짝 웃어 보인다.

캐롤 (CONT'D)

우리 딸 사주려는데 이런 인형 있을까요?

테레즈가 종잇조각을 읽는다.

테레즈

'브라이트 벳시'네요. 우는 인형이에요.

캐롤

오, 그래요?

테레즈

쉬도 하고요. 죄송하지만 벌써 품절됐어요.

캐롤

너무 늦게 왔네요.

그녀가 가방을 뒤지기 시작한다.

테레즈

다른 인형도 많아요. 종류도 다양하고...

갑자기 말문이 막힌 테레즈는 인형 진열장으로 돌아선다. 캐롤도 같이 돌아선다.

캐롤

네 살 때 어떤 인형을 제일 좋아했어요?

테레즈

저요? 전 별로... 별로 안 좋아했어요.

캐롤이 담배를 입술에 대고 불을 붙이려 하자 테레즈가 끼어든다.

테레즈 (CONT'D)

죄송하지만 판매층에선 금연이에요.

캐롤

내 정신 좀 봐. 미안해요.
(잠깐 쉬고) 쇼핑만 하면 긴장해서.

테레즈

괜찮아요. 여기선 저도 긴장해요.

캐롤이 테레즈의 위로에 고마워하며 웃는다.

캐롤

참 친절하시네요.

캐롤이 다시 가방을 뒤지기 전 그들의 눈이 잠시 마주친다. 그녀는 지갑을 꺼내 테레즈에게 열어 보인다. 캐롤의 네 살 난 딸, 린디 의 사진이다.

테레즈

손님을 닮았네요. 입 주변이랑. 눈이요.

캐롤

(테레즈를 힐끗 보며)
그래요?

테레즈가 고개를 들어, 자신을 쳐다보는 캐롤을 본 뒤 다시 고개를 숙인다. 조금 어색한 순간을 캐롤이 구제한다.

캐롤 (CONT'D)
이 나이 때 뭘 갖고 싶었어요?

테레즈
(망설임 없이)
장난감 기차 세트요.

캐롤
정말요? 놀랍네요.
(잠깐 쉬고) 기차 세트 잘 알아요?

테레즈
그럼요, 지난주에 신제품이 들어왔어요.
조립도 채색도 손으로 한 건데, 5,000개 한정판이고,
가장 세련된 전기 스위치 시스템을 사용했어요. 굉장히...

테레즈는 자신을 바라보는 캐롤의 눈을 느끼며 기차에 대한 열정을 누른다.

테레즈 (CONT'D)
엘리베이터 옆에서 보셨을 거예요.
바로 저쪽에...

테레즈가 기차를 가리키자 캐롤이 숙고하며 돌아본다. 테레즈는 그녀의 모든 움직임을 쳐다본다.

캐롤
(테레즈를 돌아보며)
배송도 돼요?

테레즈
특별 배송이 있어요. 아니면 택배요.
(잠깐 쉬고) 2, 3일이면 받으실 거예요. 이틀이요.
조립도 해서 드려요.

캐롤
그렇군요. 그걸로 하죠. 주세요.

그들은 거기 서서 잠시 서로를 향해 고개를 끄덕인다.

캐롤 (CONT'D)
계산해도 될까요?

테레즈
네, 그럼요.

테레즈는 전표를 쓰기 시작하고, 펜과 함께 그것을 내밀며 캐롤을 힐끗 올려다본다. 캐롤은 잠깐 동안 생각에 빠져, 멀어져 있다.

테레즈 (CONT'D)
계좌 번호와 주소 부탁드릴게요.

캐롤
물론이죠. (쓰기 시작한다) 난 크리스마스가 좋아요.
적어도 준비하는 건 좋아하죠. 선물 포장하고 뭐하고
하다 보면 어느 순간 칠면조가 오븐에서 타고 있죠.

그녀가 작성을 마치고 빛나는 미소를 지어 보인다. 테레즈는 잘 알아들을 수 없지만 캐롤이 말을 멈추는 걸 원치 않는다.

캐롤 (CONT'D)
됐어요.

캐롤이 펜과 전표를 테레즈에게 돌려준다.

캐롤 (CONT'D)
어떻게 기차 세트를 그렇게 잘 알아요?

테레즈
이것저것 많이 읽어서...

캐롤
재미있네요. 고마워요.
(잠깐 쉬고) 메리 크리스마스.

테레즈
메리 크리스마스.

캐롤이 멀어진다. 테레즈는 그녀의 매너, 스타일, 걸음걸이까지 모든 것을 눈에 담는다. 캐롤이 잠깐 뒤돌아 테레즈의 모자를 가리킨다.

캐롤
모자 마음에 들어요.

테레즈는 그녀가 기차 세트와 엘리베이터를 빠르게 지나치는 모습을 본다. 그리고 남겨진 빈 공간이 손님과 직원들로 채워져 가는 모습을 잠시 바라본다. 마지막으로 그녀를 보기 위해 목을 길게 빼보지만 소용없다. 그녀는 갔다. 테레즈가 한숨을 쉰다. 인형 진열대로 시선을 내린 그녀는 캐롤이 장갑을 두고 갔음을 알아챈다.

16. INT.
프랑켄베르크 백화점. 직원 라커룸. 저녁.

테레즈가 열린 라커 앞에 서 있고, 폐점을 알리는 버저 소리가 시끄럽게 이어진다. 그녀는 프랑켄베르크 유니폼을 벗고 코트와 스카프를 걸친다. 라커 문은 테레즈가 찍은 사진, 그리고 리처드와 함께 코니아일랜드에서 찍은 사진들로 덮여있다. 테레즈는 캐롤의 장갑을 자신의 핸드백에 넣고, 마침내 버저가 멈춘다. 그녀는 라커 룸 건너편에서 아주 힘겹게 겨울용 부츠를 신고 있는 루비 로비첵을 본다. 테레즈는 재빨리 파우더를 살짝 두드리고 라커를 닫는다.

17. INT.
극장 영사실. 밤.

테레즈, 리처드와 필, 대니 맥엘로이가 작고 어두운 공간에 끼어 앉아 조그만 유리 패널을 통해 영화를 보며 담배를 피우고 있다. 테레즈는 리처드의 무릎에 앉아있고, 리처드는 영화를 보기보단 그녀의 뒷목에 키스하는 데 만족하는듯하다. 호스트이자 영사기사인 필 맥엘로이가 장비 가까이 앉아있고, 그의 동생 대니 맥엘로이는 최대한 영화에 가까이 앉아 이따금 조그만 공책에 뭔가 적는다. 영화는 〈선셋 대로〉이고, 노마 데스몬드가 준비한 둘만의 새해 전야 파티에서 조 길리스와 함께 대리석 바닥에서 춤을 추는 장면이다. 테레즈는 대니의 모습에 감탄하고 있지만, 필이 그의 뒤통수를 때린다.

필
옆으로 좀 가. 아무도 못 보잖아.

리처드
(테레즈에게 입을 부비는 와중에)
아무도 안 봐.

테레즈
(웃으며)
나 보잖아.

대니
(테레즈에게) 난 여섯 번 봤어.
인물들의 대사와 실제 느끼는 감정 간의 관계를 적어보고 있어.

필
내 동생이야, 영화광.

당황한 대니가 유리 옆으로 약간 비켜 앉는다. 하지만 그는 계속
영화를 보며 여전히 뭔가 쓰고 있다. 테레즈는 그를 바라본다.

18. INT.
그리니치 빌리지 바. 밤.

리처드와 필은 꽤 마셨다. 빈 맥주병이 그들 앞 테이블에 줄지어
늘어서 있다. 대니는 코카콜라를 홀짝인다. 테레즈는 와인 한 잔을
마신다.

대니
난 맥주만 마셔. 딴 건 전부 토 나와.

테레즈
난 와인 마시면 좀 장난스러워져.

필
장난스러워질 수 있는 다른 방법은 없나?

리처드
난 내일 출근하는 거 잊으려고 마셔.

필
넌 그게 문제야, 셈코. 직장이 있다는 걸
잊으려고 마셔야지. 직장은 저주야.

테레즈
너도 직장 있잖아, 필.

필

그게 직장이야? 허상이지.

대니

돈 받잖아. 돈도 허상이야?

필

내 동생이야, 구린 철학자.

테레즈

(대니에게) 넌 어디서 일해?

리처드

(존경하는 척 놀리며)

몰랐어? 대니는 뉴욕타임스 다녀.

리처드와 필이 감탄하는 척한다.

테레즈

(그녀는 감명받았다)

설마.

필

맞아, 다만 인쇄공은 퓰리처상을 못 타지.

대니

(어깨를 으쓱하며)

그냥 일하는 거야. (테레즈에게) 진짜 하고 싶은 건 집필이야.

그래서 영화를 보는 거야.

필

(눈을 굴리며)

개나 소나 작가라지...

대니는 관심을 끌지 않으려고 노력한다. 그는 테레즈와 눈이 마주
친다. 그녀가 미소를 지어 보인다. 그는 고마워한다.

40

테레즈, 취해서 깜빡할라.

필이 커다란 메신저백을 뒤져 낡은 코닥 카메라를 꺼내 테레즈에게
건넨다.

테레즈
고쳐온 거야?

필
금방 고치더라고.

테레즈
고마워, 필!
정말 그리웠는데!

대니
사진도 찍어?

테레즈
뭐.

리처드
유럽 여행 얘기엔 시큰둥하더니
싸구려 카메라에 흥분하는 거 봐.

필
여자들이란!

리처드
내 말이!

리처드와 필은 웃으며 건배하고 마신다. 테레즈는 그리 기분이 좋지
않다. 대니는 이를 알아본다.

19. EXT.
3번가. 밤.

테레즈는 대니와 나란히 걷는다. 이제 완전히 취해 소란을 피우는 리처드와 필이 그들보다 약간 앞서간다. 리처드는 인도를 따라 비틀거리며 자전거를 끌고 있다.

필
너희가 스페인에서 가야 할 곳은 말이지... 팜플로나야.
투우 한 판 봐야지!

앞쪽으로 모두가 아는 커플이 다가온다. 잭 태프트와 그의 여자친구 도로시다. 남자들이 서로 떠드는 사이 도로시가 테레즈에게 말을 건다.

잭
젠장, 이게 누구야. 자기야
조심해, 빨갱이 떼거리야!

필 (CONT'D)
믿을 수가 없군! 정부에선
너희 빨갱이들이 길에
돌아다닌다는 거 아냐?

도로시
테리, 너 정말 백 년 만이다.
연락 좀 해, 알았지?

테레즈
도티, 그치? 전화할게,
약속해!

그들이 스쳐 가자 리처드가 방향을 바꿔 자전거를 끌고 비틀거리며 뒤로 걷기 시작한다.

리처드
저 망할 놈... 지난번 포커 칠 때 신세 아직 안 갚았다, 너!

테레즈

리처드, 조심해!

하지만 리처드가 가로등에 부딪히는 걸 막기엔 너무 늦었다. 그가 넘어지고, 자전거가 그의 위로 쓰러진다. 필이 도우려 하지만 역시 리처드 위로 넘어져 버리고, 둘은 취해서 웃음을 터뜨린다.

대니

(테레즈에게) 유럽이라. 대단한데. 운 좋다.

테레즈

그런가?

그들은 잠시 동안 필과 리처드가 일어나기 위해 무진 애를 쓰는 광경을 바라본다.

테레즈 (CONT'D)

도와줘야겠어.

대니

(잠깐 있다가)

테레즈, 타임스 놀러 와. 저녁 한 번 먹자. 난 야간 근무거든.
사진 편집부에 친구가 있어, 편집자야.
좀 건방지긴 한데 소개해줄게.

테레즈

정말? 그럼, 그럼 좋지.

대니

(기뻐하며)

그래? 그럼 된 거다.

그들은 리처드와 필에 대해선 아예 잊어버린다.

20. INT.
테레즈의 아파트. 늦은 밤.

테레즈와 리처드가 침대에 나란히 누워있다. 테레즈는 옷을 다 갖추어 입은 상태다. 리처드는 러닝셔츠와 박서만 입고 있다. 그들은 제법 열정적인 애무를 나누고 있다. 리처드가 테레즈의 블라우스 단추를 풀기 시작한다. 그녀가 부드럽게 그를 멈춘다. 그가 테레즈의 위로 올라간다. 그녀가 다시 그를 멈추게 한다. 리처드는 테레즈에게서 내려와 일어나 앉는다. 그는 그녀를 끌어안고 코에 입을 맞춘다.

> **리처드**
> 만지게 해줘.
>
> **테레즈**
> 내가 만지게 해줘.
>
> **리처드**
> 정말?

테레즈가 고개를 끄덕인다. 리처드가 테레즈의 손을 잡아 박서 위로 자신의 좆에 갖다 댄다.

> **리처드 (CONT'D)**
> 이래도 괜찮아?

그녀가 끄덕인다. 리처드는 그녀의 손을 속옷 안으로 넣는다. 그는 자신의 손을 테레즈의 손에 포개어 천천히, 그리고 꾸준히 애무를 가르친다.

테레즈
이렇게?

리처드는 테레즈의 손을 놓고 뒤로 기대어 눈을 감는다. 그가 낮은 신음을 낸다. 테레즈는 내내 리처드를 빤히 바라본다. 마치 완전히 참여하기보다는 관찰하는 것처럼. 리처드의 호흡이 빠르게 가빠진다.

리처드
(사정하며)
사랑해, 테리.

리처드가 늘어진다. 테레즈는 리처드의 속옷에서 손을 빼낸다. 그녀는 손에 묻은 정액을 내려다본다. 리처드가 일어나 웃옷을 벗고 불을 끈다.

리처드 (CONT'D)
맙소사, 테리,
그걸 뭐하러 봐.

리처드가 웃으며 테레즈의 손을 웃옷으로 닦아주고 바닥에 던져버린다. 테레즈도 같이 웃는다. 리처드가 앞으로 몸을 숙여 테레즈에게 깊고 부드러운 키스를 한다. 테레즈가 갑자기 빠져나간다.

테레즈
젠장, 네 아스피린을 깜빡했네.

테레즈가 침대에서 뛰쳐나가 화장실로 달려간다. 진이 빠지고 행복한 리처드는 침대로 다시 넘어진다.

21. INT.
테레즈의 아파트. 늦은 밤.

리처드는 잠들었다. 테레즈는 작은 부엌 식탁에 앉아있다. 테레즈는 캐롤의 장갑과 프랑켄베르크에서 받은, 그녀의 이름과 주소, 서명이 적힌 전표를 들고 있다. 그녀는 잠시 전표를 빤히 바라보다 장갑과 함께 소금 통에 기대어 세워둔다. 그녀는 무릎을 안고 앞뒤로 몸을 흔든다. 그녀는 리처드가 자는 모습을 바라본다.

22. EXT.
테레즈의 아파트. 늦은 밤.

테레즈는 잠옷 위에 코트를 걸치고 우편함 앞에 서 있다. 추운 밤 거리엔 아무도 없다. 그녀는 "H. 에어드 부인" 앞으로 보내는 작은 꾸러미를 잠시 바라보고는 우편함에 넣는다. 테레즈는 잠시 자기 집 창문을 올려다보다 한기에 몸을 떨며 건물로 뛰어 올라간다.

23. EXT.
뉴저지 교외의 거리. 늦은 아침.

우편배달부가 위엄 있는 주택가에 위치한, 박공지붕을 얹은 커다란 석조 주택 앞에 차를 세운다. 그는 한 손 가득 우편물을 쥐고 차에서 내려 진입로를 걸어가기 시작한다.

24. INT.
캐롤의 집. 현관. 늦은 아침.

테레즈가 캐롤에게 보낸 꾸러미와 함께 우편물들이 편지 구멍으로 떨어진다. 캐롤의 가정부 플로렌스가 바닥을 닦다 힐끗 그것을 쳐다본다.

25. INT.
캐롤의 집. 캐롤의 침실. 늦은 아침.

캐롤은 네 살짜리 딸 린디와 함께 화장대 앞에 앉아있다. 린디가 숫자를 세며 화장하는 시늉을 하는 동안 캐롤은 아이의 머리를 빗겨준다.

린디
오십삼, 오십사, 오십오...
(엄마를 올려다보며) 육십?

캐롤
(아이의 이마에 입 맞추며)
오십육.

린디
오십육. 오십칠...

캐롤이 아래층에 남편이 도착하는 소리를 듣는다.

캐롤
아빠 왔나 보다. 이제 내려가자. 오십팔, 오십구...

린디
아빠랑 나랑 같이 스케이트 타러 가자!

캐롤
엄마는 못 가, 아가야...

린디
왜, 엄마? 제발요!

캐롤의 남편 하지가 침실 문 앞에 나타난다. 우편물을 들고 있다.

하지
(린디에게)
안녕, 공주님.

캐롤이 고개를 든다. 그녀가 화장대 거울에 비친 하지를 본다. 린디가 돌아보고는 엄마의 무릎에서 뛰어내려 그에게 달려간다.

캐롤
일찍 왔네.
하지
우편물 왔어.

하지가 그것을 희미하게 흔들어 보이고는 작은 테이블에 앉는다.

린디
아빠! 엄마도 데려가자!

아이가 그의 품으로 뛰어오른다. 그는 아이를 들고 빙빙 돌린다. 캐롤은 화장대에서 움직이지 않는다.

하지
그래, 그래, 우리 아가.
하나씩 하자.

린디를 내려놓은 그는 자신을 바라보는 캐롤의 시선을 알아차린다. 그는 우편물을 화장대 위에 내려놓는다.

26. INT.
캐롤의 집. 부엌. 늦은 아침.

캐롤과 하지, 그리고 린디가 부엌에 앉아있다. 린디는 하지의 무릎에 앉았다. 아이가 크레용으로 그림을 그린다. 플로렌스가 뒤에서 따뜻한 식사를 준비하고 있다.

> **하지**
> 나무를 초록색으로 칠하면 어떨까?
>
> **캐롤**
> 먼저 파란색으로 하늘 칠하는 걸 좋아해.
>
> **하지**
> 그리고 싸이의 처가 당신 오는지...
>
> **캐롤**
> (그는 매번 이런다) 지네트야.
>
> **하지**
> 지네트. (잠시 침묵) 당신 가면 좋아할 거야.
>
> **캐롤**
> 안부 전해줘. 나도 보고 싶다고.

캐롤이 린디의 그림을 보고 다른 색을 아이에게 밀어준다. 하지는 손을 뻗어 캐롤의 손을 잡는다.

> **하지**
> 당신도 갔으면 해.

캐롤은 자신의 손 위에 포개진 하지의 손을 바라본다. 그리고 고개를 들어 그를 본다.

캐롤

미안해, 하지. 약속 있어.

린디

엄마랑 애비 이모는 선물 교환할 거래.

하지는 미소를 짓고 고개를 끄덕이며 캐롤의 손을 토닥이고,
손을 빼서 딸을 마주 볼 수 있게 무릎 위에서 돌려 앉힌다.

하지

요즘 애비 이모 자주 봤지, 우리 공주?
엄마랑 같이?

캐롤은 하지를 쏘아본다. 그도 포기하지 않고 캐롤을 마주 본다.
캐롤은 플로렌스의 존재를 의식하고 불편해하며 눈을 피한다.

캐롤

애비한테 연락해서 날짜 바꿔볼게.

하지

고마워.

27. INT.
프랑켄베르크 백화점. 배송부서. 낮.

테레즈가 앞에 서 있는 와중에 배송 담당 직원이 영수증이 모인
철제 파일을 자세히 살피고 있다.

테레즈 (CONT'D)

손님에게 크리스마스이브엔 도착한다고 했거든요.
늦어도 3일이면 된다고 들어서...

배송 직원
(그녀를 올려다보며)
오늘 오후에 배송됐을 거예요.

테레즈
확실히 도착한 거죠?
서명도 하셨대요?

배송 직원
(퉁명스럽고 사무적인 말투로)
도착했어요.

테레즈
다행이네요. 감사합니다. 감사해요.

28. INT.
캐롤의 집. 캐롤의 침실. 밤.

캐롤은 화장대 앞에 앉아 머리를 빗는다. 불 붙인 담배가 화장대 위의 재떨이에서 타고 있다. 얼음을 넣은 스카치 한 잔이 재떨이 옆에 놓여있다. 캐롤은 빗을 내려놓고 무릎을 내려다본다. 거기엔 프랑켄베르크 백화점에 놓고 온 장갑과 테레즈로부터 온 쪽지가 놓여있다. 그녀는 담배를 한 모금 피우고 다시 쪽지를 읽는다.

프랑켄베르크 백화점에서 인사드립니다.
직원번호 645-A.

그녀는 쪽지를 구겨 작은 쓰레기통에 던져 넣는다. 그녀는 다시 담배 한 모금을 피우고 휴지통을 힐끗 쳐다본다.

29. INT.
프랑켄베르크 백화점. 인형 진열대. 다음날. 늦은 오후.

진열대의 테레즈는 까다로운 여성 손님 때문에 진이 빠져있다. 20개 정도의 열린 상자와 인형들이 진열대 위에 아무렇게나 놓여 있다.

로버타 월스 (O.S.)
벨리벳? 벨리벳 양?

테레즈가 고개를 든다. 로버타 월스가 근처 진열대에 서서 테레즈에게 손가락을 까딱이며 수화기를 들고 있다.

로버타 월스 (CONT'D)
이쪽으로 오세요.

그녀는 다른 판매 직원을 향해 손가락을 튕겨 테레즈를 대신하도록 한다.

테레즈
(손님에게) 죄송합니다. 실례할게요.

테레즈가 서둘러 로버타 월스에게 다가가고 다른 판매 직원이 까다로운 여성 손님을 대신 맞이한다. 로버타 월스는 테레즈에게 수화기를 건네며 매서운 눈길을 보낸다. 테레즈가 전화를 받는다.

테레즈 (CONT'D)
여보세요?

교환원 (O.S.)
직원번호 645-A,
테리즈 벨리벳 씨 맞습니까?

테레즈
네.

교환원 (O.S.)
연결하겠습니다.

30. INT.
캐롤의 집. 부엌. 늦은 오후.

캐롤은 전화를 걸며 저녁을 만들고 있다. 약간 남은 수줍음을 감추기 위한 일종의 전략이다. 라디오에서는 빅 밴드 음악이 나오고 있다.

캐롤
당신이었군요.

31. INT.
프랑켄베르크 백화점. 인형 진열대. 늦은 오후.

테레즈가 전화를 받고 있고, 윌스가 굳은 표정으로 그것을 주시하고 있다.

테레즈
안녕하세요, 에어드 부인.
기차 세트 받으셨어요?

32. INT.
캐롤의 집. 부엌. 늦은 오후.

캐롤
네, 받았어요. 장갑도 정말 고마워요. 생각도 못 했는데.
그냥 고맙단 말 꼭 하고 싶었어요.

테레즈 (O.S.)
별말씀을요.

캐롤이 소스팬 뚜껑을 열려 하지만 너무 뜨거워 놓쳐버리고 만다.
뚜껑은 쨍그랑하고 바닥에 떨어진다.

캐롤 (CONT'D)
오, 젠장. 미안해요. 다른 게 아니라, 점심시간 있나요?
점심이라도 한 번 살게요. 그 정도는 해야죠.

33. INT.
프랑켄베르크 백화점. 인형 진열대. 늦은 오후.

테레즈는 세차게 눈을 깜빡인다. 로버타 월스가 그녀의 한마디 한
마디를 듣고 있는 와중에, 그녀가 긴 숨을 쉬고 대답한다.

테레즈
아, 네, 물론이죠. 하지만 그러실 건... (침묵) 내일요?
(침묵) 아뇨, 모르겠어요. 잠깐만요. (소심하게 로버타를 향해)
펜이랑 종이 좀 빌려주실래요?

로버타는 심기가 불편한 채로 테레즈에게 종이와 연필을 건넨다.
테레즈는 빠르게 주소를 휘갈겨 쓴다.

34. INT.
미드타운 레스토랑. 낮.

테레즈는 나무 서까래와 흰 식탁보로 장식된 미드타운의 작은 레스토랑 문 앞에 서 있다. 그녀는 1시 12분을 가리키는 시계를 올려다보고 자신의 손목시계와 비교해본다. 그녀는 창밖을 내다본다. 거기, 비스듬한 창문 너머로, 서둘러 길을 건너는 캐롤을 발견한다.

35. INT.
미드타운 레스토랑. 낮. 잠시 후.

캐롤과 테레즈는 조용한 테이블에 앉았다. 캐롤은 모자를 벗고, 웨이터가 서성이는 와중에 메뉴를 힐끗 본다. 테레즈는 얼어붙은 채 앉아 빠르게 시선을 움직이며 캐롤이 메뉴를 정독하는 동안 섬세한 금팔찌가 손목에 내려앉는 모습부터 그녀의 손가락이 물잔을 쥐는 모습까지, 모든 것을 눈에 담는다.

캐롤
기다리게 해서 정말 미안해요.
(웨이터에게) 크림소스 시금치에 수란 올려주세요.
올리브 넣어서 드라이 마티니도요.

캐롤과 웨이터가 테레즈를 바라보고, 그녀는 자신이 메뉴판을 열지도 않았다는 사실을 알아차린다. 잠깐 멈췄다가,

테레즈
같은 걸로 할게요.
웨이터
식사요? 아니면 음료?

55

테레즈

어, 둘 다요. 고맙습니다.

웨이터가 고개를 끄덕인 뒤 사라지고 캐롤은 테레즈의 머뭇거림을 알아챈다. 캐롤을 쳐다보고 싶지 않은 테레즈는 이제야 메뉴판을 들어 엄지로 넘겨본다.

캐롤

담배?

캐롤이 대단히 아름다운 은색 담배케이스를 내밀어 담배를 권한다. 테레즈는 자신과는 달리 캐롤의 손이 사랑스럽고, 부드럽고, 전문가의 관리를 받았다는 사실을 알아차린다. 테레즈가 케이스에서 담배를 받아든다. 캐롤이 테레즈의 담배에 불을 붙여주고 테레즈는 약간 힘들여 그것을 피운다.

캐롤 (CONT'D)

그런데 무슨 성이 벨리벳이에요?

테레즈

체코 성이에요. 바꾼 건데, 원래는...

캐롤

아주 독특해요.

테레즈

(볼이 붉어지는 게 느껴진다) 네...

캐롤

이름은요?

테레즈

테레즈.

캐롤

테레즈. 테리-자가 아니라.

테레즈

아니에요.

캐롤

테레즈 벨리벳. 예쁜 이름이네요.

테레즈

당신은요?

캐롤

캐롤.

테레즈

캐롤.

웨이터가 술을 들고 나타나자 캐롤이 자신의 잔을 들고 건배를 청한다.

캐롤

건배.

테레즈

(잔을 부딪치며)

건배.

캐롤이 마티니를 홀짝인다. 테레즈는 잠깐 그녀를 쳐다보다가 자신의 잔을 맛본다. 그녀는 독한 술에 놀란 것을 감추려고 애쓴다. 캐롤이 미소 짓는다.

테레즈 (CONT'D)

(잠시 침묵) 장갑 보낸 사람이 남자인 줄 아셨죠?

캐롤
맞아요. 스키 매장 직원인가 했어요.

테레즈
죄송해요.

캐롤
아뇨, 다행인걸요.
그 사람이었으면 안 불렀을 거예요.

테레즈는 캐롤이 목 뒤를 주무르는 모습을 잠시 바라본다.

테레즈
향수가...

캐롤
네?

테레즈
좋아서요.

캐롤
고마워요. 하지가 결혼 전에 사줬는데, 아직까지 쓰고 있네요.

테레즈
그분이 남편이세요?

캐롤
맞아요. 정확히 말하자면 이혼 중이지만.

테레즈
(잠깐 침묵) 유감이에요.

캐롤
(담배를 비벼 끄며) 그럴 거 없어요.

테레즈는 무슨 말을 해야 할지 모른다. 캐롤은 미소를 짓고, 화제
를 돌린다.

캐롤 (CONT'D)
그런데 혼자 살아요?
테레즈 벨리벳.

테레즈
네. (잠깐 쉬고) 리처드가 같이 살자고 조르고 있긴 해요.

캐롤이 고개를 들고 눈썹을 추켜올리며 미소 짓는다.

테레즈 (CONT'D)
아니, 그런 게 아니라 결혼하자고 해서요.

캐롤
그렇군요.
당신도 결혼하고 싶어요?

침묵.

테레즈
(가볍게 넘어가려 애쓰며)
전 점심 메뉴도 간신히 결정하는 걸요.

거의 테레즈 너머를 보듯 캐롤이 고개를 끄덕인다. 그녀는 무슨 생각을 하는 걸까? 테레즈에겐 갑자기 캐롤의 기분이 왠지 어두워진 것처럼 보인다. 웨이터가 음식을 들고 나타난다. 그가 접시를 놓는다. 캐롤은 은식기를 집어 든다. 겉보기에 어둠은 가신 것 같다.

캐롤
배고파 죽겠어요. 맛있게 먹어요.

캐롤은 먹고 테레즈는 그것을 쳐다본다. 억지로 포크와 나이프를 들고 캐롤과 함께 식사하려 애를 쓰는 것 같다. 캐롤은 고개를 들어 그녀를 잠시 바라본다.

캐롤 (CONT'D)
일요일엔 보통 뭐해요?

테레즈
특별한 건 없어요.
뭐하시는데요?

캐롤
요즘엔 별 거 없어요.
시간 나면 한 번 놀러 와요.
외곽에 살아서 풍경은 좋으니까.
이번 일요일에 놀러 올래요?

캐롤이 테레즈의 대답을 기다린다.

테레즈
네.

캐롤
참 신기한 사람 같아요.

테레즈
왜요?

캐롤
하늘에서 떨어진 것처럼.

테레즈는 얼굴이 붉어지는 것을 느끼며 캐롤에게서 시선을 피한다. 그녀는 점심과 마티니를 먹고 마시려 애쓴다.

36. EXT.
레스토랑. 낮.

지나가는 사람들 사이로, 레스토랑 바로 앞에 선 테레즈는 캐롤이 길 건너편에서 컨버터블에 올라타는 것을 바라본다. 캐롤의 베스트 프렌드 애비가 운전한다. 둘은 유럽식으로 볼에 키스하며 인사를 나눈다. 그리곤 캐롤이 뒤돌아 테레즈에게 손을 흔든다. 테레즈가 따라 손을 흔들고, 차는 출발하여 다른 차들 속으로 사라진다.

37. INT.
애비의 차. 낮.

애비가 6번가를 꿈틀거리며 따라간다.

캐롤
이러고 나타나면 어머님 표정 가관이겠네.
집에 가서 갈아입고 갈까?

애비
소심 떨지 마.

캐롤
그냥 가지 말까봐.

애비
그럼 내가 욕먹어.
그냥 웃으면서 꾹 참아.
(잠깐 쉬고) 그 여자 얘긴 안 할 거야?

캐롤과 애비가 짧은 시선을 교환한다.

캐롤

테레즈? (어깨를 으쓱하며) 장갑 돌려준 사람이야.

애비

그리고?

캐롤

그리고, 늦기 전에 여길 못 빠져나가면 그놈의 파티 걱정할 필요도 없겠네. (한 술 더 뜨며) 이 차 뚜껑 닫아본 적은 있어?

38. INT.
프랑켄베르크 백화점. 직원 라커룸. 낮.

테레즈가 유니폼으로 갈아입은 채 라커를 마주 보고 앉아있다. 그녀는 만년필로 수첩의 빈 페이지에 천천히, 조심스럽게 무언가 적고 있다.

캐롤 에어드 부인. 7번가 입구. 일요일 오후 2시.

그녀는 자기가 쓴 것을 골똘히 들여다보고는 잉크를 말리려 입으로 바람을 분다.

39. EXT.
뉴저지. 부유한 교외. 이른 저녁.

부유한 집들과 녹지, 광활한 땅과 오래된 부가 가득 들어찬, 잘 관리된 도로. 애비의 차가 나무들 사이에 숨은 커다란 현대식 저택의 순환도로에 들어서 멈춘다. 하지의 상관, 싸이 해리슨의 집이다. 음악소리, 웃음소리, 속속 도착하는 잘 차려입은 손님들, 문을 열어주고 차 키를 받아가는 발렛... 파티가 열리고 있는 게 분명하다. 애비는 엔진을 끄고 갑자기 불안해하며 가방을 뒤지고 있는 캐롤을 돌아본다.

캐롤

컴팩트가 어디 있지? 빌어먹을.

애비가 캐롤을 향해 몸을 뻗어 그녀의 팔에 손을 얹는다.

애비

지금도 괜찮아.

캐롤이 애비를 쳐다본다.

캐롤

같이 가자. 잠깐만 있어.

애비

말도 꺼내지 마. 약속 깬 사람이 누군데 그래, 이 바보야.

캐롤

알아, 알아. 미안해. 가면 되잖아.

캐롤이 다시 한 번 저택을 보며 정신을 차리려 한다.

애비

이따가 전화해.

40. INT.

싸이 해리슨의 집. 서재 겸 거실. 이른 저녁.

현관을 들어서자마자 손님들을 환영하는듯한 넓은 공간이 펼쳐진다. 커다란 벽난로. 웨이터들이 음식과 술을 들고 돌아다닌다. 하지

는 부모님인 존과 제니퍼, 그리고 상관인 싸이와 그 아내 지네트
와 함께 모여있다.

존
(싸이에게)
이 녀석한테 사리를 가르치려고 해봤다니까, 싸이.
자네가 골프 실력을 더 많이 감추지 않는 이상
트라이 스테이트 금융이 머리 힐 부지를
살 일은 없다고 말일세.

하지
(아버지에게, 약간 날을 세우며)
생각할 거리가 많아요, 아버지.

모두 그가 무엇을 의미하는지 알기라도 하듯 말을 아낀다. 하지가
고개를 돌리자 현관에서 코트를 맡기는 캐롤이 보인다.

하지 (CONT'D)
실례할게요.

그는 손님들을 헤치고 캐롤에게 다가간다.

41. INT.
싸이 해리슨의 집. 거실. 밤.

파티가 무르익었다. 밴드가 "Harbour Lights"를 연주하고, 하
지와 캐롤이 느리게 폭스트롯을 춘다. 캐롤의 눈에 자신보다 훨씬
제대로 차려입은 다른 여자들이 들어온다. 하지가 이것을 눈치채
고 그녀를 가까이 당긴다.

하지
당신은 세상 어디에서든 가장 아름다운 여자야.

캐롤
어머님한테나 얘기해.

그들은 건너편에서 그들을 지켜보는 제니퍼에게 시선을 돌린다. 물론 그녀는 심기가 불편한 얼굴이다.

42. INT.
싸이 해리슨의 집. 뷔페/식당. 잠시 후.

캐롤과 하지, 싸이와 제니퍼가 접시를 들고 저녁 뷔페 줄을 따라 움직이고 있다.

제니퍼는 서성대며 진열을 바로잡고, 흐트러진 잔과 냅킨을 일하는 사람들에게 건네준다.

제니퍼
크리스마스 아침에 린디를 위해 산타 역할을 해줄
동네 아이를 고용할까 한단다. 걔가 굴뚝으로 내려올
방법을 찾을 수만 있다면 말이야!(잠깐 쉬고, 캐롤에게)
전에는 어떻게 했니, 캐롤?

캐롤
뭐라고요?

제니퍼
크리스마스 아침에 말이다. 린디랑.

캐롤은 답하기 전에 하지와 잠시 시선을 교환한다.

캐롤

오, 저희는... 보통 새벽에 일어나서
같이 린디의 선물을 포장했어요. 하지랑 저랑요.
그걸 트리 밑에 두고 린디가
일어나길 기다리죠. 그럼, 보통 린디는...

하지

(캐롤을 거들며)

보통 한 달음에 계단을 뛰어내려와서 우리가 있다는 걸
알아차릴 새도 없이 모든 선물을 뜯어버려요.

캐롤

(미소 짓고, 하지에게 고마워하며)

네, 맞아요.

제니퍼

하지만 산타클로스는 없었고.

캐롤

네.

제니퍼

오, 뭐. 연출하는 거지.
내가 떠줘도 되겠니?

지네트가 '오, 맙소사'라고 말하듯 캐롤에게 위로의 표정을 지어
보인다.

43. EXT.
싸이 해리슨의 집. 잠시 후.

캐롤과 지네트가 정원에 있다. 유리문 너머로 파티 전경이 보인다.
그들은 담배를 피운다. 캐롤이 신발을 벗고 발바닥을 문지른다.

지네트

(담배를 깊이 한 모금 마시고)

망 좀 봐줄래요? 싸이가 보면 난리를 칠 거예요.

캐롤

(웃으며) 뭘 어쩌시는데요? 용돈이라도 줄이세요?

지네트

(매우 감정 없이)

내가 담배 피우는 걸 싫어해요.

캐롤

그래서요? 본인이 좋다는데.

하지만 그들 모두 원래 그런 식이란 걸 알고 있다. 아내들은 남편의 바람을 따른다.

지네트

캐롤, 저기... 오지랖 부리는 것 같지만,

크리스마스 혼자 보낼 거면 우리 부부랑 같이 보내요.

캐롤

(제의에 진심으로 감동했다)

고마워요, 지네트.

캐롤은 다시 한 번 파티를 돌아본다. 색을 입힌 플라스틱 너머로 커플들이 춤을 춘다.

캐롤 (CONT'D)

(춤 추는 커플들을 보며)

글쎄요. 혼자 여행이나 다녀올까봐요. 며칠만이라도요.

44. INT.
뉴욕타임스. 사진부 사무실. 밤.

대니가 사진 편집자의 매혹적인 세계로 테레즈를 안내한다. 라이트 보드에 매달린 인화지들, 전문 장비, 쟁반과 렌즈들. 하지만 그녀가 가장 경탄하는 건 사진들 그 자체다. 몰래 찍은 사진, 범죄 현장, 스포츠 사진, 신문의 시각적 내러티브를 만드는 모든 것들이 있다. 대니는 책상에 앉아 집에서 가져온 부실한 저녁을 준비한다. 포장한 샌드위치와 맥주 몇 병이다. 이 공간의 모든 것을 흡수하고 있는 테레즈는 감히 아무것도 만지지 못한다.

> **대니**
> 안 망가지니까 들고 봐도 돼. 샌드위치 먹을래?

테레즈는 고개를 젓고 현상지와 확대경을 집어 들고 사진들을 본다. 대니는 그녀를 지켜보고 있다.

> **대니 (CONT'D)**
> 네 사진들은 어때?
> **테레즈**
> 글쎄, 대단하진 않아. 몰라.
> **대니**
> 아니, 주로 어떤 걸 찍냐고.
> **테레즈**
> 나무, 새, 창문. 딱히 안 가려.
> (잠깐 쉬고) 너는 뭐에 대해서 써?
> **대니**
> 사람들.

침묵. 테레즈는 카메라 렌즈를 통해 대니를 본다. 대니가 고개를
들자 그녀는 렌즈를 내린다.

테레즈

난 사람들을 찍을 땐 기분이 좀 이상해.
꼭 침범하는 것 같기도 하고...

대니

사생활 침해 같아서?

테레즈

응.

대니가 맥주 한 병을 따서 테레즈에게 내민다. 테레즈가 그것을
받는다.

대니

하지만, 누구나 사람에 대한 친밀감이 있잖아.

테레즈는 대답하지 않는다.

대니 (CONT'D)

아니면 특정한 사람들에 대해서라도.
너도 어떤 사람들을 좋아하잖아.

테레즈

가끔은.

대니

싫은 사람도 있고. 그들에게 끌리거나
끌리지 않는 이유는 알 수 없어.
우리가 아는 건 그 사람에게 끌리느냐 아니냐 뿐이야.
물리학 같은 거지. 핀볼들처럼 서로 부딪치는 거야.

테레즈

(웃으며)

이젠 과학자가 됐네.

대니

내가 왜 나무 말고 사람들에 대해 쓰는지 설명하려는 것뿐이야.

테레즈

심리학 같은데.

대니

물리학이 더 위로가 돼.

테레즈가 샌드위치를 집어 든다.

테레즈

하지만 모든 게 핀볼 움직임처럼 단순하진 않아.

대니

반응조차 않는 것도 있지. 하지만 모두 살아있긴 하잖아.

잠시 침묵. 대니가 테레즈에게 다가가 그녀의 맥주병을 내려놓는 다. 그가 테레즈의 양 어깨에 손을 얹는다.

테레즈

늦었어. 그만 가야겠어.

그가 그녀에게 키스하고, 그녀는 꼼짝 않고 서서 내버려둔다. 그 리고 대니가 한 걸음 물러서고 테레즈가 고개를 떨군다.

테레즈 (CONT'D)

이러면 안 돼.

대니

불쾌했어?

테레즈

아니.

대니

리처드는 불쾌해할까?

테레즈

아마도. (잠깐 침묵) 가야겠어.

테레즈는 자기 물건을 챙겨 문으로 향한다.

대니

내일 다시 올래? 아님 수요일?

테레즈

어쩌면. 잘 모르겠어.

테레즈가 떠난다.

45. EXT.
캐롤의 집. 늦은 밤.

하지가 파티에서 캐롤을 데려다준다. 캐롤이 열쇠를 찾는 동안 그들은 함께 문 앞에 서 있다. 하지가 주머니에서 자신의 열쇠를 꺼내 문을 연다.

하지

여기.

캐롤

고마워. 술도 안 마시고 태워다 준 것도.

(그의 볼에 키스하며) 잘 가, 하지.

그녀가 집 안으로 들어가려 한다. 하지가 부드럽게 그녀를 멈춘다.

하지
크리스마스에 부모님 댁으로 와. 오늘 저녁도 좋았잖아.

캐롤
(쌀쌀맞지 않게) 하룻밤일 뿐이었잖아.

하지
혼자 둘 생각에 마음이 안 좋아.

캐롤
혼자 아니야. 린디도 있고, 또...

그녀가 말을 멈춘다. 하지는 그녀가 무슨 말을 하려 했는지 알고
있다.

하지
애비. 늘 애비지.

캐롤
(침묵 후에)
애비와는 당신보다 훨씬 전에 끝냈어, 하지.
(잠깐 쉬고) 크리스마스이브 4시까지 린디 짐 싸놓을게.

그녀가 집으로 들어가기 시작한다.

하지
이건 정말 아니야.

캐롤
알아.

그리고 그녀는 하지 앞에서 조용히 문을 닫는다.

46. INT.
캐롤의 집. 거실. 밤.

거실은 어둡고 조용하다. 린디는 소파 위에, 플로렌스는 맞은편 의자 위에 잠들어있다. 캐롤은 플로렌스의 어깨를 가볍게 두드리고 린디 옆에 몸을 굽혀 앉는다.

플로렌스
기다리고 싶어했어요.

캐롤
내 귀한 딸.

캐롤이 아이의 눈에서 머리카락 한 올을 떼어낸다. 그녀는 아이를 조심히 들어올려 계단을 오른다.

캐롤 (CONT'D)
잘 자요, 플로렌스.

47. INT.
캐롤의 집. 거실. 잠시 후.

캐롤이 조그만 플랫폼 위에 덮인 크리스마스 담요를 걷어 소파 뒤에 조립되어있는 기차 세트를 드러낸다. 그녀는 기차를 켜고 천천히 철길을 따라 달리는 것을 지켜본다. 그녀는 술 한 모금을 들이켠다.

48. EXT.
프랑켄베르크 백화점. 7번가 출입구. 이른 일요일 오후.

코트에 스카프를 두르고 장갑을 낀 테레즈가 밖에서 캐롤의 차를 기다린다. 리처드가 함께 기다리고 있다.

리처드
뉴저지 어디라고?

테레즈
외곽이라는데 나도 잘 몰라.

리처드
우리 삼촌이 유니언시티 사시는데 밤에는 꽤 위험하대.

테레즈
유니언시티 아니야.

리처드
알았어, 알았어.

캐롤이 모퉁이에 차를 세운다.

테레즈
저기 왔다.

리처드가 테레즈를 차로 배웅한다. 그가 문을 열어주자 그녀가 타고, 문을 닫은 뒤 창문을 내린다. 그가 몸을 숙여 키스한다.

리처드
여덟 시?

테레즈
여덟 시.

리처드가 차 안을 들여다보고 캐롤과 인사하려 손을 내민다.

리처드
안녕하세요.

캐롤
안녕하세요.
캐롤 에어드예요.

리처드
(테레즈 앞으로 몸을 숙여 캐롤과 악수하며)
리처드 셈코입니다.
반갑습니다.

캐롤
저도요.

테레즈
(리처드에게)
널 만나보고 싶어 하셨어.

캐롤
테레즈가 칭찬을 많이 하던데요.

리처드
(듣기 좋아하며)
그래요? 그거 멋지네요.
무사히 돌려보내 주실 거죠?

캐롤이 미소 지으며 알았다는 뜻으로 경례를 보낸다. 테레즈는 약
간 창피하다. 리처드가 차 안으로 몸을 숙여 테레즈의 뺨을 살짝
만진다.

리처드 (CONT'D)
사랑해.

하지만 테레즈는 이미 창문을 올렸고, 차는 출발하기 위해 시동을 걸었다. 리처드는 뒷창문 너머로 사라진다.

49. INT.
캐롤의 차. 링컨 터널로 접근하며. 낮.

차가운 겨울 햇살이 차창을 구석구석 쓰다듬고, 캐롤과 테레즈는 도시를 가로지른다. 캐롤은 운전대 앞에서 제자리를 찾은 것 같다. 편안하고 자신 있어 보인다. 볕에 그을린 가죽 시트와 마호가니 대시보드부터 운전자의 자연스러운 스타일과 우아함까지, 테레즈에게 캐롤의 차 안이라는 세계는 그녀에 대한 하나의 폭로와도 같다. 이 세계의 소리, 심지어 이따금 캐롤이 재잘대는 소리까지도 모두 가장 고요한 '음악'인 빛과 공기의 소리로 대체된다. 실크 스타킹을 신고 값비싼 향수를 뿌린 이 성숙하고 세련된 여인의 존재는 그녀를 취하게 하는 만큼 불안하게 하기도 한다. 테레즈 옆 시트에 놓인 캐롤의 가방마저도 그녀가 가까이에서 본 그 어떤 것보다도 미스터리하고, 그 주인의 기질과 향기로 가득한 물건이다. 테레즈의 시선은 가방으로부터 뿌연 실크 스타킹을 신은 캐롤의 다리로 옮겨간다. 둔한 울 스타킹으로 싸인 자신의 다리를 내려다보며, 테레즈는 언젠가 이런 차를 가지고 저런 옷을 입는 여자가 될 날이 오기는 할지 궁금해한다.

테레즈가 고개를 들어 앞을 보고 차가 링컨 터널에 진입함에 따라 음악이 아주 살짝 커진다. 차는 마치 그들을 한 데 감싸는 고치에 들어가듯, 열에 들뜬 하강을 하듯 어둠 속으로 고꾸라진다. 그녀는 핸들을 쥔 캐롤의 손가락을, 집중할 때면 살짝 찡그리는 캐롤의 모습을 본다.

테레즈는 작은 미소를 숨길 수 없다. 하지만 흘긋 돌아보자 문득 캐롤의 정신이 딴 데 가 있는듯하다. 캐롤이 라디오 채널을 바꾸자 조 스태포드의 "You Belong to Me"가 흘러나온다.

차가 계속해서 달리며 어두운 터널 안에서 속력을 내고, 테레즈는 좌석에 몸을 기댄다.

50. INT./EXT.
캐롤의 차. 크리스마스트리 판매장. 뉴저지. 낮.

야외 크리스마스트리 판매장. 테레즈는 차 안에 앉아 카메라에 필름을 넣고 있다. 필름을 넣은 뒤, 그녀는 10대 소년이 커다란 전나무를 묶는 것을 기다리고 있는 캐롤을 발견한다. 심한 감기에 걸린 소년에게 캐롤이 휴지를 내민다. 테레즈는 차에서 내려 캐롤을 향해 구도를 잡고 사진 몇 장을 찍는다.

51. INT.
캐롤의 차. 뉴저지 리지우드. 낮.

차가 캐롤의 집으로 향한다. 전나무는 앞 뒷좌석을 가로질러 테레즈와 캐롤 사이에 놓여있다.

테레즈는 뾰족한 잎이 피부에 닿는 느낌과 나무의 향기, 그리고 보이지는 않지만 캐롤이 옆에 있다는 사실을 사랑한다. 차가 캐롤의 집 앞에 멈춰선다. 커다란 저택이다. 테레즈가 들어가 본 집 중에 가장 크다. 캐롤이 엔진을 끈다.

캐롤
아직 살아있어요?

테레즈
네.

캐롤이 문을 열고 차에서 내린다. 테레즈가 내리려고 하는 참에 대문을 열고 엄마에게 인사하러 뛰쳐나오는 린디가 보인다. 플로 렌스가 엄마와 딸을 에스코트하기 위해 문간에 서 있다.

린디
엄마!
캐롤
안녕, 우리 아가! 엄마가 뭐 가져왔게? 못 맞힐걸?

테레즈는 엄마와 딸이 재잘대며 집 안으로 멀어지는 것을 지켜본다.

52. INT.
캐롤의 집. 부엌. 낮. 잠시 후.

테레즈가 쟁반에 차와 쿠키를 준비한다. 열린 문 너머로 거실에서 트리를 꾸미고 있는 캐롤과 린디가 보인다. 거의 마무리가 되자 캐롤은 트리 옆에 사다리를 놓는다.

캐롤
별은 어디 있어?

린디가 장식품 더미를 뒤적여 별을 찾아낸다.

린디
이거, 엄마.
캐롤
우리 딸 잘하네.

테레즈는 캐롤이 사다리를 올라 트리 꼭대기에 별을 다는 모습을 바라본다.

캐롤 (CONT'D)
정말 아름답네!

캐롤이 사다리에서 내려와 린디를 무릎에 앉힌다.

캐롤 (CONT'D)
이렇게 예쁜 트리 본 적 있니?
자, 이제... 별 다음엔 뭘 달아야 하지?

린디
별 더 많이!

캐롤
(린디를 간지럽히며)
아닌 것... 같은데!

O/S 플로렌스
필요한 것 다 찾으셨나요, 아가씨?

테레즈는 깜짝 놀라며 부엌 뒷문 근처에 서 있는 플로렌스를 돌아본다.

테레즈
맙소사, 깜짝 놀랐어요. 바보같이.

플로렌스
(미안한 기색 없이)
죄송합니다, 아가씨.
(잠깐 쉬고) 제가 에어드 부인께 내어가지요.

플로렌스가 쟁반을 들고 거실로 나간다.

53. INT.
캐롤의 집. 거실. 밤.

벽난로가 타고, 트리 밑에 앉은 캐롤이 기차 세트를 포장하려고 애쓴다. 테레즈는 피아노 앞에 앉아 이 곡 저 곡 쳐보고 있다. 반쯤 비운 화이트와인병과 잔 두 개가 근처에 놓여있다.

캐롤
아까 트리 살 때 날 찍은 거예요?

테레즈가 연주를 멈춘다. 정적.

테레즈
죄송해요. 여쭤보는 건데.

캐롤
사과할 거 없어요.

테레즈
친구가 그러는데... 사람에게도 흥미를 가져보라고 해서요.

캐롤
그래서 어떻게 되고 있어요?

테레즈
(짧은 침묵 후에)
아주 잘 되고 있어요.

캐롤
다행이네요.

테레즈가 "Easy Living"을 치기 시작한다. 캐롤이 잠깐 듣다가, 일어나, 테레즈에게 다가온다.

캐롤 (CONT'D)

아름다운 곡이네요.

그녀의 손이 테레즈의 어깨를 약하게 스친다. 테레즈가 얼어붙고, 캐롤은 그녀의 볼을 빠르게 두 번 쓰다듬으며 분위기를 가볍게 만들려고 한다. 테레즈는 연주를 계속하고 캐롤은 듣는다.

캐롤 (CONT'D)

되고 싶은 게 그거예요? 사진작가?

테레즈

그런 것 같아요. 재능이 있는지는 모르겠지만.

캐롤

그건 다른 사람들이 판단하는 거 아니에요?
내가 할 수 있는 건 계속하는 것뿐이죠.
맞다고 느껴지는 것들을 이용하고. 나머진 버리고.

테레즈가 곡을 마친다. 캐롤이 소파 근처의 테이블로 다가가 담배 상자를 열고 한 개비를 꺼내 불을 붙인다.

캐롤 (CONT'D)

나중에 작품들 보여줄래요?
(소파에 앉는다)

테레즈

네. 한 장도 못 팔았어요. 팔려고 누구한테
보여준 적도 없고. 쓸만한 카메라도 한 대 없어서…
대부분 싱크대 아래 쌓아놓고 있어요.

캐롤

한 번 초대해요.

81

밖에서 차가 진입로에 멈추는 소리가 들린다. 차 문이 열렸다가 세게 닫힌다. 분위기가 바뀌고, 캐롤은 빠르게 일어나 현관으로 나아간다.

캐롤이 거실에서 나와 입구에서 크리스마스 장식을 다시 걸어놓고 있는 하지를 발견한다.

캐롤 (CONT'D)
하지. 무슨 일 있어?
하지
없어. 아내 보러 오는 데 이유가 필요한가?

하지가 캐롤에게 다가가 인사하려다가 거실 피아노 앞에 앉은 테레즈를 발견한다. 그는 캐롤을 쳐다보고 캐롤은 시선을 피한다. 그러자 하지는 캐롤을 지나쳐 복도 끝의 부엌으로 들어간다. 테레즈는 이 모든 분위기를 눈치챈다.

54. INT.
캐롤의 집. 거실. 잠시 후.

테레즈는 거실에서 혼자 책을 뒤적이며 캐롤과 하지가 부엌에서 대화하는 소리를 듣는다. 문틈 사이로 캐롤이 불안하게 담배를 피우며 몸을 앞뒤로 흔드는 모습이 보이고, 하지가 싱크대 밑의 파이프를 고치는 소리가 난다. 테레즈는 책장에 꽂힌 책들의 제목을 따라가며 딴 데 정신을 집중하려 노력한다.

캐롤
너무하잖아, 하지. 크리스마스이브까진
내가 데리고 있기로 합의했잖아.

하지

나더러 어쩌라고? 난들 연말 연휴에 플로리다 가고 싶겠어?
어머니가 가자잖아.

캐롤

애 가방도 안 쌌어. 지금 잔단 말야!
난 크리스마스를 딸도 없이 보내?

하지

미안해, 캐롤. 아침 비행기라는데 뭘 어떡해. 난 짐 쌌겠어?...
(공구가 떨어지는 소리) 염병할!

55. INT.
캐롤의 집. 부엌. 계속.

하지는 손을 다친 채 싱크대 밑에서 빠져나온다. 캐롤이 그를 일
으켜주러 간다. 하지만 그때 하지가 문틈으로 테레즈를 발견한다.
그는 성큼성큼 다가가 문을 활짝 연다. 테레즈는 깜짝 놀라 들킨
얼굴이다. 정적.

하지

내 아내랑 어떻게 아는 거요?

캐롤

하지, 제발...

테레즈

프랑켄베르크 백화점 직원이에요.

캐롤

물건 사러 갔다가 장갑 놓고 왔는데 돌려주길래
고마워서 초대했어.

하지

(캐롤에게) 대담하군.

하지는 테레즈를 잠시 훑어보고 부엌으로 돌아간다. 그는 캐롤을 지나쳐 뒤쪽의 창고로 향하고, 그가 치우는 소리가 들려온다. 분노한 캐롤은 거실 입구로 다가간다.

테레즈
제가... 어떻게...

캐롤
그냥... 내버려둬요.

캐롤이 살며시 문을 닫는다. 테레즈는 거기 남겨진 채 서 있다.

56. EXT.
캐롤의 집. 밤.

유니폼을 입은 하지의 운전기사가 긴장한 채로 조용히 운전대를 잡고 있고, 캐롤이 린디를 뒷좌석에 밀어 넣는다. 하지가 대문 앞에서 담배를 피우고 술을 마시며 기다리는 동안 플로렌스가 린디의 짐을 트렁크에 싣는다.

캐롤
기억해, 일곱 시엔 자는 거다.
할머니랑 있을 때 떼쓰는 거 다 알아. (잠깐 쉬고) 됐다,
우리 눈송이. 엄마 안아줘야지? (린디를 꼭 안고 뽀뽀한다)
세상에서 제일 즐거운 크리스마스가 될 거야, 엄마가 약속할게.

린디가 포옹에서 빠져나온다. 좋은 생각이 있다.

린디
차에 자리 있어. 엄마도 같이 가!

캐롤
우리 아가, 엄마도 그러고 싶어. 하지만 어떨 땐...

84

엄마 아빠가 같이 있기에 자리가 부족하다고
판단할 때가 있어... (말을 잇지 못하고)
엄마는 남아서 산타의 요정들이
선물 못 가져가게 지키고 있을게. 가져가면 싫지?

린디가 캐롤을 향해 활짝 웃고 캐롤은 아이를 끌어안고 눈꺼풀에 입을 맞춘다. 캐롤은 운전기사가 백미러로 자신을 쳐다보다 황급히 시선을 돌리는 것을 눈치챈다.

57. INT.
캐롤의 집. 거실. 계속

축음기에서 부드럽게 음악이 흐른다(자비에르 쿠가와 그 오케스트라의 "El Americano"). 테레즈는 할 일을 찾으려 노력하며 이것저것을 바로잡는다. 퇴창 밖으로 얇은 스웨터만 어깨에 두른 채 차 문을 닫고 집 쪽으로 돌아오는 캐롤이 보인다.

그녀는 하지가 현관 계단에서 내려와 담배를 비벼 끄고 캐롤을 향해 걸어가는 것을 본다.

58. EXT.
캐롤의 집. 계속.

캐롤은 현관문으로 향하지만 하지가 그녀를 자기 쪽으로 당겨 멈춰 세운다. 그가 캐롤의 손을 잡고, 침묵이 이어진다. 집안에서 흐르는 음악이 하지에게 들려온다. 그는 약간 비틀거린다.

하지
향기 좋군.

캐롤
당신 취했어.

그는 그녀를 가까이 당겨 눈을 감고, 그녀와 춤을 추려 한다.

캐롤 (CONT'D)
하지, 나 추워.

59. INT.
캐롤의 집. 거실. 계속.

열린 현관문 사이로 테레즈는 살짝 헛디디며 캐롤에게서 떨어지는 하지를 본다. 캐롤은 그의 팔을 잡아준다.

캐롤
커피 갖다 줄게.
하지
(약간 취해서) 나 안 취했어.

하지가 캐롤을 향해 한 걸음 내디딘다. 테레즈는 거실로 피하며 더 이상 엿들을 수 없기를 바란다.

하지 (CONT'D)
지금이라도 짐 싸서 같이 가자.
캐롤
그건 안 돼.
하지
갈 수 있어, 쉬워. 아침에 표만 사면 돼.

60. EXT.
캐롤의 집. 계속.

하지가 그녀의 손을 잡으려 하지만 그녀가 물러선다.

하지
왜? 애비랑 크리스마스 보내려고?
그런 거야?
아니면 저 종업원이랑?

캐롤
그만해, 하지.

하지
당신 같은 여자가 이럴 줄은 몰랐어.

캐롤
나 같은 여자랑 결혼한 건 당신이야.

61. INT.
캐롤의 집. 거실. 계속.

테레즈가 축음기로 다가가 밖에서 들리는 목소리의 높낮이만 들리도록 볼륨을 살짝 높인다.

62. EXT.
캐롤의 집. 계속.

하지가 캐롤을 잡으려고 다가서지만, 그녀가 물러선다. 그가 발을 헛디디다 무릎이 꺾어지며 넘어진다. 그가 숨을 고르고 정적이 이어진다.

하지

나랑 같이 가. 지금, 내가, 차 문을 열테니까...
지금 같이 가지 않으면...

캐롤

(그를 가로막으며)
않으면 뭐? 끝이라고?

하지가 대답하려 하지만, 캐롤 앞에서 술에 취해 바닥에 넘어져 있는 자신의 모습을 문득 깨닫는다. 그녀는 매우 차분하고 조용하다.

하지

빌어먹을...
이 정도로 잔인하진 않았잖아.

캐롤

하지...

캐롤이 하지를 향해 한 걸음 내디딘다. 이런 상태의 그를 차마 보고 있기 힘들다. 하지만 하지는 지금 캐롤의 도움을 받을 생각이 없다. 그는 일어나서 린디를 뒷좌석에 태운 채 기다리고 있는 차에 짧게 시선을 던진다. 하지는 심호흡을 몇 번 하고, 옷을 가다듬은 뒤, 손바닥으로 얼굴을 쓸어낸다. 캐롤이 한 걸음 더 다가선다.

캐롤 (CONT'D)

미안해.

딱딱하게 굳어 움츠러든 하지는 포켓 주머니에 깊이 손을 찔러 넣고 빠르게 차로 걸어간다. 캐롤은 그가 차에 타서 문을 닫는 모습을 바라본다. 차가 떠난다. 캐롤은 추위에 팔짱을 낀다.

63. INT.
캐롤의 집. 저녁. 계속.

축음기 앞에 가만히, 조용히 서 있는 테레즈에게 현관문이 조심스럽게 닫히는 소리가 들린다. 고개를 들자 캐롤이 그녀를 바라보며 서있지만, 거의 자신을 못 본 척하는 것 같다. 캐롤이 축음기로 가 전원을 끄고 술을 따르러 간다. 그녀가 담배 상자를 연다.

테레즈
택시 부를게요.
캐롤
더 이상 나빠질 수 없겠다 싶을 때 꼭 담배가 떨어지지.
테레즈
담뱃가게 가르쳐주시면 제가 나가서...
캐롤
(폭발하며)
이렇게 아무것도 없는 데서 담배 사러 뛰어나갈 필요 없어요.
나 때문에 그럴 거 없다고요. 난 괜찮아요.

침묵. 캐롤이 술을 마신다. 테레즈가 화를 누른다.

캐롤 (CONT'D)
6시 50분 기차 있어요. 역에 데려다줄게요.

64. INT.
캐롤의 차. 밤.

캐롤이 테레즈를 역으로 태워다준다. 도로는 텅 비었다. 완벽히 고요하다. 이 순간 둘 사이는 한없이 멀다.

65. INT.
기차 객실. 밤.

테레즈가 차창에 기대 캐롤의 차가 출발하는 모습을 바라본다. 크리스마스를 맞은 취객들이 웃고 떠들며 복도를 지나가다 테레즈의 좌석에 부딪친다. 테레즈는 그들의 즐거움을 감당할 수 없다. 테레즈는 창문 쪽으로 최대한 몸을 웅크린다. 그녀는 울고 있다.

66. INT.
셈코의 아파트. 밤.

넘치는 짐과 어울리지 않는 가구들, 볼링 트로피로 가득한 따뜻하고 낡은 아파트. 부엌에서는 리처드가 저녁 먹은 접시들을 씻고, 테레즈와 셈코 부인이 테이블에 앉아있다. 셈코 부인이 테레즈의 입에서 체온계를 빼내 불빛에 비추어 읽으려 한다.

셈코 부인
(체온계를 가리켜) 몇이라는 거야?
읽을 수가 없네, 아이고 눈이야.

테레즈가 대신 체온계를 읽어준다.

테레즈
37도요. 정상이에요. 열 없어요.

리처드
들었죠, 엄마. 열 없대요.

셈코 부인
눈이 안 좋지, 귀는 괜찮다. 국수 한 접시 줄까?
큰 접시 너 주려고 남겨뒀단다.

테레즈

정말 배가 안 고파요.

셈코 부인

(농담인 척하지만 진심이다)

똑똑한 줄 알았더니.

시어미의 마음은 그게 아니라는 거 알잖니.

리처드와 테레즈가 시선을 교환한다. 엄마가 그를 창피하게 한다.

리처드

엄마, 그만 좀 해요.

셈코 부인

뭘? 뭘 그만해?

셈코 씨가 부엌 입구에 나타난다. 그는 볼링 셔츠를 입고 볼링 가
방을 들고 있다.

셈코 씨

(테레즈에게)

나타났구나. 잘 됐네. 이 녀석 꿍꿍거리는 걸 참을 수가 없더니.

테레즈, 부탁이니 이 녀석한테 정착 좀 하렴.

리처드는 더욱 창피해진다.

리처드

제발, 왜 이래요? 심문하는 거예요?

테레즈

(상황을 진정시키려) 알았어요, 먹을게요.

셈코 부인이 활짝 웃으며 테레즈의 볼을 꼬집는다.

셈코 부인
아이고 기특해라!

그녀가 테레즈의 접시를 준비한다. 리처드와 테레즈가 시선을 교환한다. 그는 도와준 테레즈가 고맙다.

67. INT.
셈코의 집. 밤.

리처드의 방. 테레즈와 리처드가 침대에 앉아있다. 테레즈가 무릎 위에 포장된 상자를 들고 있다.

테레즈
지금 열어볼 순 없어. 크리스마스까진 며칠이나 남았잖아.

리처드
빨리 열어봐. (어깨를 으쓱하며) 나 참을성 없잖아.

테레즈가 포장을 뜯고 상자를 연다. 안에는 프랑스 안내 책자와 배표 두 장이 들어있다. 1953년 3월 1일 출발이다. 침묵.

테레즈
리처드... 이게 뭐야?

리처드가 활짝 웃으며 테레즈에게서 표 한 장을 가져간다.

리처드
이건 내 거야. 같이 포장하는 게 더 로맨틱할 것 같아서.

테레즈가 자기 손의 표를 빤히 보다 파리의 사진으로 가득한 책자

한 권을 집어 든다.

리처드 (CONT'D)
맙소사, 테리, 좀 더 좋아할 수도 있잖아.
크리스마스 선물로 유럽 여행을 받는 게
매일 있는 일은 아니라고.

테레즈가 고개를 들어 리처드를 본다.

테레즈
7월에 가기로 돼 있었잖아.

리처드
알아. 근데, 크리스마스에 얘기하려고 했는데,
프랑켄베르크에서 승진 제의가 왔어.
침구류 부매니저로.

테레즈는 말문이 막혀 그냥 그를 쳐다본다.

리처드 (CONT'D)
월급도 많이 올라.
그리고 3월에 한 달간 휴가도 준대.
2주는 유급이야. 여름은 성수기니까...

테레즈
3월엔 못 가.

리처드
왜 못 가? 넌 다음 주면 그만두잖아.
무슨 큰 계획이 있는 것도 아니면서.

테레즈는 기분이 상하고, 리처드는 후회한다.

리처드 (CONT'D)

그게 아니라, 테리. 내가 너 정말 존경하는 거 알지?
난 네가 프랑스 가고 싶어 하는 줄 알았어. 나랑.
그래서 뭐 어때, 더 빨리 가면 좋지 싶어서...

테레즈

가고 싶어. 가고 싶었어.
(잠깐 쉬고) 하지만 3월은 너무 일러.

침묵. 테레즈는 표와 책자를 다시 상자에 넣고 뚜껑을 닫는다.

68. INT.
테레즈의 아파트 건물. 늦은 밤.

창밖으로 택시에서 내리는 테레즈가 보인다. 그녀는 어두운 건물
로 들어와 녹초가 된 채 계단을 오른다. 문을 열고 집으로 들어가
려 할 때 복도의 전화기가 울리기 시작한다. 테레즈가 돌아서 한
숨을 쉬고 그것을 받으러 간다.

테레즈

여보세요?

복도 끝의 문이 소리를 내며 열린다. 집주인이 테레즈를 내다본
다.

집주인

지금 몇 시인지 알아요, 벨리벳 양?

테레즈

죄송해요. 전화가 울리길래...

집주인은 불만스러운 표정으로 문을 닫는다. 테레즈는 다시 전화로 주의를 돌린다.

테레즈 (CONT'D)

여보세요?

말이 없다.

69. INT.
캐롤의 집. 침실. 계속.

전화의 반대편에서 캐롤이 담배를 피우며 숨을 내쉰다.

70. INT.
테레즈의 아파트 건물. 계속.

문득 테레즈는 전화 건 사람이 누구인지 깨닫는다. 그녀는 눈을 감는다.

테레즈

캐롤.

캐롤 (O.S.)

(잠깐 침묵하다)

아까는 내가 심했어요. 용서해줄래요?

테레즈

네, 저는... 그게 아니라...

캐롤 (O.S.)

그럼... 내일 저녁에 보러 가도 될까요?

테레즈

네... 네. (잠깐 침묵) 알고 싶은 게... 그러니까,
궁금한 것들이 있는데 물어봐도 될지 모르겠어요.

71. INT.
캐롤의 집. 침실. 계속.

캐롤

(잠깐의 침묵 후)
뭐든 물어봐줘요. 제발.

72. INT.
테레즈의 아파트 건물. 계속.

테레즈가 눈을 감는다. 침묵. 들뜨고 취한 젊은이들이 갑자기 건물
에 들어서며 정적을 깬다. 화들짝 놀란 테레즈는 그들이 비틀거리
며 들어오는 모습을 내려다본다. 그녀가 다시 수화기를 들자 캐롤
은 이미 전화를 끊었다.

73. INT.
프랑켄베르크 백화점. 직원 식당. 낮.

직원 크리스마스 파티가 열리고 있다. 평소와 똑같은 점심에 크리
스마스 쿠키와 음악, 장식을 더한 것이다. 테레즈는 길게 한 줄로
늘어선 직원들 사이에 루비 로비첵과 나란히 서 있다. 루비의 차
례가 되자 배식원이 도시락에 모든 음식을 두 배로 담아준다. 테
레즈가 이를 눈치채고, 루비도 그녀가 눈치챘다는 사실을 안다.

루비 로비첵

혼자 살면 한 푼이 아까워. 아껴야 해.

너도 알게 될 거야.

테레즈

제가 혼자 사는 거 어떻게 아셨어요?

루비 로비첵

(매우 덤덤하게)

그렇게 보여.

테레즈와 루비가 테이블에 앉는다. 루비는 가방을 뒤져 종이쪽지와 펜을 찾아 자신의 주소와 전화번호를 휘갈겨 쓰고 테레즈에게 건넨다.

루비 로비첵 (CONT'D)

난 여기서 알아야 될 모든 걸 알아.

내가 가르쳐줄게.

테레즈

전 며칠밖에 안 남았어요.

루비 로비첵

그래? 어디로 가는데?

메이시 백화점? 그럴 줄 알았어!

그렇게 사치스러운 데로 갈만한

타입일 줄 알았다니까!

루비는 만족스러워하고 입맛을 다시며 열심히 점심을 먹기 시작한다. 정적. 테레즈는 그녀가 먹는 모습을 바라본다. 그곳의 모든 사람들이 먹는 모습을 바라본다. 겉으로는 조화로워 보인다. 테레즈는 자신의 쟁반을 루비에게 민다.

테레즈
드릴게요. 입맛이 없네요.

루비 로비첵
정말? 좋은 양지인데.

테레즈가 끄덕인다. 루비가 테레즈의 식사를 받아 자신의 도시락에 욱여넣는다.

루비 로비첵 (CONT'D)
넌 좋은 애야. 이걸로 사흘은 버티겠어.

테레즈는 무슨 말을 해야 할지 모른 채, 대답을 대신해 애써 미소 짓는다.

74. EXT.
맨해튼 미드타운. 같은 날.

우리는 캐롤의 차가 프레드 헤임즈 변호사 사무소 근처 주차장에 급히 서는 모습을 멀리서 바라본다. 캐롤은 차에서 내려 복잡한 거리를 빠르게 가로질러 건물로 들어선다.

75. INT.
헤임즈 변호사 사무소. 잠시 후.

캐롤의 변호사인 프레드 헤임즈는 막 사무실로 돌아오는 길에 자신의 비서에게 크리스마스 선물을 건네는 캐롤을 마주친다.

캐롤	**비서**
메리 크리스마스, 캐서린.	오...

캐롤

정말 별거 아니에요. (고개를 들어) 드디어 오시네요.
이젠 저랑 이야기해주실 건가요?

프레드 헤임즈

이렇게 먼 걸음 하실 건 없었는데...

캐롤

그냥 솔직히 얘기해요, 프레드.
무슨 일인데 연휴 끝나고 걱정하자고 해요?

그들이 프레드의 사무실 안에 자리를 잡고, 프레드가 문을 닫는다.

프레드 헤임즈

(잠깐 쉬고)
제리 릭스가 아침에 예상 밖의 문서를 보내왔더군요.
일단 앉으시죠.

캐롤

왜 사람들은 앉아서 나쁜 소식을 듣는 게
더 나을 거라고 생각하죠?

어색한 침묵. 프레드가 헛기침을 한다.

프레드 헤임즈

하지가 양육권 심리 전까지 당신이 린디에게 어떠한 연락도
할 수 없도록 하는 명령을 청구하려 했어요.
공동 양육권에 대한 생각이 바뀐 것 같습니다.
린디에 대한 단독 양육권을 원해요.

캐롤

뭐라고요?

캐롤은 정신이 아득하다. 그녀가 앉는다.

캐롤 (CONT'D)
공동 양육권은 이미 합의했잖아요.
갑자기 이러는 이유가 뭐죠?

프레드 헤임즈
이번 29일에 지방 가정법원에, 음,
영구 양육권 신청서를 제출하겠답니다.

캐롤
그가 이렇게 할 수 있나요?
이게... 맞는 거예요?

프레드 헤임즈
맞는지는 모르겠지만, 합법이에요.

캐롤
무슨 근거로요?

프레드 헤임즈
(둘러대며)
이러지 마시고 연휴 후에 처리합시다. 그때 해결할...

캐롤
(그의 말을 가로막으며)
무슨. 근거로요.

프레드 헤임즈
판사에게 윤리 조항을 감안하라고 청원한다더군요.

캐롤
윤리요? 그게 무슨 소리예요?

프레드 헤임즈
(잠깐 후에)
알겠습니다. 돌리지 않고 말씀드리죠.
애비 게르하르트 씨요.

                          캐롤
                   애비는 린디의 대모예요.
                애비는... (혼잣말로, 진심을 담아)
          그가 날 가질 수 없다면 나도 린디를 가질 수 없다는...

정적.

                       프레드 헤임즈
                안타깝지만 진지해 보이던데요.

캐롤이 고개를 들어 프레드를 보고 끄덕인다.

                          캐롤
                   양육권 심리가 언제죠?
                       프레드 헤임즈
          연휴도 있고 일이 밀릴 테니 장담하기가 어려운데...
                       프레드 헤임즈
                   어림잡아 말해봐요, 프레드.
                       프레드 헤임즈
          3월 중순 전엔 힘들어요. 4월이 될 수도 있습니다.

정적.

                          캐롤
                    애를 볼 순 있어요?
                       프레드 헤임즈
                     (불친절하지 않게)
          그게... 이렇게 말해보죠. 감독관을 동반한 만남도 권하지는...
                          캐롤
          학교에서도요? 사무실에서 감독 하에라도...?

프레드 헤임즈
문제는 장소가 아니라…

캐롤
물론 선생님이나 누군가 감독하는 방문이라면야…

프레드 헤임즈
캐롤, 이건 심각한 혐의예요. 심리 전에 접촉을 강행하는 건
당신의 행실에 대한 정밀 조사를 불러올 뿐입니다.

캐롤
행실? 맙소사. 난 린디의 엄마라고요.
(잠깐 쉬고) 윤리 조항이라니. 알만하군요.

프레드 헤임즈
아시겠어요?

캐롤
아뇨. 린디와 날 떼어놓는 건 윤리적인 줄 아는지.

캐롤은 차가운 불신을 담아 그를 본다.

76. EXT.
5번가. 같은 날 오후.

캐롤은 멍한 상태로 길에 나온다. 갈 곳이 있고 할 일이 있는 크
리스마스 쇼핑객 무리가 스쳐간다. 그녀는 그렇지 않다. 캐롤은
자기도 모르게 겨울 햇살을 가르며 차가 서있는 방향으로 걸어간
다. 그녀는 담배를 입에 물고 라이터를 찾으려 애쓰며 가방을 뒤
지기 시작한다. 마침내 고개를 든 그녀의 눈앞에 주차장에서 후진
해 나오는 트럭이 보이고, 그녀는 길을 비키던 행인과 충돌한다.

목소리
앞 좀 보쇼!

캐롤
미안해요.

캐롤은 가게 창문 쪽으로 비켜서서 마침내 담배에 불을 붙이고 깊게 몇 모금을 마신다. 고개를 든 그녀는 가게의 진열대로 잠시 눈을 돌린다. 휴가 테마다. 마네킹에는 선글라스가 씌워져 있고, 목에는 카메라가 걸려있다. 짐은 기교 있게 쌓여있다. 그녀는 갈색 투톤 여행 가방에 시선을 고정한다.

77. INT.
레코드 가게. 이스트 50번가. 같은 날 늦은 오후.

테레즈가 미드타운의 레코드 가게 계산대에서 주문한 음반을 기다리고 있다. 점원이 음반을 갖고 돌아온다. "Easy Living"이 커버를 크게 장식하고 있는, 빌리 홀리데이의 음반이다.

테레즈
네, 이거예요. 감사합니다.

그녀가 5달러짜리를 건네자 점원이 입력을 시작한다. 거스름돈을 기다리던 테레즈는 청취 코너에서 헤드폰 하나를 귀에 나눠 대고 음악을 듣고 있는 두 명의 짧은 머리 여성을 발견한다. 뿔테 안경을 쓴, 더 남성스러운 쪽의 여자는 버튼다운 셔츠 위에 맞춤 재킷과 바지를 입고 난간에 기대어 있다. 다른 쪽은 무척 전문적으로 보이는, 매끄럽게 재단된 여성 정장을 입었다. 그들은 한눈에 보기에도 뉴욕의 레즈비언 커플 중 하나다. 테레즈는 잠시 그들을 바라보다, 바지를 입은 여자가 시선을 돌리자 황급히 고개를 숙인다.

78. EXT.
레코드 가게. 이스트 50번가.

밖에서 자전거를 세워두고 기다리던 리처드가 레코드 가게에서 서둘러 빠져나오는 테레즈를 발견한다.

테레즈
걸어가자. 이거 집에 두고 나올래.
리처드
분부대로 하겠습니다

그들은 테레즈의 아파트가 있는 블럭으로 걸어간다.

리처드 (CONT'D)
찾던 거 구했어?
테레즈
(별일 아닌 척)
어... 백화점에 누구 주려고 뭐 좀 샀어.
리처드
나중에 재즈 클럽 갈 거지?
테레즈
오, 잘 모르겠어.
리처드
그래, 괜찮아. (잠깐 침묵) 그래도 크리스마스엔 한 번 들러.
엄마가 계획이 있나 봐.
테레즈
크리스마스는... 가족들끼리 보내야지. 내가 끼기엔...
리처드
넌 우리 가족이야, 테리.

그들은 작은 진입로로 꺾어 공터를 질러간다. 테레즈는 주제를 바꾸려 애쓴다.

테레즈
포트폴리오를 만들 생각이야. 내 사진들 정리해서.
사람도 찍어보려고. 직장도 알아보고. 신문사에 갈까 봐, 타임스나.
대니가 거기 아는 사람이...

리처드
유럽 여행 생각은 해보긴 했어?
(답이 없다) 테리?

테레즈가 생각을 곱씹으며 멈추자 리처드도 멈춰 그녀를 돌아본다.

리처드 (CONT'D)
왜?

테레즈
사랑을 몇 번이나 해봤어?

리처드
(웃으며, 왜 이러는지 모르겠다는 듯)
와. 한 번도 없어. 너 전엔.

테레즈
거짓말하지 마. 들은 것만 둘인데.

리처드
왜 이래. 걔들은... 걔네랑은 섹스한 거야. 이거랑은 달라.

테레즈
우린 (조용히) 끝까지 안 가서 다르다는 거야?

리처드
아니, 아니야. 내 말은 그게 아니... 왜 이러는 거야?
난 널 사랑해. 그게 다른 거야.

테레즈가 끄덕인다. 그들은 다시 걷는다.

> **테레즈**
> 남자랑 사랑에 빠져본 적 있어?

> **리처드**
> (긴 침묵 뒤에)
> 아니.

> **테레즈**
> 들어본 적은 있지?

> **리처드**
> 당연하지. 그런 사람들에 대해서 들어봤냐고? 물론.

> **테레즈**
> 그런 사람들이 아니라. 그냥 두 사람이...
> 서로 사랑에 빠지는 거. 남자 둘이서라든가.
> 갑자기 말야.

> **리처드**
> 그런 건 못 들어봤어. 근데 그런 건 꼭 이유가 있어.
> 환경이라거나.

> **테레즈**
> 그냥 누구한테 일어날 수 있는 일은 아니란 거지?
> 아무한테나?

> **리처드**
> 아니지. 무슨 소리야?
> 여자랑 사랑에 빠지기라도 했어?

> **테레즈**
> 아니.

그들이 테레즈의 건물에 도착한다. 리처드가 난간에 자전거를 세우고 테레즈의 손을 맞잡는다.

리처드
내가 너랑 평생을 보내고 싶어 하는 거 몰라, 테리?
같이 프랑스 가자. 결혼도 하고.

테레즈
리처드, 난 준비가 안 됐어. 그런 결정을...

리처드
뭐? 말해봐.

테레즈
난 그냥... 가야겠어.

리처드
테리.

테레즈
미안해.

테레즈가 건물 입구의 계단을 뛰어 올라, 리처드가 뭐라고 말하기
도 전에 들어가 버린다.

79. INT.
칵테일 바. 같은 날 늦은 오후/이른 저녁.

애비와 캐롤이 좋아하는 술집에서 조용히 마티니를 마신다. 캐롤
이 가게에서 본 갈색 투톤 여행 가방이 테이블에 기대어 있다.

캐롤
아침에 내 베개 밑에서 린디의 빗을 찾았어. 머리칼이
잔뜩 붙어선. 자주 그랬어. 착하게 머리 빗었다고 엄마한테
티 내느라고. 보통은 빗을 청소하는데, 오늘은 왠지...

짧은 침묵.

애비
어떻게 이런대? 어떻게 감히... 윤리 뭐?

캐롤
조항이래.

애비
캐롤, 만에 하나 내 책임이 있다면...

캐롤
그런 말 하지 마. 절대로.

캐롤이 잔을 비운다. 채워달라는 의미로 빈 잔을 애비에게 내민다. 애비가 둘의 잔을 모두 채운다.

애비
야. 호보켄에 그 파산한 양복점 알지?

캐롤
그럼. 그... 그... 유리 비슷한 뭐시기로...

애비
맞아. 유리 비슷한 뭐시기. 바로 그거야.

캐롤이 웃는다.

캐롤
헛소리하네. 내가 무슨 얘기하는지 하나도 모르면서.

애비
맞아. 그래도 너 웃는 거 들으니 좋다.

애비가 캐롤에게 담배를 권하자 캐롤이 받아들고, 애비가 불을 붙여준다. 캐롤은 의자에 기대 긴장을 푼다.

애비 (CONT'D)

아무튼, 집주인이 임대를 해주겠다고 했어.
가구점을 다시 해볼까 싶어서.
고치려면 도움이 좀 필요할 것 같은데,
네가 광택 내는 덴 전문가니까...

캐롤

너 진심이구나.

애비

나 진지해.
(잠깐 침묵) 우리가 했던 가게보다 재앙일 순 없겠지.

침묵. 애비는 다른 곳을 본다. 캐롤이 그녀에게 몸을 기울인다.

캐롤

우리가 재앙은 아니었어. 그냥...

캐롤은 단어를 찾을 수 없다.

애비

알아. 타이밍. 늘 안 좋았지.
아무튼, 요새 꽂힌 빨강 머리가 있는데,
퍼래머스 외곽에 있는 스테이크집 사장이야.
리타 헤이워드는 저리 가랄 정도야.

캐롤

정말? 빨강 머리를 감당할 자신은 있고?

그들은 빨강 머리들을 생각하며 짓궂은 미소를 나눈다. 그들이 건배한다. 애비가 수트케이스를 가리킨다.

애비

어디 갈 거야?

캐롤

서부로 갈까 해. 몇 주 정도... 심리 전까지.
할 게 뭐 더 있겠어?

침묵.

애비

너 혼자 운전하는 거 싫어하잖아. 그래서.
(짧은 침묵, 애비가 숨을 깊게 들이쉬었다 내쉰다) 걔는 어려.

캐롤이 끄덕임으로 동의한다. 전혀 부정하지 않는다.

애비 (CONT'D)

뭐하는 건진 알고 있는 거지?

캐롤

몰라. (침묵) 언제는 알았나.

80. INT.
테레즈의 아파트. 같은 날 밤.

누군가 테레즈의 문을 두드린다.

테레즈가 화장실에서 고개를 내밀고 빠르게 방을 둘러본다. 그녀는 계속 머리를 빗고 블라우스를 정돈하며 황급히 나온다. 문으로 걸어가는 와중에 빌리 홀리데이 음반을 재빠르게 베개 밑에 밀어 넣고 축음기를 켠다(레스 폴 & 메리 포드의 "Smoke Rings"

가 시작된다). 그녀는 새로 깨끗하게 정돈한 아파트를 마지막으로 둘러보고 문을 당겨 연다.

캐롤이다. 여행 가방이 그녀 옆에 놓여있다.

캐롤

집주인이 열어줬어요.

캐롤이 담배에 불을 붙인다. 테레즈는 이 순간 바라보는 것밖에 할 수 없다. 이윽고 테레즈가 여행 가방의 존재를 알아차리고, 캐롤이 한 발로 그것을 문지방 너머로 민다.

캐롤 (CONT'D)

메리 크리스마스.
(잠깐 쉬고) 열어봐요.

테레즈는 몸을 굽혀 여행 가방을 연다. 안에는 새 카메라와 필름이 가득하다.

81. INT.
테레즈의 아파트. 잠시 후.

캐롤이 테레즈의 사진들을 본다. 시간을 충분히 들여, 아주 자세히 들여다본다. 테레즈는 멀찍이 떨어져 그것을 바라본다. 좋은 반응을 열렬히 바라고 있다. 캐롤은 테레즈가 트리 판매장에서 자신을 찍은 사진이 벽에 걸려있는 것을 본다. 그녀는 그 사진에, 그리고 테레즈가 그것을 제일 좋은 자리에 걸어둔 데에 감동한다.

테레즈
별로예요. 급하게 찍어서…
더 잘 찍을 수 있어요.

캐롤
완벽해요.

작은 테이블에 기댄 캐롤이 마분지 테두리가 붙은 조그만 사진을 집어 든다. 수녀원 부속 학교에서 찍힌 다섯 살 난 테레즈다.

캐롤 (CONT'D)
당신이에요?

테레즈
네.

캐롤이 돌연 그것을 내려놓고 테레즈의 부엌 겸 암실로 들어선다.

캐롤
냉장고에 인화액 말고 다른 것도 있어요? 목이 좀…

테레즈
그럼요.

테레즈가 냉장고로 가 맥주 두 병을 꺼낸다. 그녀가 캐롤을 향해 돌아서자, 캐롤은 한 걸음 더 물러서 애써 눈물을 참고 있다.

테레즈는 어쩔 줄 모르고 잠시 얼어붙는다. 그녀는 캐롤에게 다가서지만 망설이며 손에 든 맥주를 바라보다 테이블에 내려놓는다. 그녀는 조심스럽게 다가가 머뭇거리는 손을 캐롤의 어깨에 얹고 쥔다. 여전히 돌아선 캐롤이 아주 조용히 무너진다. 테레즈가 좀 더 다가오자 그녀는 고개를 숙인다.

82. EXT.
테레즈의 아파트 옥상. 밤.

캐롤은 머그잔에 든 커피를 마시며 옥상 둘레를 따라 서성이고,
테레즈는 자리에 앉아 그것을 지켜본다. 대단한 뷰는 아니지만 인
상적인 빌딩들의 꼭대기와 빛, 흐린 밤하늘을 볼 수 있다.

테레즈
싸워보는 게 의미가 있나요?

캐롤
접근 금지 명령요?
(잠깐 침묵) 아뇨.

테레즈
석 달이라니. 무력감이 들어요. 아무 도움도 못 되고...

캐롤
당신과는 상관없는 일이에요.

짧은 침묵. 그 발언은 테레즈에게 상처가 되지만, 그녀는 그것을
감추려 한다.

캐롤 (CONT'D)
당분간 떠나있을 거예요.

테레즈
언제요? 어디로요?

캐롤
발길 닿는 곳으로요. 서부로. 곧.

테레즈는 가슴이 내려앉는 걸 감추려 애쓴다.

캐롤 (CONT'D)
혹시...
당신이 같이 가고 싶을지도
모른다고 생각했어요.

짧은 침묵. 캐롤이 테레즈를 똑바로 본다.

캐롤 (CONT'D)
그래 줄래요?

테레즈가 결정을 내리기 전, 길고 조용한 시간이 이어진다.

테레즈
네. 네, 그럴게요.

눈발이 날리기 시작한다.

83. INT.
프랑켄베르크 백화점. 직원 라커룸. 크리스마스이브. 낮.

테레즈가 자신의 물건들(스타킹 몇 개, 스카프, 책들)을 라커에서 꺼내 가방에 넣는다. 프랑켄베르크 백화점 직원 지침서와 언뜻 피가 묻은 산타 모자는 따로 빼서 라커 선반에 올려둔다.

라커룸 반대편에서 여자들이 다가오는 소리가 들린다. 그들 너머로 루비 로비첵이 어느 때보다도 피곤하고 외로운 모습으로 벤치에 앉아 종아리 길이의 스타킹을 말고 있다. 테레즈가 조심스레 라커를 닫는다.

84. EXT.
프랑켄베르크 백화점. 잠시 후.

크리스마스 장식이 된 창문들 너머로 테레즈가 짐을 들고 백화점을 벗어나 길에서 택시를 잡는 모습이 보인다. 택시가 빠르게 그녀를 싣고 가고, 그녀는 마지막으로 한 번 뒤를 돌아본다.

85. INT.
테레즈의 아파트. 크리스마스이브. 낮.

테레즈와 리처드가 식탁에 앉아있다. 테레즈의 옷과 여행 가방이 침대 위에 펼쳐져 있다.

리처드
이해가 안 돼. 이해가 안 된다고, 테레즈.
이 여자가 너한테 뭔데?

테레즈
친구야.

리처드
내가 네 친구지, 테리. 필이나 대니가 네 친구고.
어떤 여자인지도 모르잖아.

테레즈
(잠깐 있다가)
편지 전해줄 거 있으면 시카고 우체국으로 보내.
근데 2월까지만 사서함 빌렸어.
뭐 좀 하려고 모아둔 돈이 조금 있어서...

리처드가 날카롭게 그녀를 쳐다본다. 테레즈는 시선을 피한다.

리처드
우리 여행 갈 돈이잖아.
우리 여행, 테리.
근데 넌 지금... 믿기지가 않네!

테레즈
설명할 수가 없어. 그냥...

리처드
뭐? 이 여자한테 반했다는 거 아냐.
무슨 고등학생처럼!

테레즈
그게 아니라, 그냥 마음에 드는 거야.
그 사람이랑 얘기하는 게 좋아.
말이 통하는 사람이면 누구든 좋아.

리처드는 상처 받고, 그들은 매서운 눈빛을 주고받는다.

리처드
잘났네. 내가 하나 말해줘?
2주만 지나면 넌...
그 여잔 너한테 질릴 거고
넌 차라리 안 갔었으면 하고...

테레즈
넌 이해 못 해!

리처드
이해해. 아주 잘 알지.
너 지금 미쳤어!

테레즈
평생 오늘처럼 머리가 맑은 적이 없었어.
(잠깐 쉬고) 그러니까 내버려 둬.

테레즈가 자신의 대담함에 스스로 놀란다.

리처드
우리 끝난 거야? 그런 거야?

테레즈
그런 말 한 적 없어.
하지만 이걸로 싸우기만 할 거면
뭐하러 너랑 만나겠어?

리처드
그러니까... 그러니까 요약하면,
멍청하게 반한 것 가지고
나한테 헤어지자는 거야?

테레즈
난 그런 말 안 했어. 네가 말했잖아.

리처드가 재킷을 움켜쥐고 현관으로 향한다.

리처드
나한테 배표까지 사게 만들고,
널 위해 승진까지 했어...
난 너한테 청혼을 했다고.

86. INT.
테레즈의 아파트 건물. 복도. 낮.

테레즈
내가 그렇게 만든 적 없어,
아무것도 해달라고 한 적 없다고.
그게 문제인가 보네.

그가 계단을 뛰어 내려가고 집주인이 문틈으로 고개를 내밀어 싸움을 구경한다.

리처드
장담하는데 2주만 있으면 없던 일로 해달라고
애걸하게 될 거야!

테레즈
리처드... 리처드!

리처드
즐거운 여행 돼라, 테리!

그는 빌딩을 뛰쳐나가고 테레즈는 자신의 집을 돌아보다 집주인의 눈빛과 마주친다.

87. INT.
테레즈의 집. 잠시 후.

짧은 클로즈업들: 테레즈가 새 여행 가방에 옷을 담는다. 캐롤에게 줄 선물을 포장한다. 카드를 쓴다.

88. INT.
캐롤의 집. 손님 방. 크리스마스 이른 아침.

테레즈는 가까워지는 차 소리에 잠에서 깬다. 그녀는 눈을 뜨고 주변을 바라본다. 캐롤의 집, 편안한 손님 방이다. 바깥에서 들리는 목소리에 그녀는 창을 내다본다.

깨끗한 눈이 쌓여있고 애비의 차가 언제나처럼 지붕을 연 채 진입로에 섰다. 캐롤은 가운 위에 코트만 걸친 채 밖에 나와 있다.

캐롤
이제 자러 가는 거야?
아니면 지금 일어난 거야?
애비
둘 다야.

애비는 웃음을 참으려 하지만 잘 안 된다. 캐롤이 입에 검지를 갖다 댄다. "쉿."

애비 (CONT'D)
드라이브 갈래?
캐롤
이 바보야.
애비
그래도 떠나는 건 보겠다고 왔다, 그치?
캐롤
나 혼자 있는 거 아니야.
애비
오 이런....
캐롤
(웃고는)
들어와. 커피 끓여놨어.

애비가 차에서 내린다.

89. INT.
캐롤의 집. 복도. 잠시 후.

애비와 캐롤이 집에 들어선다.

애비
이 집은 아침에도 무슨 탄광처럼 우울하네.

그들은 파자마 차림으로 계단 꼭대기에 앉아 있는 테레즈를 본다.

캐롤
우리가 깨웠군요. 다시 자요,
아직 시간이 일러요.
테레즈
괜찮아요. 저... 내려가도 될까요?

애비가 코웃음을 참는다. 캐롤이 가볍게 애비의 옆구리를 쿡 찌른
다. 테레즈는 둘의 모습을 신중하게 바라본다.

캐롤
물론이죠. 옷장에 가운 있어요.

테레즈가 일어서고, 애비가 그녀를 훑어본다.

캐롤 (CONT'D)
여긴 애비 게르하르트예요.
애비
내가 예의라곤 없네.

캐롤
전혀.

애비
그래도 만나서 반가워요, 테레즈.

테레즈가 미소 지으며 고개를 끄덕이고는 살그머니 복도로 돌아
간다.

90. INT.
캐롤의 집. 부엌. 잠시 후. 낮.

애비가 샌드위치 준비를 마무리하고, 테레즈가 그것을 싸고 있다.

테레즈
캐롤을 오랫동안 아셨어요?

애비
맞아요.

그들이 일하는 동안 짧은 침묵이 흐른다.

테레즈
여행 가보신 적 있어요?
캐롤이랑요.

애비
두세 번 정도.

테레즈는 표정이 일그러지는 걸 막을 수 없다. 애비가 눈치챈다.

애비 (CONT'D)

엘리자베스 외곽에서 2년 정도 가구점을 했어요.
그래서 골동품이나 중고 같은 걸 구하려고 늘 돌아다녔죠.

그녀가 테이블에서 담뱃갑을 집어 들고 한 대를 꺼내 불을 붙인다.
테레즈가 그녀를 지켜본다. 애비가 담배를 권하고 불을 붙여준다.

애비 (CONT'D)

담배 피울 수 있는 나이예요?

침묵이 흐르다 애비가 미소를 짓는다. 테레즈는 따라 미소 짓기로 한다.

테레즈

그렇군요...

잠깐의 침묵. 그리고:

애비

지금 걔는 걱정할 거리가 많아요. 그건 알죠?

테레즈

알아요.

애비

외롭고요.

테레즈

그래서 저한테 같이 가자고 하는 건가요?

애비

그게 아니라...

애비가 부엌 창문 밖을 살피고 담배를 피운다.

애비 (CONT'D)

그냥...
재가 상처 받는 건 보고 싶지 않아요.
그게 다예요.

테레즈

전 캐롤에게 절대 상처 주지 않을 거예요.
제가 그럴 거라고 생각하세요?

애비

아뇨. (솔직하게 테레즈를 바라보며)
그렇게 생각 안 해요.

테레즈가 커다란 소풍 바구니에 음식과 마실 거리를 넣기 시작한다.

테레즈

가구점은 어떻게 됐어요?

애비가 한숨을 쉰다. 테레즈의 눈에 그녀는 갑자기 약간 슬퍼 보인다.

애비

그건... (다시 일을 하며) 일이 뜻대로 되지 않을 때도 있어요.
얼마나 원하든 간에.

91. EXT.
캐롤의 집. 잠시 후. 낮.

테레즈와 캐롤은 트렁크에 짐을 다 싣고 차창에 남은 눈을 털어낸다. 캐롤이 트렁크를 쾅 닫고 운전석으로 걸어가 문을 열고 차에

탄다. 캐롤이 시동을 걸어 엔진을 깨우자 테레즈는 급히 뒷 유리의 눈을 치운다. 부드러운 음악이 시작되고 뜨거운 배기관에서 김이 올라온다. 테레즈는 잽싸게 조수석으로 가 마지막으로 주변을 둘러보고 차에 올라탄다.

92. INT.
캐롤의 차 / 펜실베이니아행 출구. 잠시 후. 낮.

차 안을 비추는 쇼트들 위로 음악이 계속된다: 미리 크림을 타 보온병에 담아 온, 몹시 뜨거운 커피를 캐롤에게 따라주는 테레즈. 담배 두 개비에 불을 붙여 하나를 캐롤에게 건네는 테레즈. 그들은 필라델피아로 향하는 흑백의 눈 내린 고속도로를 가로지른다.

93. INT.
필라델피아 식당. 잠시 후.

캐롤과 테레즈는 휑한 도시의 식당에 거의 유일한 손님으로 앉아 토마토 수프와 크래커를 먹는다. 크리스마스 분위기를 내려고 두른 몇 가닥의 우울한 반짝이 장식과 화관이 '메 크리 마스'라고 적힌 녹색과 빨간색 골판지 배너를 둘러싸고 있다. 테레즈는 자기 접시를 옆으로 치워놓곤 텅 빈 거리를 내다본다.

테레즈
도시 하나를 독차지해도 되겠어요.

테레즈는 동의한다는 듯 미소 짓고 있는 캐롤에게 고개를 돌린다. 테레즈가 더는 기다리지 못하고 의자 밑에서 예쁘게 포장한 선물을 꺼낸다.

테레즈 (CONT'D)

선물이에요. 메리 크리스마스.

캐롤

세상에, 이럴 거 없는데.

하지만 캐롤은 기뻐하고, 테레즈는 그녀가 기뻐하는 모습에 기쁘다.

테레즈

열어봐요.

그녀는 캐롤이 포장을 뜯는 모습을 지켜본다. "Easy Living"이 들어있는 빌리 홀리데이 음반이다.

테레즈 (CONT'D)

집에 놀러 갔을 때 피아노로 친 곡이에요.

캐롤

기억나요. (잠깐 있다, 테레즈를 보며) 고마워요.

테레즈가 카메라를 들고 캐롤에게 초점을 맞춰 사진을 찍는다. 캐롤이 손으로 얼굴을 가린다.

캐롤 (CONT'D)

맙소사, 꼴이 엉망인데! 찍지 말아요.

테레즈

아니에요. 얼마나... (그녀는 앞으로 몸을 기울였다가
도로 무른다) 멋진데요. 그렇게 있어요.

테레즈는 자신이 캐롤의 손을 잡고 있음을 깨닫는다. 그녀는 약간

창피해하며 빠르게 식당 안을 둘러보지만 아무도 그들을 보지 않는다. 캐롤이 이것을 알아채고 테레즈의 손을 쥐었다가 부드럽게 빠져나온다.

캐롤
리처드 그리워요?

테레즈
(생각해본다)
아뇨. 오늘 한 번도 생각 안 했어요.
집 생각도요.

캐롤
집.

테레즈는 캐롤의 기분이 조금 어두워지는 것을 보며 그 단어를 쓴 걸 후회한다.

94. INT.
필라델피아 시내. 식당. 잠시 후.

테레즈가 식당 뒤편의 화장실에서 돌아오다 세 아이를 챙기고 있는 30대 여성을 지나친다. 테레즈는 캐롤을 찾아 두리번거리다 창밖의 공중전화에 있는 그녀를 발견한다. 캐롤은 동전을 넣고 빠르게 번호를 누른다.

신호음이 울린다. 한 번, 두 번, 세 번. 캐롤은 식당 안을 힐끗 본다. 눈발 너머로 아이들 중 하나가 우스꽝스러운 표정을 지어 보인다. 그 바로 뒤에서 테레즈가 계산을 하고 있다. 캐롤은 전화가 연결되기도 전에 수화기를 내려놓는다. 테레즈가 식당을 나서려고 돌아보자 캐롤이 담배를 피우는 모습이 보인다.

95. INT./EXT.
캐롤의 차. 밤.

캐롤이 운전한다. 테레즈는 조수석 창문에 기대 웅크린 채 자고 있다. 담요가 대충 덮여 있다.

라디오 V.O.
마지막으로 대통령 당선인과 아이젠하워 부인의
명절 인사를 들으시겠습니다.
여기는 WOR 피츠버그 방송입니다...

캐롤이 핸들에서 한 손을 떼고 담요를 당겨 테레즈를 덮어준다.

96. EXT.
피츠버그 외곽 왕복 2차선 고속도로. 밤.

캐롤의 차가 빈 도로를 달린다. 뒤로는 피츠버그 산업 단지의 스카이라인이 뿜어내는 기이한 빛이 보인다. 차 앞에는 빽빽한 어둠뿐이다.

97. EXT.
애비의 집. 밤.

기사가 대기하고 있는 차에서 하지가 내린다. 어둠 속을 걸어 정면이 벽돌로 된 집으로 뛰어들어간다.

98. INT.
애비의 집.

맹렬히 문을 두들기는 소리가 나고 애비가 가운을 여며 묶으며 서둘러 계단을 내려온다. 그녀가 문을 연다. 흥분한 하지가 숨을 몰아쉬고 있다.

하지
아내랑 얘기해야겠어.

애비
여기서 뭐 하는 거야? 플로리다에 있어야 하잖아.

하지
(잠시 멈췄다가)
갈 수가 없었어. 나는... 린디가 크리스마스에 엄마를
보고 싶다고 해서. 당신이 상관할 일 아니야.
가서 데려오기나 해. 여기 있는 거 다 알아.

애비
어디라고 뻔뻔하게 명령을 해대는군. 여기 없어.

하지
그럴 리가 없어. 집에도 없고 나랑 같이 있지도 않으니
당신이랑 있겠지.

애비
(잠깐 있다가)
그래, 하지. 맞는 말이야. 빌어먹을 10년 동안 당신은
걔 인생을 당신 중심으로 돌게 만들었지.
당신 직장, 당신 친구들, 당신 가족, 당신...

하지
어디 있냐고. (잠깐 침묵, 그가 스스로를 진정시킨다)
아직 내 아내야, 애비. 나한테 책임이 있다고.

애비

그래, 접근 금지로 뒤통수 치는 것도

책임지는 방법이지,

하지. 문 닫겠어.

애비가 문을 닫으려 하지만 하지가 막아선다.

하지

난 그녀를 사랑해.

애비

내가 해 줄 일이 없네.

애비가 조용히 문을 닫는다. 하지만 양쪽 모두 잠시 어둠 속에서
움직이지 않는다.

99. EXT.

모텔. 피츠버그 외곽. 낮.

테레즈가 옷을 갖춰 입고 여행 가방을 든 채 자신의 방을 나선다.
그녀는 옆방으로 가 조용히 문을 두드린다.

테레즈

캐롤?

대답이 없자 그녀가 문을 열어본다. 열려 있다.

100. INT.
모텔 방. 피츠버그 외곽. 낮.

테레즈가 방 안으로 고개를 들이밀자 욕실에서 물소리가 들린다. 캐롤의 가방은 침대 위에 열려 있고 그녀의 물건이 방에 널려있다.

캐롤 (O.S.)
테레즈, 당신이에요?

테레즈
네!

캐롤 (O.S.)
자기 내 빨간 니트 스웨터 좀 갖다 줄래요?
작은 가방에 있어요. 왼쪽 위에요.

테레즈
네.

테레즈는 가방을 찾아 연다. 그녀는 잠시 가방에 담긴 캐롤의 옷들을 살펴보곤, 실제로 만지고, 실크와 캐시미어의 촉감을 느끼고, 파우더 향을 맡아본다. 가방 아래쪽의 무언가가 그녀의 시선을 끈다. 스타킹 밑에서 번뜩이는 금속. 그녀가 스타킹을 치우자, 손잡이가 자개로 된 작은 권총이 보인다. 그녀가 망설이며 손을 뻗어 그것을 만지려는 순간, 캐롤이 욕실에서 그녀를 부른다.

O/S 캐롤
느림보 아가씨.

테레즈가 재빨리 손을 치우고 급히 캐롤의 옷가지를 바로 놓는다.

그녀가 빨간 스웨터를 집는다.

테레즈

찾았어요.

테레즈가 스웨터를 들고 가볍게 욕실 문을 두드린다. 문이 열리고, 수건을 두른 캐롤이 나타난다. 욕실 안에서 김이 새어 나온다. 테레즈는 잠시 머뭇거리다 스웨터를 건넨다.

캐롤

괜찮아요?

테레즈

네… 그냥… 갑자기 배가 고파서요.

캐롤

(문을 닫으며) 금방 나갈게요.

101. INT.
캐롤의 차. 도로. 낮.

캐롤은 차를 몰며 점점 더 얼어붙고 있는 바깥 풍경을 바라본다. 테레즈는 뒷좌석의 바구니에서 샌드위치를 꺼낸다. 캐롤의 여행 가방이 바구니 옆에 놓여있다. 테레즈는 다시 자리에 앉는다.

테레즈

안심이 돼요? 저랑 있으면?

캐롤

(웃으며)

볼수록 놀라운 사람이네요.

테레즈는 샌드위치를 먹으며 계속 생각에 잠겨있다.

테레즈
어때요?

캐롤이 그녀를 힐끗 본다. 테레즈가 마주 본다. 캐롤은 다시 도로에 집중한다.

캐롤
질문이 틀렸어요.
테레즈
하지만 말해줄 거죠, 무서운 게 있으면.
내가 도울 수 있게요.

캐롤이 미소 지으며 고개를 젓는다.

캐롤
난 두렵지 않아요, 테레즈.

테레즈가 그 말을 곱씹다가 캐롤을 바라본다. 도로를 내다보는 그녀의 얼굴을 차가운 겨울 햇살이 가로지른다.

102. EXT.
맥킨리 모텔. 오하이오 주 캔턴. 해 질 녘.

캐롤의 차가 작은 모텔 진입로에 멈춰선다. 윌리엄 맥킨리의 초상이 나무 간판에 크고 세밀하게 그려져 있다.

103. INT.
맥킨리 모텔. 오하이오 주 캔턴. 해 질 녘.

밝은색 목재로 된 모텔 사무실의 프런트. 몹시 고지식한 타입의
매니저가 캐롤의 체크인을 돕는다.

매니저
스테레오 라디오가 설치된 스탠더드 룸이 있고,
원하신다면 스위트룸도 저렴하게 드려요.

캐롤
(잠시 생각하고는) 스탠더드 룸 두 개 주세요.

테레즈
스위트룸 쓰면 어때요?

캐롤과 테레즈가 시선을 주고받는다.

테레즈 (CONT'D)
저렴하다니까...

104. EXT.
맥킨리 모텔. 오하이오 주 캔턴. 밤.

테레즈가 제빙기 앞에 서 있다. 스카프와 장갑, 코트로 싸맨 모습
이지만 토끼 슬리퍼를 신고 있다. 그녀는 덜덜 떨며 얼음통을 채
우려 애쓰고 있다.

젊은 남자
제가 잡아드릴까요?

테레즈가 고개를 든다. 안경을 낀, 키 크고 상냥한 인상의 남자가 옆에서 나타나 그녀가 얼음통을 채우는 동안 제빙기의 뚜껑을 잡아준다.

테레즈
고맙습니다. 너무 춥네요.

젊은 남자
너무 추워서 안경에 김 서렸어요.

테레즈
감사합니다. 잘 가요.

젊은 남자
들어가세요.

그가 모자를 까딱하고 테레즈는 방으로 돌아간다.

105. INT.
맥킨리 모텔 방. 밤.

이름값을 하듯 윌리엄 맥킨리와 부인의 사진이 액자에 담겨 트윈 침대 위에 걸려있다. 부채꼴 거울이 달린 화장대와 침대 협탁, 금박 알갱이가 박힌 테이블과 줄무늬 벽지 또한 스위트룸을 장식하고 있다. 테레즈의 휴대용 턴테이블에서 음악이 흘러나온다.(빌리 홀리데이의 "Easy Living" 1933년 버전) 캐롤이 화장대에 앉아 옆에 앉은 테레즈의 속눈썹에 조심스럽게 마스카라를 칠하고 있다.

캐롤
깜빡이지 말아요.
(잠시 후에) 이제 봐봐요.

그녀는 테레즈가 거울을 볼 수 있도록 돌려 앉힌다.

테레즈
립스틱도 바를래요.

캐롤이 립스틱을 골라주고, 바르는 모습을 지켜본다. 캐롤이 테레즈에게 티슈를 건넨다. 테레즈가 묻은 걸 닦아내고 휴지를 도로 준다.

테레즈 (CONT'D)
다음은요?

캐롤이 테레즈에게 향수병을 건넨다.

캐롤
맥박 뛰는 곳에만 살짝 발라주시겠습니까, 아가씨?

테레즈가 손목, 팔꿈치 안쪽, 그리고 목에 향수를 문지른다. 그녀가 캐롤을 돌아본다. 캐롤이 테레즈에게 손목을 내민다.

캐롤 (CONT'D)
나도 해줘요.

테레즈가 같은 곳에 향수를 발라준다. 캐롤이 눈을 감고 살짝 고개를 뒤로 젖힌다.

캐롤 (CONT'D)
정말 좋은데요. 맡아봐요.

잠깐 침묵했다가, 테레즈가 캐롤의 향기를 맡기 위해 몸을 기울인다.

106. INT.
맥킨리 모텔 방. 늦은 밤.

테레즈는 옆 침대에서 캐롤이 자는 모습을 지켜본다. 그녀는 아주 조심스럽게 침대에서 빠져나와 캐롤의 침대 가장자리에 앉아 그녀가 숨 쉬는 모습을 지켜본다. 그녀는 조용히 손가락을 들어 캐롤의 볼을 가볍게 쓸어본다. 캐롤은 잠든 채 돌아눕는다. 테레즈는 캐롤이 깨지 않도록 기다렸다가 자신의 침대로 돌아간다.

107. INT.
맥킨리 모텔 사무실. 아침.

짝이 맞지 않는 테이블과 의자 몇 개, 보잘것없는 커피와 주스, 롤빵이 놓인 간이 아침 식당에 테레즈가 앉아있다. 그녀는 커다란 검은색 가방을 든, 어제 제빙기 앞에서 만났던 젊은 남자를 알아본다. 그도 테레즈를 발견하고 활짝 미소를 짓는다.

젊은 남자
안녕하세요.
안 얼어죽으신 걸 보니 반가운데요.
테레즈
저도요.

테레즈가 반응하기도 전에 그는 컵을 내려놓고 의자를 뺀다. 테레즈는 캐롤이 지도를 들고 도착해 커피 쪽으로 가는 모습을 발견한다.

테레즈 (CONT'D)
안타깝지만 최고의 커피는 아니네요.

젊은 남자

따뜻하면 됐죠.

테레즈

가방엔 뭐가 들었어요?

젊은 남자

오. 잡화예요. 들고 다니면서 팔거든요.
적어도 팔아보려고는 하죠.

캐롤이 테레즈 맞은편으로 와 털썩 앉는다.

캐롤

커피가 엉망이네.

젊은 남자

(깜짝 놀라며)
죄송해요. (일어나려 한다)

캐롤

누구시죠?

테레즈

그냥 얘기 중이었어요.

젊은 남자

토미 터커라고 합니다.

테레즈

(손을 내밀며)
테레즈 벨리벳이에요. 이쪽은 캐롤 에어드.

토미 터커

(악수하며)
만나서 반갑습니다.

테레즈

터커 씨는 잡화를 파신대요.

테레즈는 가방을 가리키고, 캐롤은 유심히 본다.

캐롤

그렇군요.

토미 터커

(짧은 침묵 후) 정확히 그게 뭔지도 모르겠어요.
회사에서 그 단어를 쓰라고 해서요. 그래야 여성들에게 먹힌다고...
(잠깐 후에) 어제 휠링에 있는 형씨한테 구둣주걱을 하나 팔았죠.

테레즈

(그를 도우려 애쓰며)
립스틱도 있어요?

토미 터커

아뇨, 하지만 반짇고리는 있어요. (잠깐 후에) 필요 없으시군요.

캐롤은 정중하게 미소를 짓고, 다시 지도에 집중한다.

캐롤

(테레즈에게)
일찍 출발하면 시카고에 대여섯 시쯤 도착할 거예요.

토미 터커

저도 거기로 가는데요. 주 경계를 넘는 지름길이 있어요.
두 시간은 당기죠.

캐롤

두 시간이면 대단한데요?

테레즈

가다가 잡지나 사 갈까요?

토미 터커

(가방에 손을 뻗으며)
저한테 '필드&스트림', '내셔널 지오그래픽' 있어요.

테레즈

'포퓰러 포토그래피'는요?

토미 터커

(잠시 미소를 짓다가)

없어요. 물론이죠.

여기서도 뭐 하나 못 팔 운명이군요.

토미는 고개를 젓고 테레즈는 캐롤에게 살며시 미소를 보낸다. 음악이 커져 다음 장면들로 이어진다.

108. EXT.

탁 트인 도로. 잠시 후. 낮.

넓게 트인 도로가 펼쳐져 있고 캐롤의 차가 스쳐지나간다.

109. INT.

캐롤의 차. 잠시 후. 낮.

차 안에서 테레즈가 남는 건 시간과 옆에 있는 캐롤 뿐인 달콤한 지루함을 즐기고 있다. 그녀는 라디오 버튼을 살펴본다.

110. EXT.

도로변. 잠시 후. 낮.

코트와 스카프를 동여맨 캐롤과 테레즈가 도로 바로 옆 낮은 나뭇가지에 앉아 샌드위치와 보온병에 든 커피를 나눠 먹는다.

111. EXT.
드레이크 호텔. 시카고. 밤.

아른하게 빛나는 시카고 드레이크 호텔의 입구가 택시와 투숙객, 벨보이들로 북적인다. 여정에 지친 캐롤과 테레즈가 차를 세우고 빠르게 짐을 챙기기 시작한다.

112. INT.
드레이크 호텔 방. 잠시 후.

벨보이가 호화로운 방으로 캐롤과 테레즈의 짐을 들고 들어간다. 캐롤이 팁을 주며 인사하는 소리가 들리고, 우리는 테레즈를 따라가 그녀가 호텔의 호화로움과 처음 마주하는 순간을 본다. 캐롤이 침대에 쓰러진다.

캐롤
드디어 진짜 침대네. 천국 같아라.

테레즈는 마치 형사처럼 방을 탐문한다. 그녀가 허리를 굽혀 카펫을 쓸어본다.

테레즈
이 카펫... 감촉이 실크 같아요.
밟으면 안 될 것처럼.
이 가구들!

테레즈가 캐롤을 돌아보자... 그녀는 침대에서 잠들어 있다.

113. INT.
드레이크 호텔. 레스토랑. 잠시 후.

캐롤이 직원과 얘기하는 동안 테레즈는 바쁜 호텔 레스토랑을 살펴본다. 웨이터들이 활기차고 효율적으로 움직이고 있다.

캐롤
두 자리 부탁해요. 저녁 식사 할 거예요.

직원
투숙객이신가요?

캐롤
네, 방 번호가... (그녀가 열쇠를 찾는다)

테레즈
623호요. 에어드 부인.

직원
곧 준비해드리죠, 에어드 부인.

캐롤
고마워요.

테레즈가 카운터의 선물과 기념품들을 발견한다. 화려한 사탕 상자, 열쇠고리, 펜들. 그녀가 버지니아 햄 한 캔을 집어 든다.

테레즈
나이 든 여자분이 이거 좋아할까요?

캐롤
아마도요. 누구냐에 따라 다르겠지만.

테레즈
프랑켄베르크에서 같이 일하던 루비라는 분이 있는데...
보면 좀 우울했어요.

캐롤
왜요?

테레즈
늙고, 혼자고, 돈도 없고.
바보 같은 생각이죠, 알아요.

캐롤
다정한 것 같은데요. 보내요. 여기.

캐롤이 주문서와 연필을 집어 테레즈에게 건넨다.

직원
에어드 부인, 테이블 준비됐습니다.

캐롤
고마워요.

테레즈는 종이와 펜을 받아들고, 그들은 테이블로 안내받는다.

114. INT.
중앙 우체국. 전화 부스. 시카고. 낮.

캐롤이 공중전화에서 전화를 걸고 있다. 부스 밖으로 일반 우편을
받으러 줄을 서서 기다리는 테레즈가 보인다.

115. INT.
중앙 우체국. 시카고. 낮. 계속.

테레즈가 우편물을 받기 위해 줄을 서 있다. 그녀가 캐롤을 찾아
두리번거리다가 전화 부스에서 번호를 누르는 캐롤을 발견한다.

116. INT.
하지의 사무실. 뉴욕. 낮.

개인회선이 울린다. 그가 받는다.

하지
하지 에어드입니다. 여보세요.

전화에선 아무 말이 없다.

하지 (CONT'D)
캐롤. 할 만큼 했어.
젠장, 지금 대체 어디야? 여보세요?

117. INT.
중앙 우체국. 전화 부스. 시카고. 낮.

갑자기 대답을 잃은 캐롤이 잠시 부스에 머리를 기댔다가 조용히 전화를 끊는다.

118. INT.
중앙 우체국. 시카고. 낮.

캐롤이 우편 창구에서 테레즈와 합류한다. 테레즈는 편지 몇 통을 받는다.

캐롤
(편지들을 가리켜) 인기 많네요.

테레즈
다 리처드가 보낸 거예요.
(편지를 가방에 넣는다)
우편물 없으세요?

캐롤
여기 온 거 아무도 몰라요.

테레즈
아까... 전화하고 오셨어요?

캐롤
네? 아뇨. 화장실 다녀왔어요.

캐롤이 머리에 스카프를 두르며 밖으로 향한다. 테레즈는 잠시 그녀가 가는 걸 지켜보다가, 이윽고 따라간다.

119. EXT.
레이크 쇼어 드라이브. 시카고. 새해 전야. 낮.

캐롤과 테레즈가 타이어 펑크로 얼어붙은 길가에 서 있다. 캐롤이 가방을 뒤지다 고개를 들자 차 소리가 들린다.

캐롤
한 대 오네요.

테레즈가 다가오는 운전자를 향해 정지 신호를 보내려 애쓴다. 어두운 색의 42년식 크라이슬러 세단이 속도를 줄여 그들 앞에 멈춰선다. 차가 후진하자 보이는 운전자는 잡화 판매원, 토미 터커다.

테레즈

어머, 세상에. (캐롤에게) 누군지 봐요.

토미 터커

이게 누구야?

두 분이실지도 모른다고 생각했어요.

토미가 차에서 내려 여성들에게 다가온다. 그가 타이어를 살핀다.

토미 터커 (CONT'D)

네, 제대로 터졌네요.

바퀴 테두리가 멀쩡해야 할 텐데요.

캐롤

뭔가 끌리고 갈리는 느낌이 났는데...

토미 터커

그럼, 뭐. 제가 잭으로 들어올려 드릴까요?

테레즈

잭이... 잭이 없는 것 같아요.

토미 터커

잭이 없어요?

테레즈

(캐롤을 힐끗 보며) 집에 두고 온 것 같아요.

캐롤

얘기가 길어요.

테레즈

더 큰 문제는, 스페어타이어도 터진 것 같아요.

토미 터커

알았어요. 저한테 잭이 있어요.

제가 해드릴게요.

제 스페어를 쓰시죠.

테레즈
당신은 어떡하고요?

토미 터커
저는 여기서 집으로 가니까요.
집에 스페어 잔뜩 있어요.
(타이어를 살피며) 휠은 괜찮은 것 같군요.
그렇게 오래 걸리지 않을 겁니다.

테레즈
저 그게... 부탁이 하나 더 있는데...

토미 터커
뭔데요?

120. INT./EXT.
토미의 차. 레이크 쇼어 드라이브. 잠시 후. 낮.

앞 좌석에서 테레즈가 캐롤에게 보온병 커피를 따라준다. 라디오
가 살짝 켜져 있다. 앞쪽에서 토미가 후드 위로 몸을 굽히고 있
다. 오랜 작업으로 손이 까매졌다.

캐롤
배가 고파 죽을 것 같아.

테레즈
저도요.

캐롤
(그가 일하는 모습을 보며) 저 사람 만나서 다행이에요.

테레즈
그렇겠죠.

정적.

테레즈 (CONT'D)

온 거 후회하세요?

캐롤

이 여행요? 아뇨. 후회해요?

테레즈

아뇨.

캐롤의 차에 시동이 걸리는 소리에 그들이 고개를 든다. 토미가 운전석에서 기어 나와 먼지를 털며 다가온다. 캐롤과 테레즈가 차에서 내린다.

캐롤

대단해요!

토미 터커

다음 목적지까진 갈 겁니다. 하지만 정비소 가시는 게 좋아요.
호스를 갈아야 해요. 거기서도 똑같이 말할 겁니다.

테레즈

정말 감사해요.

캐롤

토미, 얼마 드리면 될까요?

토미 터커

오, 제발요. 아닙니다, 부인.

캐롤

타이어값이라도요.

토미 터커

아니에요. 스페어 컬렉션이 있다니까요.
직업 덕분이죠.

캐롤

다시 한번 고마워요. 전부 다요.

토미 터커

천만에요, 부인.

캐롤이 차에 시동을 걸고, 토미와 테레즈 사이에 잠깐의 침묵이 돈다.

토미 터커 (CONT'D)

새해 복 많이 받으시고요.

테레즈

아, 맞아요. 새해 복 많이 받으세요.

토미 터커

네, 오늘 좀 팔릴까 기대하고 있어요.
모자와 폭죽을 가득 챙겨 왔죠.

테레즈가 미소를 짓고 그가 뒤로 물러나 모자를 까딱하고 자기 차로 돌아간다. 그녀는 캐롤을 힐끗 보고 차에 탄다. 그리고 갑자기 강한 갈망이 밀려든다.

121. EXT.

아이오와 주 워털루. 이른 저녁.

워털루로 향하는 길, 캐롤은 넬슨에게 목이 졸리고 있는 나폴레옹을 만화로 그려놓은 광고판을 지난다. 그림 아래 화려한 글씨로 다음과 같이 적혀있다.

워털루 베컨스 방송국. 팝. *12,070*.

하늘은 무척 붉다.

122. INT.
객실. 조세핀 모텔. 밤.

어김없이 퀼트로 장식된 트윈 침대다. 라디오에서는 월도프 아스토리아 호텔에서 가이 롬바르도가 진행하는 새해 전야 방송이 나오고 있다. 자정이 다 됐다. 남은 햄 앤 치즈 샌드위치가 담긴, 이 빠진 쟁반 두어 개가 한쪽 침대에 놓여있다. 캐롤은 머리에 수건을 두르고 앉아 샴페인 잔에 맥주를 마시고 있다. 둘 다 가운을 입은 채, 캐롤은 테레즈가 화장대에 앉아 머리를 빗는 모습을 바라본다. 라디오에서는 새해 카운트다운이 시작되었다. 오. 사. 삼. 이. 일. 해피 뉴 이어! 그리고 롬바르도 특유의 "Auld Lang Syne"이 시작되지만, 둘 중 누구도 눈치채지 못한다. 대신 캐롤은 침대에서 일어나 테레즈의 손에서 빗을 가져가 천천히, 조심스럽게 그녀의 머리를 빗겨주기 시작한다. 빗질이 끝나자, 그녀는 빗을 내려놓고 테레즈가 자신과 마주 보도록 돌려 앉힌다.

캐롤
해피 뉴 이어.

테레즈
해피 뉴 이어.

그들은 조용히 서로를 마주 보고, 멀찍이서 들려오는 라디오 소리를 듣는다. 무슨 일이든 일어날 수 있는 순간이다. 테레즈가 처음으로 손을 뻗어 몹시 조심스럽게 캐롤의 손가락을 쓸어본다. 캐롤은 맞닿은 둘의 손끝을 내려다본다.

캐롤
하지와 난 새해 전야를 같이 보낸 적이 없어요.
늘 사업 때문에 행사가 있고, 늘 비위 맞춰야 할 손님들이 있었죠.

테레즈
전 늘 새해를 혼자 보냈어요.
많은 사람들 틈에서요.
(잠깐 후에) 올해는 혼자가 아니에요.

테레즈가 캐롤의 손을 몹시 조심스럽게 쥔다. 가이 롬바르도 밴드가
밝은 새해 음악을 연주하기 시작한다.

캐롤이 자신의 가운을 풀어 열리도록 두고 테레즈에게 자신의 벗
은 모습을 드러낸다. 너무 고요해서, 마치 방 안의 모든 숨이 멈
춘 것 같다. 테레즈가 일어나 그녀에게 다가가고, 캐롤이 양손으
로 부드럽게 테레즈의 얼굴을 감싼다. 그녀가 테레즈의 입술에 키
스한다. 느리고 서두르지 않는 키스는 둘 모두에게 경이롭다. 그
리고는 캐롤이 테레즈의 얼굴에서 손을 떼고, 머리의 타올을 푼다

캐롤
미안해요.
테레즈
뭐가요?
캐롤
앞으로 있을지도 모르는 모든 일에 대해.
테레즈
(잠깐 있다가)
침대로 데려가 줘요.

캐롤이 테레즈에게 다가서 그녀를 팔에 안고 침대로 이끈다.

캐롤
누워요.

테레즈가 눕는다. 캐롤은 자신의 가운을 바닥에 떨어뜨리고 침대 위에서 테레즈의 가운을 연다. 그녀의 젊은 아름다움을 느낀다.

캐롤 (CONT'D)
내 몸은 이랬던 적이 없어요.

그녀는 침대로 올라가 테레즈 위에 올라앉는다. 그녀가 테레즈의 얼굴과 머리를 쓰다듬는다. 테레즈는 눈을 감지만, 자기도 모르게 떨기 시작한다.

캐롤 (CONT'D)
떨고 있네요.

캐롤은 몸을 숙여 이마에 가볍게 키스하고, 침대 옆으로 손을 뻗어 불을 끄려고 한다. 테레즈가 막는다.

테레즈
끄지 말아요.
당신을 보고 싶어요.

캐롤은 고개를 끄덕이고 테레즈의 몸을 스쳐 내려가 배꼽 아래서 멈춘다. 그녀는 테레즈의 배꼽에 키스하고, 입으로 그녀의 몸을 훑어 내려간다. 테레즈는 천장을 올려다보며 긴장으로 떨리는 몸을 진정시키려 애쓴다. 캐롤이 위로 올라와 테레즈의 젖꼭지를 혀로 건드린다. 테레즈가 살짝 신음한다. 그녀가 캐롤을 위로 당기고 그들은 간절히, 열정적으로 키스한다. 테레즈가 눈을 떠 아주 가까이에서 캐롤의 얼굴을 바라보고, 미소 짓는다.

캐롤

(속삭임)

나의 천사. 하늘에서 떨어진 사람.

그들은 처음으로 사랑을 나누기 시작한다.

FADE TO BLACK

123. INT.

객실. 조세핀 모텔. 낮.

드리워진 커튼을 통해 아침 햇살이 테레즈에게 비친다. 아직 침대에 누워 짐을 싸고 있는 캐롤을 보고 있다. 하지만 문득, 오늘, 세상의 모든 것이 완전히 달라졌다.

테레즈

여기가 어디라고요?

캐롤

여기요? 워털루. 끔찍하지 않아요?

124. INT.

사무실. 조세핀 모텔. 잠시 후.

황량한 방에 빈 맥주병과 싸구려 새해 장식이 널려있다. 캐롤은 직원을 찾으려 돌아보다 벨을 울린다. 나이 든 여자가 뒷방에서 발을 끌며 나온다. 고깔모자를 쓰고 있다.

나이 든 여자

13번 방이에요?

캐롤

체크아웃 하려고요.

나이 든 여자

어젯밤에 전보 왔어요.

나이 든 여자가 발을 끌며 나갔다가 전보를 들고 돌아온다. 그녀가 그것을 캐롤에게 건넨다. 캐롤이 전보를 연다. 읽는다. 좋은 소식이 아니다.

캐롤

언제 도착했죠?

나이 든 여자

내가 시계요? 일찍. 일곱 신가. 아홉 시나.

125. EXT.
조세핀 모텔. 아침.

캐롤이 사무실을 박차고 나가 드문드문 쌓인 잔설을 지나쳐 테레즈가 짐을 싣고 있는 차로 달려간다. 캐롤은 운전석을 열어 뭔가를 찾다 실패하고 문을 세게 닫는다. 그녀는 그들이 방금 비운 객실로 달려가 문을 열었다가 거의 바로 다시 나와 문을 쾅 닫는다. 그녀는 분노했다.

테레즈

캐롤! 왜 이래요!

캐롤

(테레즈를 보며)

내 가방 어딨어요?

테레즈

캐롤, 잠깐만요. 무슨 일이에요?

캐롤

(그녀가 폭발한다)

빌어먹을 여행 가방 어딨어!

캐롤이 트렁크로 달려가며 테레즈를 휙 스쳐 지나간다. 가방을 찾은 그녀는 그것을 열고 뒤지기 시작한다. 그녀가 권총을 찾았다. 테레즈는 가로막으려 애쓴다.

테레즈

그걸로 뭘 하려고요? 캐롤, 무슨 일이에요?!

캐롤이 테레즈를 밀치고 지나간다.

126. EXT. / INT.
객실. 조세핀 모텔. 아침.

캐롤이 자신들이 묵었던 옆방 문을 발로 찬다.

캐롤

문 열어! 내 말 들려? 당장 열어!

테레즈가 캐롤에게 달려온다.

테레즈

캐롤, 무섭게 왜 이래요. 이러면...

캐롤

비켜요, 테레즈.

캐롤이 문으로 손을 뻗어 잠기지 않은 것을 확인한다. 그녀는 문을 발로 차서 열고 총을 겨눈다. 토미 터커가 옷을 입고 있다. 바지를 반쯤 올린 채, 모자는 쓰고 있다. 그가 안경을 집어 들고 코끝에 얹는다. 흐트러진 침대 위에 그의 큰 검은색 가방이 열려 있어 그 안의 정교한 오픈릴식 녹음기와 세련된 마이크들이 드러나 있다. 테레즈는 상황을 이해하지 못한 채 그 장비들을 바라본다. 캐롤은 공이치기를 당기고 토미의 머리를 정확히 겨냥한 채 사격 자세를 취한다.

캐롤 (CONT'D)
(토미에게)
테이프 어딨어, 이 개새끼야.

그녀가 방으로 들어가 토미를 겨눈 채 가방과 장비를 잡아 뜯기 시작한다. 토미는 침착하게 계속해서 옷을 입는다.

캐롤 (CONT'D)
하지한테 얼마 받았어?
내가 두 배, 세 배, 원하는 대로 주지.

토미 터커
돕고 싶지만, 부인,
테이프는 이미 남편분께 가고 있어요.

캐롤
그럴 리가 없어.

토미 터커
(으쓱하며)
전 효율적이기로 유명하답니다,
에어드 부인.

긴장된 침묵. 캐롤이 토미에게 다가선다. 그는 여전히 무척 침착하다. 하지만 내내 그녀를 주시하고 있다. 캐롤이 더 가까이 가서 그의 머리에 총을 겨눈다.

캐롤
거짓말이 아닌 걸 어떻게 알지?

토미 터커
(잠깐 있다) 알 수 없죠, 부인.

캐롤은 긴장을 더해 검지를 방아쇠에 놓는다. 그리곤 갑자기 녹음 장비를 향해 돌아서 그것을 겨누고 방아쇠를 당긴다. 하지만 총은 딸깍 소리를 낼 뿐이다. 그녀는 총을 장비에 던져버린다. 문간을 맴돌던 테레즈가 캐롤에게 다가선다.

테레즈
캐롤...

지치고 얼이 빠진 캐롤이 테레즈에게 전보를 건네고 객실 밖으로 나간다. 그녀가 난간에 털썩 쓰러진다.

테레즈는 여전히 몹시 침착한 토미와 시선을 교환한다. 테레즈는 총을 되찾아 밖의 캐롤에게 간다. 캐롤은 담뱃불을 붙이고 고속도로를 내다본다. 테레즈는 전보를 읽고, 여전히 옷을 반만 입은 채 방 안에 있는 토미를 노려본다.

테레즈 (CONT'D)
(토미에게) 어떻게 이런 짓을.

토미 터커
난 프로예요, 벨리벳 양. 악감정은 없어요.

침묵. 담배를 피우는 캐롤. 테레즈가 역겨움으로 토미에게 고개를 저어 보인다. 이 모든 일이 일어났다는 사실을 믿고 싶지 않다. 토미가 테레즈에게 모자를 까딱해 보인다.

캐롤
여기서 나가요.

127. EXT.
골목. 워털루. 잠시 후.

테레즈가 권총과 전보를 들고 골목에서 쓰레기통을 찾는다. 그녀는 뚜껑을 열고 권총을 던져 넣지만 위에 걸리고 만다. 그녀는 한 손으로 권총을 쑤셔넣고 전보로 최대한 손을 닦는다. 그녀는 다시 뚜껑을 닫고 모퉁이를 꺾어 황급히 도로로 나간다. 캐롤이 공중전화를 쓰고 있다. 테레즈는 본능적으로 물러서지만, 캐롤과 애비의 통화를 듣게 된다.

캐롤
... 라과디아로 가는 제일 빠른 비행편이 내일 오후야...
애비, 어쩌면 좋아. 못 버티겠어...

테레즈는 지금 캐롤을 안아줄 수 있길 간절히 바란다. 하지만 그럴 수 없다는 것을 알고 있다.

128. INT.
캐롤의 차. 이른 저녁.

캐롤이 조용히 차를 몰아 시카고에 접근한다. 테레즈는 담배를 피운다. 긴장이 터질듯하다.

캐롤
담배 피우지 말아요. 기침하잖아요.
(침묵) 무슨 생각 해요?...
이걸 하루에 몇 번이나 물어보는지 알아요?

테레즈
미안해요. 무슨 생각 하냐고요?
내가 너무 이기적이어서
이렇게...

캐롤
이러지 말아요. 몰랐잖아요.
어떻게 알았겠어요?

테레즈
내가 거절했어야 하는데 난 거절해본 적이 없어요.
그리고 이기적으로 다 받기만 해요.
내가 뭘 원하는지 난 몰라요.
무조건 알았다고만 하는데 어떻게 알겠어요?

테레즈가 조용히 울기 시작한다. 캐롤이 얼어붙은 눈 더미 옆으로 갓길에 차를 세운다. 그녀는 자신을 마주 보도록 테레즈를 돌려 앉힌다. 눈물을 닦아준다. 캐롤과 테레즈는 조용히, 흔들림 없이 서로를 바라본다.

캐롤
난 당신이 기꺼이 준 걸 받은 거예요.

짧은 침묵. 캐롤이 테레즈의 볼을 손가락으로 쓸어내린다. 그녀는 운전대로 돌아간다. 차에 다시 시동이 걸린다.

캐롤 (CONT'D)
당신 잘못이 아니에요, 테레즈. 알았죠?

더 깊은 정적. 상황을 개선하는 데 실패한 캐롤이 빠르게 속력을 내 고속도로로 들어선다.

129. INT.
드레이크 호텔. 시카고. 밤.

캐롤이 트윈 침대 중 하나에 앉아 담배를 피우며 애비와의 통화를 마무리한다. 테레즈가 욕실에서 나와 불을 끈다. 그녀는 잠시 어둠 속에 서 있다가 다른 침대로 올라간다.

캐롤
고마워... 오, 알잖아.
완전히 지쳤어. 지겨워...
그래야지. 아냐... 내일 얘기해.
고마워, 그럴게. 잘 자.

그녀가 전화를 끊고 잠시 고개를 숙인다. 그리고 슬픔에 찬 다정함으로 테레즈를 돌아본다.

캐롤 (CONT'D)
거기서 잘 필요 없어요.

정적. 테레즈가 일어나 캐롤의 침대로 간다. 캐롤이 팔다리로 테레즈를 감싸고 눈과 입술에 부드럽게 키스한다. 테레즈는 그녀를 빤히 바라보다가 키스로 답한다. 길게 이어지는, 깊은 키스.

130. INT.
드레이크 호텔. 시카고. 아침.

한 줄기 햇살이 테레즈의 얼굴에 비친다. 그녀는 눈을 감은 채 캐롤을 찾지만 그녀는 거기 없다. 욕실에서도 아무 소리가 들리지 않는다. 그녀는 고개를 들어 시계를 본다. 아침 8시다. 테레즈가 침대 위에 일어나 앉는다. 거기, 반쯤 어두운 방에 놓인 의자에 애비가 앉아있다. 그녀는 담배를 피우고 있다. 그리고 테레즈는 일순간 캐롤의 부재가 무엇을 의미하는지 깨닫는다. 정적.

> **테레즈**
> 갔어요?
> **애비**
> 아침 일찍.
> **테레즈**
> 다시 와요?
> **애비**
> 아뇨.

날카로운 침묵.

> **테레즈**
> 다 내 잘못이에요.
> **애비**
> 말도 안 되는 소리.

애비가 담배를 끄고 일어나 커튼을 걷는다. 밝고 차가운 햇살이 방으로 흘러든다.

가야 해요.

131. INT.
시카고 외곽 도로변 식당. 낮.

테레즈가 창밖을 응시한다. 식사에는 손도 안 댔다.

애비
뭐라도 먹어요.
(답이 없다) 맘대로 해요.

애비가 테레즈의 그릇을 당겨 마저 먹기 시작한다. 테레즈가 그녀를 돌아본다.

테레즈
왜 저를 싫어하세요? 당신한텐 잘못한 게 없는데.

짧은 침묵. 애비는 뭔가 말하려 하다가 한 번 더 생각한다. 그녀가 테레즈에게 몸을 기울인다.

애비
당신이 미워서 괴로워하는 걸 보려고
나라의 반을 날아와 태우고 가겠어요?

테레즈
내가 아니라 캐롤을 위해서잖아요.

애비
(짧은 침묵 후에)
그건... 정말 그렇게 믿는다면
당신은 내가 생각한 만큼 똑똑하지 않군요.

161

테레즈는 이 말을 받아들이고, 고개를 들어 애비를 본다. 정적.

테레즈
캐롤하고는... 어떻게 된 거예요?

애비
그건 전혀 달라요.
난 열 살 때부터 캐롤과 알고 지냈어요.
(긴 침묵 후)
가구점 할 때였어요. 하루는 늦게까지 있었죠.
엄마 집 근처에서 내 포드가 망가졌어요.
우린 둘 다 깨어있으려고 노력했지만...
내 옛날 트윈 침대에서 안고 자게 됐죠. 그게 끝이었어요...
한동안은. 그러다 변했죠. 변하게 마련이에요.
누구의 잘못도 아니에요. (잠깐 쉬고) 그래서...

그녀가 자신의 가방을 열어 안을 뒤진다. 그녀는 봉투 하나를 꺼내 든다.

애비 (CONT'D)
여기. 걔가...

테레즈
뭔데요?

애비가 편지를 건넨다.

132. EXT.
도로변 식당. 잠시 후.

넓고 외로운 프레임으로, 밖에 나와 편지를 열어보는 테레즈가 보인다. 그녀가 편지를 읽자 캐롤의 목소리가 들린다.

캐롤 (V.O.)

내 사랑. 세상에 우연이란 건 없어요.
하지는 어떻게든 찾아냈을 거예요.
모든 건 원점으로 돌아오게 마련이에요.
차라리 일찍 이렇게 된 걸 감사히 생각해요.
이렇게 말하는 내가 모질다고 생각하겠지만,
당신을 납득시킬 말이 없어요.

애비가 나오는 모습이 보이고, 테레즈는 계속해서 편지를 읽는다. 애비는 차에 타고 시동을 건다. 부드럽고 어두운 음악이 시작된다.

133. INT.
다른 모텔. 밤.

애비는 화장실에서 옷가지를 빨고 있다. 열린 문틈으로 울다 진이 빠져 표정 없이 침대에 앉아있는 테레즈가 그녀의 눈에 들어온다.

캐롤 (V.O.) (CONT'D)

당신이 젊기 때문에 해결책과 설명을 찾는 거라고 말해도
화내지 말아줘요. 언젠간 이해하게 될 거예요.

134. INT./EXT.
시골길. 낮.

애비가 도로에서 벗어나 작은 수풀과 녹아가는 눈더미 옆에 차를 세운다. 테레즈가 차에서 뛰어내려 토하기 전에 나무 사이로 몸을 숨기려 한다. 애비는 차에 남아 멀리서 테레즈를 바라보며 담배에 불을 붙인다.

그때가 오면, 영원한 일출을 맞이하는 아침의 하늘처럼,
그곳에서 당신과 우리 앞에 펼쳐진 삶을 반겨줄게요.

135. INT.
캐롤의 차. 밤.

운전대를 잡은 애비가 룸미러로 뒷좌석에 몸을 뻗고 잠든 테레즈를
힐끗 본다. 멀리서 지나가는 불빛들이 그녀의 휴식을 비춘다.

캐롤 (V.O.) (CONT'D)

하지만 그때까진 어떠한 연락도 있어선 안 돼요.
난 할 일이 많아요. 그리고, 내 사랑, 당신은 훨씬 많겠죠.
당신의 행복을 위해선 뭐든 할 거라는 걸 믿어줘요.
그래서 내가 할 수 있는 유일한 일을 해요.
당신을 놓아줄게요.

136. INT.
테레즈의 아파트. 뉴욕. 낮.

코트 차림에 여행 가방을 든 테레즈가 집 한복판에 서 있다. 자신
의 물건으로 가득하지만 다른 나라처럼 느껴진다. 벽에 붙은 사진도
전부 다른 사람이 찍은 것 같다.

137. INT.
테레즈의 아파트. 같은 날 밤.

테레즈는 붉은 조명을 받으며 싱크대로 몸을 굽힌다. 짧게 담배를

한 모금 빨고 재떨이에 끈다. 네거티브 필름들이 찬장 아래, 현상액
이 담긴 쟁반들 위로 걸려있다. 그녀는 확대기로 한 장의 사진을 찾
아내 표시하고, 초점을 맞춘다. 그녀는 현상 작업을 계속한다.

마침내, 그녀는 사진이 현상액 속에서 천천히 나타나는 것을 본
다. 여기저기 그림자가 지며 모양이 잡힌다. 캐롤이다. 등을 대고
누워 헝클어진 시트 아래 몸을 구부리고 있다. 한 손이 섬세하게
놓여있다.

138. INT.
테레즈의 아파트 건물. 복도. 늦은 밤.

테레즈가 어둑어둑한 계단을 살금살금 내려온다. 그녀는 소리 없
이 수화기를 들고 다이얼을 바라본다. 전화를 끊는다. 이번에는
한 번에 수화기를 들고 번호를 누른다. 그녀는 얼어붙은 채 서 있
다. 긴 신호음. 정적. 다시 긴 신호음. 그리고 누군가 전화를 받는
다. 하지만 아무 소리도 들리지 않는다.

아무 말도 없다. 테레즈는 얼어붙었다.

테레즈
여보세요?(짧은 침묵)
캐롤?

이어지는 정적이 마치 대답 같다. 테레즈는 소중한 것인 양 수화
기를 들고 있다.

139. INT.
캐롤의 집. 부엌. 밤.

전화의 반대편, 캐롤이 어둠 속에 조용히 서 있다. 그녀는 뭔가 말할 듯 움직였다가 말하지 않는다. 수화기 버튼을 살짝 스쳤다 누르는 캐롤의 손가락이 보인다.

140. INT.
테레즈의 아파트 건물. 복도 전화기. 밤.

캐롤이 전화 끊는 소리를 듣고도 빈 수화기를 들고 있는 테레즈가 익스트림 클로즈업으로 보인다.

테레즈
(기도하듯이) 보고 싶어요.
보고 싶어요.

141. INT.
하지 부모의 집. 뉴저지. 낮.

하지, 캐롤, 제니퍼와 존이 모든 것이 명백하게 제자리에 갖춰진 평일 점심을 함께하고 있다. 아이젠하워의 취임식이 진행되는 소리가 들리고, 거실의 텔레비전 세트가 언뜻 보인다.

제니퍼
으깬 감자 더 먹을래, 캐롤?
캐롤
네, 감사합니다. 맛있어요.

캐롤이 감자가 담긴 그릇으로 손을 뻗지만 하지가 먼저 들고 캐롤에게 떠준다. 분위기는 정중하지만, 편안함과는 거리가 멀다.

캐롤 (CONT'D)
고마워. (잠깐 있다) 제가 알기로는... 아마...
체스터랑 마지가 올 때가 된 줄 알았는데요. 린디랑...

제니퍼
마지가 먼저 먹으라더구나.
기다리지 말고.

하지
(캐롤에게) 곧 도착할 거야.

캐롤이 하지의 작은 친절에 고마워한다.

존
하지한테 듣기로는 의사가 아주 잘 봐준다더구나, 캐롤.

제니퍼
당연히 잘 봐주겠지. 아주 비싼 의사잖아.

캐롤
의사가 아니고 심리치료사예요.

제니퍼
평판 좋은 분이란다.

존
(하지에게) 네 삼촌처럼 예일 출신이지.

캐롤
(아주 희미하게 날을 세우며)
그렇다고 의사가 되는 건 아니에요.

하지가 약간 눈치를 준다.

캐롤 (CONT'D)
마음에 들어요. 무척요.
큰 도움이 되고 있어요.

제니퍼와 존이 침묵 속에서 식사를 계속한다.

142. INT.
하지 부모의 집. 잠시 후.

캐롤이 거실 창가에 혼자 앉아 멍하니 밖을 보고 있다. 그녀는 제니
퍼가 차를 들고 다가오는 소리에 정신을 차린다. 캐롤이 돌아본다.

캐롤
감사하지만 전 정말 괜찮아요.

제니퍼
네 신경을 진정시켜 줄 거다.

제니퍼가 작은 테이블에 차를 내려놓고 캐롤의 어깨에 손을 얹는
다. 바로 그때 진입로에 차가 들어오는 소리가 들린다.

캐롤
왔나 봐요.

캐롤이 일어서, 잽싸게 머리를 가다듬고 현관으로 향한다.

제니퍼
잠깐만, 아가야.

캐롤이 멈춰서 돌아선다. 제니퍼가 캐롤의 옷깃을 바로잡아준다.

캐롤은 평정을 유지하려 애쓰고, 제니퍼에게서 돌아서 문으로 향한다.

143. EXT.
하지 부모의 집. 늦은 오후/이른 저녁. 계속.

캐롤이 고모와 고모부의 손을 잡고 걸어오는 린디를 맞으러 달려간다. 엄마를 본 린디는 그들의 손을 놓고 캐롤에게 달려온다. 그들이 만난다. 캐롤은 무릎을 꿇고 린디를 자신의 품에 안는다. 그녀는 아이를 꼭, 필사적으로 끌어안는다.

캐롤
오, 아가... 우리 아기...

144. INT.
테레즈의 아파트. 오후.

대니가 와서 집을 새로 칠하는 테레즈를 돕고 있다. 테레즈는 사다리에 올라가 천장 근처의 몰딩을 칠하고 있고, 대니가 그 밑에 있다. 라디오가 나오고(조지 시어링의 "Lullaby of Birdland"), 대니는 눈썹의 땀을 닦는 테레즈를 본다. 꽤 오랜만에 만났다.

대니
좀 쉬자. 맥주 좀 가져올게.

테레즈
좋아.

대니는 주방에서 맥주와 병따개를 가져온다. 테레즈는 더 많은 사진을 인화했다. 대부분이 여행에서 캐롤과 찍은 사진이다. 대니는 보지 않을 수 없다.

뒤에서 인기척을 느낀 그가 돌아본다. 테레즈다.

                          대니
                  이 사진들 진짜 좋은데.
            누군지 몰라도 정말 잘 담았어.
                          테레즈
                    그냥 습작이야.

테레즈가 방을 가로질러 와 사진들을 주우며 그곳을 치우기 시작한다.

                          대니
            꼭 사진 정리해서 포트폴리오 만들어.
            말만 하면 타임스에 소개해줄게.
                  사무직은 늘 있거든.

테레즈가 고개를 젓고 사진을 다른 방으로 가져가 서랍장에 넣어
둔다.

                     대니 (CONT'D)
                  저 여자랑 다녀온 거지?
                          테레즈
                          응.
                          대니
                    무슨 일 있었어?
                          테레즈
            별일 없었어. 그게, 설명하기가...

대니
(잠시 후에)
그때 내가 키스하려고 해서 이러는 거야?
그것 때문이라면, 생각할 것도 없어.
내 말은, 두려워할 건...

테레즈
난 두렵지 않아.

테레즈는 자신의 말에 잠시 다른 기억이 떠오른다. 그녀는 다시 그를 바라본다.

테레즈 (CONT'D)
해 지기 전에 마무리하자, 알았지?

대니는 어깨를 으쓱하고 다시 일을 시작한다.

대니
그래도 포트폴리오는 만들어야 해.

145. INT.
테레즈의 아파트. 늦은 밤.

테레즈가 부엌 바닥에서 사진을 분류하고 있고, 그 옆의 재떨이에서 담배가 타고 있다. 그녀는 사진을 차곡차곡 쌓느라 분주하다. 우리는 그녀의 예전 사진들을 본다. 풍경, 정물, 건축물의 디테일들. 그리고 최근의 사진도 본다. 길에서 놀고 있는 아이들, 쇼핑 카트를 끄는 늙은 여인, 도시의 얼굴들. 사실상 최근에 찍은 모든 사진이 사람들을 그리고 있다. 사진 더미 맨 밑에서 그녀는 크리스마스트리를 사는 캐롤의 사진을 발견한다. 그녀는 그 사진을 한참 들여다보다 빼낸다.

146. EXT.
센트럴 파크. 며칠 뒤. 오후.

회색의 비 오는 날이다. 우산을 쓴 행인들. 리처드가 테레즈의 물건을 상자에 담아왔다.

> **리처드**
> 다 들어있어. (잠깐 후에)
> 엄마가 네 블라우스들 빨고 다려서 넣어놨어.

> **테레즈**
> 감사하다고 전해줘.

> **리처드**
> 직접 말해.

> **테레즈**
> 리처드...

> **리처드**
> 내가 뭐라고 하길 바래?
> 넌... 편지 한 통 안 썼잖아.

테레즈가 시선을 돌린다.

> **테레즈**
> 쓰려고 했어. 그냥... 뭐라고 해야 할지 몰랐어.

그녀가 그의 어깨를 만지려고 하지만 그가 몸을 피한다.

리처드
제발 나 만지지 마. (그가 고개를 젓는다)
우리가 가졌던...
네가 했던... 모든 걸 던져버린 거야.

테레즈
우리가 뭘 했는데?

리처드
고맙다. 그것 참...

테레즈
아니, 말해봐!

리처드
네가 말해봐, 테리.
너 날 조금이라도 사랑하긴 했니?

그들이 서로를 마주 본다. 하지만 테레즈는 그에게 이렇게 상처를 줄 수 없다. 그녀가 몸을 돌린다.

테레즈
제발, 제발 날 미워하지마.
난 여전히... 나야.
원래랑 똑같은 사람이라고.

리처드
아니. 아냐, 알았어?
넌 이제 다른 사람이야.
그리고 난 못해. 너 용서 못 해.
(잠시 후) 잘 가, 테리.

리처드가 떠나기 전 짧은 정적이 흐른다. 테레즈는 움직이지 않는다.

147. INT.
캐롤의 집. 해 질 녘.

캐롤이 계단 위 자리에 앉아 밤 풍경을 내다보고 있다. 아래층에서 요란하게 스탈린의 죽음을 보도하는 라디오 소리가 들린다.

라디오 소리가 줄어들고 캐롤이 아래를 내려다본다. 애비가 커피 두 잔을 들고 계단을 오르기 시작한다. 캐롤이 그녀를 돕기 위해 내려간다.

> **애비**
> 앉아 있어.

> **캐롤**
> 걱정은.

그녀가 애비에게 자신의 컵을 받아 앉아 있던 곳으로 다시 올라간다. 애비는 그녀 아래 계단에 앉는다. 애비는 집 밖에서도 캐롤의 상심을 알아볼 수 있을 것 같다.

> **캐롤 (CONT'D)**
> 이렇게는 못 버티겠어, 애비. 내가 뭘 더 하겠어?
> 말도 안 되는 점심을 몇 번이나 더 먹어야...
> 매일 린디 없이 집으로 돌아오기 위해서? 이러려고?

> **애비**
> 테레즈는?

> **캐롤**
> 테레즈가 왜?

> **애비**
> 들은 거 있어?

캐롤

아니. 아니. 전화 온 것도 한 달이 넘었고. 그 뒤론 없어.
나도 정말... (하지만 말을 멈췄다가, 이윽고)
무슨 소식이라도 들은 거야?

애비

테레즈한테? 아니.
(잠깐 있다) 근데 타임스에 취직한 것 같더라. 잘 됐어.

캐롤

테레즈한테 말할 걸 그랬어.
기다리라고.

애비가 손을 뻗어 캐롤의 팔에 얹는다. 난데없이 헤드라이트 한 쌍이 창문을 밝히고, 그들은 가슴이 내려앉는다. 캐롤은 돌아앉고 애비는 깜짝 놀라 일어난다. 그들이 시선을 교환한다. 누가 있나? 무슨 일이 생긴 건가? 이윽고 헤드라이트가 사라진다.

캐롤 (CONT'D)

누가 내 집 앞에서 차를 돌리는 거야?

애비

가야겠어.

캐롤

그럴 필요 없...

애비

있어.

애비가 캐롤의 손을 쥔다. 용기를 주는 것이다.
그리고 그들은 함께 계단을 내려간다.

148. EXT.
허드슨 부두. 뉴욕. 밤.

대니와 테레즈가 부두에 앉아 강 건너 뉴저지를 바라보고 있다.

대니
전화해줘서 고마워. 도통 볼 수가 없잖아!
근무 시간 좋은 그럴듯한 직장도 생기고.
네가 퇴근하면 내가 출근하잖아.

테레즈
커다란 현상액 병을 들고
하루 종일 뛰어다니는 게 그럴듯한 것 같진 않은데.
그래도 정말 좋긴 해. 알지?

대니
그럼. (잠깐 쉬고) 야, 나 무슨 일 있었게?
모르겠어? 전혀?

테레즈가 미소를 지으며 고개를 젓는다.

대니 (CONT'D)
여자를 만났어. 루이즈라고.
녹색 눈에다가, 완전 영화 백과사전이고,
제일 좋은 점은 걔가 날 진짜 멋지다고 생각하는 거지.

테레즈
(그녀가 기뻐한다) 말도 안 돼.

대니
(그녀가 기뻐해서 기쁘다)
맞아. (잠시 후에) 너만 괜찮으면 한 번 같이 보자.
영화도 보고.

테레즈
좋은 생각인데? 만나보고 싶어. (침묵) 혹시 너...
리처드 본 적 있어?

대니
만났어. (잠깐 쉬고) 얘기하고 싶어 하는 것 같아, 아마도.
근데... 모르겠어. 마음이 안 좋아.
하지만 끼어들고 싶지는...

그가 말을 멈추고, 테레즈를 힐끗 봤다가, 시선을 돌린다. 테레즈의
생각이 멈추고 짧은 어둠이 그녀 위로 쏟아진 것 같다.

테레즈
맞다고 느껴지는 것들을 쓰고.
나머진 버리고.

대니
(웃으며) 갑자기 무슨 소리야?

테레즈
캐롤이 그렇게 말한 적 있어.

대니
(짧은 침묵 후에) 너한테...
그렇게 한 거야?

테레즈가 애를 쓴다...

테레즈
돌아갈 수는... 없어. 슬픔과 수치를 감추고,
사람들을 실망시키고, 스스로한테 실망하던 때로.
울고, 숨어서... 말도 안 되는 생각만 계속하던 때로는.
전화기를 계속 쳐다보고 있으면 혹시...

아니면 그냥 기차를 타고 가서 숨어 있을까,
그런 생각들 말야. 그 모든 게 돌아올지도 모른다고. (침묵)
그러다 어느 날 전화기는 그냥 전화기가 되고,
뉴저지행 기차도 그냥 기차가 돼.
울고 숨는 걸 멈추는 거야.
그리고 나면 뭔가를 쓰고 내다 버릴 수
있다는 걸 알게 되는 거지.

강이 검은 셀로판지처럼 이어진다.

149. EXT.
41번가 브로드웨이 교차로. 아침.

지나가는 차들과 차창 너머로 출근을 위해 말쑥한 정장을 차려입
은 테레즈가 보인다. 통근자들 사이를 서둘러 가로질러 뉴욕타임
스 건물로 들어간다. 그녀의 머리와 옷에서 드러나는 세련됨과 성
숙함에서, 우리는 어쩔 수 없이 캐롤을 연상하게 된다.

150. EXT.
택시. 타임스퀘어. 아침.

프레드 헤임즈의 사무소로 향하던 캐롤이 창밖을 내다보다 문득
테레즈를 발견한다. 신호가 바뀌고 택시가 움직이기 시작한다. 테
레즈가 멀리서 나타났다 사라졌다 한다. 캐롤은 반사광 너머로 고
개를 돌려 바라본다.

151. INT.
엘리베이터. 제리 릭스 변호사 사무소. 낮.

엘리베이터 안에서 뒤돌아있는 캐롤의 모습이 보인다. 그녀가 돌아서고, 잠깐 밖을 보다가 문을 나서 복도를 걸어간다. 안에 모여 있던 하지, 릭스, 프레드 헤임즈와 속기사가 모두 그녀가 도착하는 모습을 돌아본다.

152. INT.
제리 릭스 변호사 사무소. 낮. 잠시 후.

모두 회의실 탁자에 둘러앉아 있다.

제리 릭스
(헛기침) 사안의 중대성과 증거의 명확성으로
미루어볼 때, 저희 고객이 좋은 결과를 기대할 이유가
충분하다고 봅니다.

프레드 헤임즈
서두르지 맙시다, 제리.
심리치료사에 따르면 제 고객은...
겨울의 그 사건으로부터 훌륭하게 회복했고 양육 능력이
충분합니다. 테레즈 벨리벳과는 완전히 연락을 끊었습니다.
또한 새들브룩 심리치료사 두 분의 진술도 있습니다.
남편이 촉발한 일련의 사건들이 의뢰인을 신경쇠약으로
몰고 가 이러한... 문제의 행동을 보이게 되었다는 명백한
소견을 밝히고 있습니다.

하지
(자신의 변호사를 보고 도움을 청하며)
말도 안 되는 소리!
진심입니까?

제리 릭스
좋아요, 프레드. 이렇게 나올 거라면...

프레드 헤임즈

나아가, 이 테이프를 입수하고 녹음한 방식을 볼 때,
증거 채택도 거부되리라 확신...

제리 릭스

알았어요, 알았어요.
먼저 이 진술부터 봅시다. 그리고...

캐롤

(그의 말을 자르며)
프레드, 제발요. 그렇게... 제가 얘기해도 될까요?

정적과 함께 방 안의 모든 사람이 캐롤을 쳐다본다.

캐롤 (CONT'D)

테이프 내용의 진위를 부인하진 않을 거예요.

프레드 헤임즈

(속기사에게 신호하며) 비공식 진술이에요.

캐롤

이것도 기록하세요.

짧은 침묵이 흐르고 제리가 속기사에게 계속하라고 고개를 끄덕
인다. 캐롤이 물을 한 잔 따른다.

캐롤 (CONT'D)

저는... 원래... 의무와 희생에 대해서 이야기하고 싶었어요.
그 이야기를... (잠깐 쉬고) 하지만 여기 오니까...
제가 뭘 믿는지... 심지어 내가 뭘 알고 있는지도... 모르겠네요.
딸을 보고 싶다는 거... 목소리를 듣고 싶다는 것 밖에는요.
항상 아이 곁에 있고 싶다는...

그녀가 말을 멈추고 눈물을 참는다. 우는 건 스스로 용납할 수 없다.
정신을 차리고 하지에게 똑바로 눈을 맞추고 직접 이야기한다.

캐롤 (CONT'D)
하지, 난 당신이... 행복했으면 해.
내가 행복을 주지 못했고, 내가 당신을 실망시켰어,
우리 둘 다 서로에게 좀 더... 줄 수 있었는데 말야.
(잠깐 쉬고) 하지만 우린 서로에게 린디를 줬어.
세상에서 가장 아름답고... 커다란... 선물을. (잠깐 쉬고)
그런데 왜 서로 뺏어가려고 이 많은 시간을 낭비해?
(잠깐 쉬고) 테레즈와 있었던 일은...내가 원했던 거야.
부인하거나 후회하지 않을 거야.

하지가 고개를 숙인다.

캐롤 (CONT'D)
... 하지만 우리가 아이의 인생을 망치려 하고 있다는 사실은
후회해, 통탄스러워. 하지... 우리 둘 다 책임이 있어.
우리가... 바로 잡자. (잠깐 쉬고)
저는 하지가 영구적인 양육권을 가졌으면 해요.

갑자기 시작된 혼돈 속에서 하지의 시선은 캐롤에게 고정되어 있다.

프레드 헤임즈
잠깐 쉬시죠. 의뢰인과
상의하고 다시 시작...

제리 릭스
아뇨, 프레드. 당신의 의뢰인이
분명하게 자신의 의견을...

캐롤
아뇨, 프레드. 말하게 둬요. 왜냐하면... 지금 막으면...
말할 수가... 없을....

캐롤이 일어나 진정을 찾기 위해 테이블 밖으로 걸어나간다. 그녀
가 말을 계속하기 전까지 정적이 흐른다.

캐롤 (CONT'D)

난 순교자가 아니에요.

날 위한 최선이 뭔지도... 모르겠어요.

하지만 내 딸을 위한 최선이 뭔지는 알아요,

뼛속 깊이 느낄 수 있어요.

그녀가 다시 돌아서 서성이며 하지에게 말한다.

캐롤 (CONT'D)

(잠깐 쉬고) 방문은 할 수 있어야 해, 하지.

감독이 있어도 상관없지만 정기적이어야 돼.(잠깐 쉬고)

린디와 함께 있기 위해서는 무슨 짓이든 하려 했던 때도 있었어.

하지만 날 부정하며 산다면... 린디에게...

우리에게 무슨 도움이 되겠어?

린디는... 기쁨을 누릴 자격이 있어.

나조차 기쁨이 뭔지 모른다면 어떻게 기쁨을 줄 수 있겠어.

그녀가 물 한 잔을 더 따른다.

캐롤 (CONT'D)

이게 내 제안이야. 더는 못 물러나. 협상 못... 안 할 거야.

거절하면 법정으로 가서 추하게 되겠지.

우린 추한 사람들 아니잖아, 하지.

갑자기 떨기 시작한 캐롤은 돌아서 방을 나선다. 프레드가 그녀의
이름을 부르며 쫓아 달려가는 사이, 하지는 일어서서 그녀가 가는
모습을 바라본다.

153. EXT.
커피숍. 7번가. 낮.

반사광 너머로 테이블에 앉아 뭔가를 쓰고 있는 캐롤이 보인다. 그녀 옆에 커피 한 주전자와 담배가 타고 있는 재떨이가 놓여있다. 그녀가 서명한다. 봉투에 넣고 봉한 뒤, 물건을 챙기기 시작한다.

154. INT.
뉴욕타임스. 사진부. 낮.

큰 테이블에 모인 사진 편집자들과의 미팅에서 테레즈가 흑백 프린트들을 정리하고 있다. 담배연기가 자욱하다. 창문을 통해 사무원과 이야기를 나누는 배달부가 보인다. 사무원이 회의실 안의 테레즈를 발견하고 봉투를 가져간다.

사무원
벨리벳.

테레즈가 고개를 들어 보고 급하게 문간의 사무원에게 달려온다. 그가 봉투를 건넨다.

사무원 (CONT'D)
직접 배달온 거야. 죽이네.

테레즈가 봉투를 받아 테이블로 돌아간다. 힐끗 내려다본 그녀가 캐롤의 손글씨를 알아본다.

155. INT.
뉴욕타임스. 사진부. 잠시 후.

테레즈가 자기 자리에서 라벨을 만들고 있다. 책상 위에 편지가
펼쳐져 있다. 그녀가 타자를 멈추고 편지를 본다. 그녀가 그것을
집어 잠깐 들고 있다가 구겨서 책상 서랍에 던져 넣는다. 그녀는
다시 타자를 친다.

Dearest Therese,
   Would you possibly be free to
meet me for tea this evening?
Ritz Tower Hotel, Friday, April 17,
6:30 pm.
I understand if you cannot.

                    Carol

156. INT.
리츠 타워 호텔. 밤.

캐롤이 도로 쪽 입구를 통해 호텔에 들어서 스카프를 풀고 머리를 매만진다. 공중전화로 다가가 부스로 들어간다. 그녀가 번호를 누르고 짧은 통화를 하는 모습이 보인다. 전화를 끊고 컴팩트를 꺼내 파우더를 두드린다. 그녀가 부스에서 나와 갑자기 멈춘다.

157. INT.
리츠 타워 호텔. 바/라운지. 밤.

거기, 홀 반대편 구석 테이블에 테레즈가 나타났다. 훨씬 성숙하고 안정된 모습의 테레즈, 웨이터에게 감사를 표하는 테레즈, 자리에 앉는 테레즈... 캐롤이 숨을 고르고 홀을 가로지른다.

테레즈가 고개를 들어 그녀를 본다.

캐롤
올 줄 몰랐어요. 만나줘서 고마워요.
테레즈
그런 말 마세요.

캐롤이 테레즈 맞은편에 자리를 잡고 코트를 치운다.

캐롤
내가 미워요? 테레즈?
테레즈
아뇨. 어떻게 당신을 미워하겠어요?

캐롤
그랬을 텐데요, 아니에요? 한동안은?

테레즈가 고개를 떨군다. 그녀가 차를 따른다.

캐롤 (CONT'D)
잘하고 있단 얘기 애비한테 들었어요.
얼마나 기뻤는지 모를 거예요. (잠깐 후에)
보기에도 정말 근사해요. 갑자기 만개한 꽃처럼.
나한테서 벗어나면 이렇게 되는 건가요?

테레즈
(빠르게 대답한다) 아뇨.

테레즈는 너무 황급히 대답한 것을 후회하며 인상을 쓰고, 고개를 떨군다. 다시 고개를 들자 그녀를 빤히 바라보고 있는 캐롤이 보인다.

테레즈 (CONT'D)
왜요?

캐롤
아니에요. 그냥 그 날에 대해 생각하고 있었어요.
인형 코너.

테레즈
항상 궁금했어요...
왜 나한테 왔어요?

캐롤
미친 듯이 바쁘지 않은 유일한 사람이었으니까요.
(잠깐 쉬고) 실망했어요?

테레즈가 아니라고 고개를 젓는다. 캐롤이 기억에 미소를 짓고 담배에 불을 붙인다.

캐롤 (CONT'D)
하지와 난 집을 팔기로 했어요.
매디슨 가에 아파트를 얻었어요.
믿기 힘들겠지만 직장도 구했고요.
4번가에 있는 가구점에서 바이어로 일하기로 했어요.
우리 집안에 목수가 있었던 게 분명해요.

테레즈가 캐롤에게 미소를 지어 보인다. 조금 긴장이 풀렸다.

테레즈
린디는 만났어요?

캐롤
(잠깐 있다가) 한두 번. 변호사 사무소에서요.
아이가 무릎에 앉아서...
(테레즈의 시선을 마주 보며) 하지와 지낼 거예요,
지금으로선 그게 옳아요.

캐롤은 아픔을 감출 수 없지만, 노력한다.

캐롤 (CONT'D)
아무튼, 아파트가 크고 좋아요,
둘이 써도 될 정도로.
같이 살면 좋겠는데 아무래도 거절하겠죠?
(잠깐 있다) 그래 줄래요?

숨이 멈춘다.

테레즈

아뇨. 안 될 것 같아요.

캐롤

당신이... 결정할 일이죠.

테레즈

네.

정적.

캐롤

오크룸에서 9시에 가구점 사람들을 만나기로 했어요.
저녁 같이 하고 싶으면... 혹시 마음 바뀌면...
그 사람들 좋아할 것 같아요.
(잠깐 쉬고) 그럼... 이게 다예요.

캐롤이 담배를 끄고 테이블에 놓인 자신의 라이터를 물끄러미 바라본다.

캐롤 (CONT'D)

사랑해요.

정적. 테레즈는 뭔가 말하고 싶지만, 할 수 없다.

O/S 잭 태프트

테레즈? 너야?

분위기가 깨진다. 테레즈가 고개를 들고 인사가 들린 쪽을 돌아본다.
홀 중간쯤, 바 근처에 있는 잭 태프트다.

잭
이게 누구야!
(걸어오기 시작하며)
어쩐지 아는 사람 같더라고.

테레즈는 잭이 걸어오는 모습을 본다. 그녀가 캐롤에게 짧은 시선을 보낸다. 캐롤은 테이블을 내려다보며, 어쩔 줄 모르고, 나약하게... 테레즈가 잭에게 인사하기 위해 일어난다.

테레즈
잭.
잭
이렇게 반가울 데가! 본 지 몇 달 됐지?
테레즈
응.

캐롤이 담뱃불을 붙인다. 테레즈가 그녀를 돌아보고, 그들은 테레즈가 입을 떼기 전까지 잠시 서로를 바라본다.

테레즈 (CONT'D)
잭, 이쪽은 캐롤 에어드 씨.

잭이 손을 내민다. 캐롤이 맞잡고 악수한다.

잭
반갑습니다.
캐롤
저도요.

캐롤은 다시 담배를 피우며 생각에 빠져든다.

잭
저기, 테드 그레이가 오기로 했어.
필이 파티 열어서 가기로 했거든. 너도 가지?

테레즈
응, 난 그냥 좀 있다 가려고...
(캐롤을 바라보며)

캐롤
둘이 가요.

잭
같이 가실래요?

캐롤
아뇨, 아뇨. (테레즈에게) 어차피 저녁 식사 전에
연락할 데가 있어서. 나도 일어나야 해요.

테레즈
정말 괜찮아요?

캐롤
그럼요.

테레즈
(잭에게) 그럼 가는 길에 나도 태워줘.

캐롤은 테레즈를 향해 한 걸음 내딛지만, 더는 나아가지 않는다.

캐롤
둘이 즐거운 밤 보내요. 반가웠어요, 잭.

잭
반가웠습니다.

그리고 캐롤은 간다. 테레즈는 움직이지 않는다. 뒤돌아 캐롤이 떠나는 것을 쳐다보지 않는다.

잭 (CONT'D)
그럼 이 녀석들 오는 중인지 확인하고 올게.
금방 올게.

그리고 잭이 전화 부스로 향한다. 테레즈는 잠시 그대로 있다가 몸을 돌린다. 바 너머를 둘러보며 캐롤을 찾지만, 그녀는 없다. 로비 입구로 가 로비를 둘러본다. 하지만 캐롤은 영영 떠났다. 그리고 이제야, 캐롤을 가게 내버려 두었다는 사실이 테레즈를 덮친다. 테레즈는 약간 어지러움을 느끼며 여자 화장실로 향한다.

158. INT.
리츠 타워 호텔. 여자화장실. 밤.

테레즈가 물을 틀어놓은 채 세면대 앞에 서 있다. 그녀는 차마 거울을 바라보기도 힘들다. 그녀가 얼굴에 찬물을 끼얹는다.

159. INT./EXT.
택시. 뉴욕. 밤.

테레즈가 여전히 생각에 잠겨 창밖을 본다. 앞에서는 잭이 웨스트 빌리지의 아파트 빌딩을 가리키고 ("여기, 여기, 여기요!") 택시가 끼익 멈춘다. 잭이 택시비를 내는 동안 모두 차에서 내린다. 테레즈는 자기도 모르게 필 맥엘로이가 사는 건물 계단을 오르고 있다. 그들 위로 열린 창문에서 헝클어진 머리를 한 필 맥엘로이가 몸을 내민다.

####### 필
시간 맞춰 왔네, 벨리벳.
인사라도 해줘, 오랜만인데!
####### 테레즈
안녕, 필, 미안. 내가 좀…

필의 동생, 대니가 그의 옆에서 창 밖으로 몸을 내민다.

####### 대니
테레즈잖아! 올라와!
(그녀의 말을 듣고) 뭐라고?
####### 테레즈
아니야! 위에 맥주 있겠지?
아니면 와인.
####### 일행
아니면 맥주!

누군가 현관을 열어주고 일행이 들어간다. 거슬리는 버저 소리에
테레즈가 얼굴을 찌푸린다. 그녀가 계단을 올라감에 따라 회상으
로 이어진다.

160. INT.
필의 아파트. 밤.

몇몇 커플들이 춤을 추는 와중에 여기에도 "You Belong To Me"
가 흐르고 있다. 그들 가운데는 리처드와 그가 꼭 붙든 젊고 예쁜
여자도 있다. 테레즈는 맥주를 마시며 거실 바로 앞 복도에서 그들
을 지켜본다.

리처드는 테레즈의 시선을 알아차리고 잠시 신경을 곤두세웠다가 파트너를 돌려 테레즈의 시야를 벗어난다. 테레즈는 고개를 숙이고 가방에서 담배를 꺼내 불을 붙인다. 그녀는 어두운 머리의 매력적인 여성이 거실 반대편에서 자신을 빤히 바라보는 것을 발견한다. 테레즈는 그녀와 잠시 시선을 마주하지만, 얼굴이 붉어지는 걸 느끼고 다시 고개를 숙인다. 다시 고개를 들자 그 여성은 사라졌다. 테레즈는 잠시 서성이다 옆방으로 시선을 던진다. 대니와 그의 여자친구 루이즈가 느리게 춤을 추고 있다. 새로 사랑에 빠진 사람들이 흔히 그렇듯, 그들은 거의 움직이지 않고 서로를 안고 있다.

161. INT.
필의 아파트. 밤.

파티는 정점에 이르렀다. 사람도, 웃음소리도, 취기도 한창이다. 테레즈는 창가에 서 있고 그 옆에서 몇 사람이 어울리고 있다. 그중에는 아까 테레즈가 쳐다보던 여자, 제네비에브 칸트렐도 있다. 테레즈는 눈에 띄지 않게 제네비에브를 쳐다보느라 애쓰고, 한 남자가 대화를 주도한다.

남자 손님
글쎄다. 만나려면 만나.
그리니치 빌리지 시늉만 하고 다니는 애야.
(다른 사람에게) 어디 가, 데이브? 더 있다 가.

제네비에브
필의 친구죠?

테레즈
네, 대니도 알아요.

제네비에브
어떻게 아느냐고 안 물어봐요?

테레즈
여기 대부분이 필의 친구 아니에요?

제네비에브가 인정한다는 듯 미소 짓는다. 테레즈도 긴장을 풀고, 추파를 즐기며 미소 짓는다.

제네비에브
필이 좋게 보는 이유를 알겠네요.

테레즈
그래요?

제네비에브
그럼요. 아주 잘 알겠어요.

테레즈
정말요? 어떤 건데요?

제네비에브
(그녀를 유심히 바라보다)
엄청난... 잠재력이요.

제네비에브가 테레즈에게 맥주 한 병을 건네고, 그들은 병을 부딪쳐 건배한다. 테레즈가 미소 짓는다. 그녀는 제네비에브의 관심을 즐기지만 시선을 계속 마주볼 수 없다. 그 대담함이 테레즈를 그 순간으로부터, 그 파티로부터 먼 곳으로 데려간다.

162. INT.
필의 아파트. 밤.

테레즈가 욕조 가장자리에 걸터앉아 열린 창문에서 들어오는 바깥공기를 마시고 있다. 파티가 이어지고 사람들이 즐거워하는 소리가 들리지만, 그녀는 다시 합류할 준비가 안 됐다. 문을 빠르게 두드리는 소리가 들린다.

테레즈
죄송해요. 잠시만요.

테레즈가 정신을 차리고 일어나 문을 연다. 제네비에브다. 그녀는 코트에 스카프 차림이다.

테레즈 (CONT'D)
오. 가시는군요.

제네비에브
가려던 참이에요. 나 보고 싶어 할 거예요?

테레즈는 이번엔 시선을 피하지 않는다. 제네비에브가 가까이 다가와 그녀의 귀에 속삭인다.

제네비에브 (CONT'D)
테레즈, 이따 우리 집에서 '사적인' 모임이 있어요.
아무나 들이는 게 아니에요. 무슨 뜻인지 알겠어요?
(잠깐 쉬고) 빨리, 손 줘봐요.

테레즈
손금 봐주게요?

제네비에브
행운을 주려고요.

제네비에브가 테레즈의 손을 잡고 손바닥에 자신의 주소를 적어준다.

제네비에브 (CONT'D)
잊어버리지 않게요.

제네비에브가 떠난다. 테레즈는 문으로 향하는 그녀의 뒷모습을
지켜본다.

163. INT.
필의 아파트. 밤.

테레즈가 필의 손님들 사이를 이리저리 빠져나가 현관으로 향한
다. 누구도 그녀를 알아차리지 못하고 흠뻑 자기 시간에 취해있어
방향을 잡기 쉽지 않다. 마침내 현관에 다다른 테레즈는 인사를
빼먹은 사람이 있는지 뒤를 돌아본다. 대니와 루이즈가 무릎을 안
고 바닥에 앉아 작은 흑백 텔레비전으로 집중해서 영화를 보고 있
다. 주변의 소음도 들리지 않는 듯하다. 대니가 작은 수첩에 가끔
뭔가를 끄적인다. 이곳의 모든 게 꼭 맞는 자리에 있는 것 같다.
적어도 다른 사람들에겐 그렇다. 테레즈가 문을 빠져나간다.

164. EXT.
그리니치 빌리지 거리. 밤.

테레즈가 자갈이 깔린 운치 있는 길을 걷는다. 사랑스러운 밤이다.
다양한 행인들이 길을 거닌다. 오직 테레즈만이 웃지 않고, 이 사랑
스러운 밤에 곁에 있어 줄 사람이 없는 것처럼 보인다. 그녀가 손
바닥을 들여다보고 주소를 확인한 뒤 계속 걷는다. 주소에 다다를
즈음 그녀는 팔짱을 끼고 서로를 지탱하며 마주 오는 노부부를 발
견한다. 그들은 영원히 함께해온 것 같다. 테레즈를 지나치며 부인
은 남편에게 기대고, 남편은 테레즈에게 모자를 까딱해 보인다.

근처 아파트에서 날카로운 웃음소리가 들린다. 테레즈가 돌아보자 제네비에브 칸트렐이 뒤돌아 창밖으로 등을 기울이고 있다. 그녀가 손에 든 병에서 거리로 샴페인이 쏟아진다. 제네비에브가 안에 있는 누군가에게 손짓하자 다른 여자가 창가로 나와 제네비에브와 키스하기 시작한다. 테레즈는 그들의 키스를 잠시 지켜본다. 믿을 수 없이 섹시하다. 제네비에브가 여자를 아파트 안으로 이끌어 들어가고, 그들 뒤로 창문이 닫힌다. 문득 밤이 아주 조용해진다. 테레즈는 노부부가 지나간 방향을 돌아본다. 그녀는 제네비에브를 지나쳐 무언가 다른 것을 향해 걷기 시작한다. 그녀는 점점 더 빨리, 더 빠르게 걷는다. 낯선 이들의 세상을 스쳐 지나며.

165. INT.
오크룸. 플라자 호텔. 밤.

숨이 찬 테레즈가 레스토랑에 들어온다. 웨이터가 그녀를 막는다.

웨이터
예약하셨습니까?
테레즈
누굴 좀 찾아왔어요.
웨이터
죄송합니다만, 예약 없이는...

그녀가 웨이터를 지나쳐 북적이는 실내를 둘러본다. 없다. 이윽고, 테레즈의 시야 끝에, 처음에는 거의 알아볼 수 없는 곳에, 뒤쪽에 있는 테이블에, 웃으며 고개를 젖히는 금발 여성이 보인다. 그녀는 빛과 연기에 묻힌 듯, 혹은 보호받고 있는 듯하다. 캐롤이다. 테레즈가 언제나 봐온, 그리고 언제나 볼 바로 그 캐롤. 슬로우 모션으로 마치 꿈처럼, 혹은 단 하나의 유일한 기억처럼, 분명하지만 규정하기 어려운 모습으로 그녀가 보인다. 테레즈가 그녀를 향해 움직인다.

캐롤이 와인잔을 들어 입술에 갖다 대며 몸을 약간 돌리자, 테레즈가 보인다. 그녀는 놀라지 않는다. 우리는 그녀의 얼굴이 풀어지는 것을 볼 수 있다.

테레즈가 계속 다가온다. 캐롤이 타는 듯한 눈으로 미소 지으며 지켜본다. 테레즈가 거의 다 왔다.

THE END

CAROL

By PHYLLIS NAGY

Based on the novel 'THE PRICE OF SALT' by PATRICIA HIGHSMITH

FINAL - FOR PUBLISHED VERSIONS

1. EXT.
NYC SUBWAY STATION. APRIL 1953. NIGHT.

Out of the darkness, the screeching moan of an arriving
train. A dark swarm of bodies file out of the LEXINGTON and
59TH ST STATION. We descend upon the crowd, singling out a
young man in coat and hat, JACK TAFT, late 20s, who weaves
through the line of COMMUTERS, some opening umbrellas to
the patchy skies. JACK buys an evening paper at a newsstand
and makes his way across 59th.

2. EXT. / INT.
RITZ TOWER HOTEL. NIGHT.

JACK enters the hotel and we follow him as he walks through
the lobby to the bar. JACK easily finds a stool, nods to
the BARTENDER and tosses him the newspaper. The BARTENDER
points to a bottle of Dewars and JACK gives him a thumbs up.
He scans the cocktail lounge adjacent to the bar - not much
activity in there, either: a FEW TABLES OF BUSINESSMEN
getting drunk, an ELDERLY COUPLE, TWO WOMEN tucked away in
a corner table. JACK checks his watch and the BARTENDER
sets down his drink.

JACK

Not much going on for a Friday.

BARTENDER

It's early yet.

JACK downs his scotch, slides his empty glass over to the BARTENDER, taps out a rhythm along the edge of the bar.

JACK

Say Cal, make it a double, would you?
And one for yourself. I gotta make a call.

JACK gets up.

3. INT.
RITZ TOWER HOTEL. BAR/LOUNGE. NIGHT.

JACK makes his way through the lounge on his way to a
telephone booth. He takes another look at the TWO WOMEN
tucked away in the corner, deep in conversation, and thinks
he recognizes one of them. He begins approaching them.

JACK

Therese? Is that you?

THERESE, the younger of the women, turns to look at JACK.

JACK (CONT'D)

What do you know!
(he starts over)
I'm saying to myself, I know that girl.

It seems to take her a split second to react, to stand and greet JACK
with a short hug.

THERESE

Jack.

> JACK

Gee it's great to see you, Therese.
It's been, well, months.

> THERESE

Months.

The OTHER WOMAN at the table lights a cigarette. THERESE glances at her, and they hold a brief, tense look before THERESE remembers her manners.

> THERESE (CONT'D)

Jack, this is Carol Aird.

JACK holds out his hand. CAROL shakes it.

> JACK

Pleased to meet you.

> CAROL

Likewise.

CAROL retreats back to her own thoughts, smokes.

> JACK

Hey, Ted Gray's meeting me here and a bunch of us are heading down
to Phil's party. You're going aren't you?

> THERESE

Well - yes. I just planned to get
there a little... (looking to Carol)

CAROL

You should go ahead.

JACK

You coming along?

CAROL

No, no. (to THERESE) I should make a few calls
before dinner, anyway.
I should really run.

THERESE

You sure?

CAROL

Of course.

THERESE

(to JACK)
Well… it would be great to
catch a ride.

CAROL takes a step towards THERESE, but no more.

CAROL

You two have a wonderful night.
Nice meeting you, Jack.

JACK

Nice meeting you.

And she's gone. THERESE doesn't move, doesn't turn around
to watch CAROL leave.

JACK (CONT'D)

Alright, well let me go make sure the loaf is on his way.
Back in a flash.

JACK takes off. A beat before THERESE turns and scans the
bar and beyond for CAROL. But she's gone.

4. INT.
RITZ TOWER HOTEL. BAR
LOUNGE. MOMENTS LATER

JACK, through the glass of the phone-booth door, is
finishing his call. He emerges from the booth, passing the
bar on the way, where the bartender spots him, and holds up
the paper.

JACK

Keep it!

JACK returns to where he left THERESE but stops when he doesn't
see her, glancing around. He's about to ask a WAITER if he's seen
her when he spots THERESE emerging from the ladies lounge. She
looks pallid.

JACK (CONT'D)

There you are! Thought you ditched me.
You alright? He said he'd meet us out front.

5. INT./EXT.
NYC TAXI CAB. NIGHT.

THERESE sits against the window in the back of a taxi,
crowded with JACK and OTHER 20-somethings, MALE AND FEMALE,
all involved in animated conversation we can't hear.
The taxi stops for a light and THERESE catches sight of an
ELEGANT COUPLE, arm-in-arm at the corner, crossing the
avenue as the light changes. A strong gust of wind gives the woman
some difficulty as she tries to knot a green silk scarf around her head.
As they reach the sidewalk, she turns back to face the avenue,
and then recedes, swallowed by swirling lights and reflections.
CUT TO:

6. FLASHBACK: DECEMBER, 1952
BRIEF SHOTS
(INT. TOY DEPARTMENT – FRANKENBERG'S)

A toy train whizzes by the faces of miniature pedestrians
on a department store display. CAROL AIRD, seen from a
distance, in winter coat, stands watching. She wears a
green silk scarf over her head, loosely tied.
She turns, smiles.

7. INT.
THERESE'S APARTMENT. EAST 50'S.
DECEMBER 1952. MORNING.

An alarm blares over the sleeping face of THERESE BELIVET,
huddled under covers. THERESE doesn't stir though the alarm

continues. Finally, THERESE, in one skilled maneuver,
pushes herself up and out of bed, still cocooned within the
blankets. She finds the alarm clock and shuts it off. She
looks at the alarm clock. It reads 7.00 A.M.

THERESE moves through her morning rituals: she throws
open her window shades, moves on to a small gas stove, strikes
a match and lights the stove to take the chill off, moves on
to the kitchen sink set in one corner of the room, which
doubles as a partial home darkroom - developer and fixer
trays stacked to the side of the sink, an Argus C3 camera
from the late 1930s set on a shelf above the sink, along with
a collection of red or amber light bulbs and photo paper.

The room is sparsely furnished, and much of the wall space
is taken up with THERESE'S B&W photos,
mostly NY CITY STREET SCENES and URBAN LANDSCAPES.
THERESE is brushing her teeth when the doorbell rings.
Once. Twice. Three times.
She sheds her blankets and goes to the window, opens it, leans out.

8. EXT.
THERESE'S APARTMENT BUILDING. CONTINUOUS.

THERESE'S boyfriend, RICHARD SEMCO, looks up at her from
the street, striding his bicycle. He's well-bundled in scarf and hat.

THERESE

I like your scribbles.

RICHARD looks around to the street behind him covered in children's chalk scribblings.

RICHARD

Yeah - I've been busy! (grinning at her):
I don't know how you look a million bucks first thing
in the morning.

THERESE

I won't be a minute.

9. EXT
CENTRAL PARK. NY CITY. MORNING.

RICHARD rides THERESE to work through the park.
She sits with her arms wrapped around his hips while he stands
pumping away at the pedals.

RICHARD

So I got the schedules. In the mail.
You listening to me?

THERESE

I'm listening!
You got the schedules.

RICHARD

And there are two sailings to
France in June, one in July.

THERESE

Wow.

RICHARD

So whaddya think?

> THERESE

I think…
I think it's so cold I can't think straight.

> RICHARD

Oh yeah? Well let's get you warmed up.

RICHARD accelerates. THERESE laughs, holds on tighter.
RICHARD begins to sing: "I love Paris in the… summer- time!"
as they speed away.

10. EXT.
FRANKENBERG'S DEPARTMENT STORE. MORNING.

Outside the employee's entrance, RICHARD and THERESE stand
in a longish line of MOSTLY YOUNG STAFF waiting to begin
their work day. Everyone looks exactly the same: a lot cold,
a little Soviet-factory-worker glum.

> RICHARD

Anyway she wants to make it for you
so there's no use fighting it,
once she gets an idea in her head…
She's just going crazy with no girls in the family but Esther-

A SECURITY GUARD has opened the door and the line has begun
to move.

Upon entering, each employee is handed a Santa Cap, which
they dutifully put on. RICHARD reaches the door, takes his cap,
wordlessly puts it on, moves inside. He holds out a cap to THERESE.

212

SECURITY GUARD

Compliments of the season
from the management.

THERESE takes her cap, doesn't put it on, moves inside.

RICHARD

I gotta open the floor.

11. INT.
FRANKENBERG'S. EMPLOYEE CAFETERIA.
MORNING.

From a table in the corner, THERESE sips at a cup of coffee and watches a sea of Santa-capped and uniform-smocked STAFF move wordlessly along the breakfast line, accepting gooey eggs and cups of coffee. THERESE looks down at a Frankenberg's employee handbook. We glimpse bits and pieces of information: ...2 weeks vacation after 5 years, 4 weeks vacation after 15 years... full pension, benefits..." She turns a page: "Are YOU Frankenberg Material?"

It's too depressing to take in. THERESE slips the handbook back into her purse and removes a copy of Joyce's "Portrait of the Artist as a Young Man." But just as she settles in ROBERTA WALLS, an officious supervisor in bright red harlequin glasses, swoops by THERESE planting a Santa cap firmly onto her head.

ROBERTA WALLS

You're needed upstairs, Miss
Belivet. Make it snappy.

213

12. INT.
FRANKENBERG'S. DOLL STOCK ROOM. MORNING.

THERESE, surrounded by rows of identical Christmas dolls,
counts stock. THERESE watches a very middle-aged, wheezing
employee, RUBY ROBICHEK, struggle with carrying seven or
eight large boxes across the stock room floor. RUBY can't
see in front of her, and as she attempts to peer around the edge
of the boxes, most of the boxes tumble out of RUBY'S arms
and onto the floor.
THERESE quickly determines she's the only help on the floor,
and goes to assist RUBY, who has great difficulty in kneeling
to pick up the boxes.

> THERESE
>
> (kneels to help RUBY)
> Please- let me help.

RUBY is grateful to avoid kneeling, and places each box THERESE
hands to her on the display counter.

> RUBY ROBICHEK
>
> Thanks an awful lot, honey.
> I keep telling them upstairs we need more
> stock boys come the holidays,
> but they haven't listened in 18 years.

> THERESE
>
> You've been here 18 years?

> RUBY ROBICHEK
>
> Oh, sure. And when you're here long enough,
> you'll get inventive with juggling boxes, like me.

THERESE

I'm just a temporary.
For the holiday.

RUBY ROBICHEK

(shrugs)
I said that once.

13. INT.
FRANKENBERG'S. TOY DEPARTMENT. MORNING.

Just before opening: a surreal calm and silence. THERESE,
in Santa cap, and makeshift bandage, stands beside an elaborate
model train set. She flips a switch and the train set comes
to life - the tiny lights, the tinny whir of the engine
as the train chugs its way along the track. A LOUD BUZZER
sounds. Behind THERESE, we can see the analogue lift indicator
start to move: 5th floor, 4th floor, 3rd floor… as the lift descends
to accept its first load of daily customers and a voice bellows
from the intercom:

STORE ANNOUNCER (V.O.)

Good morning, Happy Holidays and welcome,
shoppers, to Frankenberg's.
Be sure to take advantage of our Congratulations
Ike and Mamie Inaugural Early Bird special
in our Beds and Bedding Department on the second floor.
(MORE)

STORE ANNOUNCER (V.O.) (CONT'D)

And on your way there, you won't want to miss
our brand new General Electric television and
stereophonic display on the first floor,

just past the haberdashery.

Behind THERESE, the lift doors open and all at once THERESE
is swallowed up by the rush of MANAGERS, STAFF and
CUSTOMERS.

14. INT.
FRANKENBERG'S. DOLL DEPARTMENT. LATER

THERESE sits behind a display case full of dolls. She tries
to make herself invisible while she surreptitiously reads
her book. The department is full of MOTHERS buying
Christmas gifts for their children. THERESE'S reading is
interrupted by a SHARP WAILING. She looks up to see a
TODDLER throwing a tantrum and an EMBARRASSED MOM
trying to get the situation under control. Just then,
ROBERTA WALLS bustles through the department, sees THERESE,
points to THERESE'S head - where's the Santa cap? ROBERTA
WALLS seems to say without saying it. THERESE hurriedly stashes
her book into her handbag and pulls out the cap. She tries to
hide the bloodstains. ROBERTA WALLS nods to THERESE and
moves on.

THERESE settles back down, bored. A CUSTOMER looks
expectantly to THERESE; THERESE pretends she doesn't see
the CUSTOMER and ducks down to her handbag to retrieve her
book. She looks up above the desk to see where the CUSTOMER
went and instead spies a glance of another woman - a woman
whose green silk scarf tied loosely around her neck and
head catches THERESE'S attention. This WOMAN appears to be

the only customer surrounded by no one else. This is CAROL AIRD. CAROL bends down to examine the train set, and inadvertently toggles the on/off switch - the train shuts down. CAROL stands up, turns around towards the doll department, smiling, as if asking for help.

THERESE meets CAROL'S eyes for a strange split second - until the EMBARRASSED MOM and the screaming TODDLER appear in front of THERESE, blocking her view of anything else.

EMBARRASSED MOM

Where's the ladies room, honey?

THERESE

To the left, past men's shoes,
then right at the tie racks.

EMBARRASSED MOM nods her thanks and hoists TODDLER away. THERESE looks for CAROL, but she's no longer there. The train set is back on, and being admired by several sets of FATHERS and SONS.

15. INT.
FRANKENBERG'S. DOLL DEPARTMENT.
MOMENTS LATER

Behind and below the desk, THERESE contemplates sneaking a read of her book, but decides against it. She glances back up and sees a pair of black leather gloves tossed onto the desk. THERESE looks and sees CAROL standing before her.

CAROL

I'm looking for a doll.
She's about-(she gestures)- this high
and this wide and... (rethinking):
Let's begin again, shall we?

As CAROL steps away from the desk a moment to rummage
through her purse, THERESE can't stop staring - at her well-
tailored suit, her blonde hair, her green silk scarf. CAROL
produces a crumpled slip of paper, steps back up to the desk,
gives THERESE a big smile as she hands it to her.

CAROL (CONT'D) (CONT'D)

I wonder if you might help me find
this doll for my daughter.

THERESE reads the slip of paper.

THERESE

Bright Betsy. She cries.

CAROL

Oh she does?

THERESE

And wets herself.
But we're out of stock.

CAROL

I've left it too long.

She begins to rummage through her purse.

We have plenty of other dolls.
All kinds, umm…

THERESE, suddenly tongue-tied, turns toward the doll
display, which CAROL turns to as well.

CAROL

Right. What was your favorite doll
when you were four?
Do you remember?

THERESE

Me? I never…
Not many, to be honest.

CAROL raises a cigarette to her lips, begins to light it,
THERESE interrupts

THERESE (CONT'D)

Sorry. No smoking on the sales floor.

CAROL

Oh, of all the - forgive me.
(beat) Shopping makes me nervous.

THERESE

That's okay.
Working here makes me nervous.

CAROL laughs, appreciating THERESE'S commiseration.

CAROL

You're very kind.

Their eyes meet for a moment, before CAROL rummages inside
her purse again. She produces a billfold, opens it, shows
it to THERESE. It's a photo of RINDY, CAROL'S 4-YEAR-OLD
DAUGHTER.

THERESE

She looks like you.
Around the mouth. The eyes.

CAROL

(glancing at THERESE)
You think so?

THERESE looks up, clocks CAROL watching her, looks down.
A bit of an awkward moment that CAROL rescues:

CAROL (CONT'D)

So what did you want? When you were that age?

THERESE

(no hesitation)
A train set.

CAROL

Really. That's a surprise. (beat)
Do you know much about train sets?

THERESE

I do actually. And there's a new model,
just in last week. Hand- built with hand-painted cars -
it's a limited edition of five thousand,

with the most sophisticated electric switching system
- it's quite...

THERESE checks her own enthusiasm, noticing CAROL'S eyes on her.

THERESE (CONT'D)

You may have seen it.
Over by the elevators? Just there-

THERESE points towards the train set and CAROL turns to look,
mulling it over. THERESE watches her every move.

CAROL

(turns back to THERESE)
Do you ship?

THERESE

Special delivery. Or courier.
(beat) You'll have it in two,
three days. Two days. We'll even assemble it.

CAROL

Well. That's... that. Sold.

They stand there, nodding at each other for a moment.

CAROL (CONT'D)

Shall I pay now?

THERESE

Oh - yes, of course.

THERESE begins writing out a sales slip, then slides it
over to CAROL with a pen, glancing up at her. CAROL snaps
out of a brief moment of thought, a distance.

We'll need your account details,
your shipping address.

CAROL

Of course. (she begins writing)
I love Christmas. At least I love the preparation.
Wrapping gifts, all that. And then… you somehow
wind up overcooking the turkey anyway.

She finishes, flashing a bright smile. THERESE doesn't quite
follow her, but she doesn't want CAROL to stop talking.

CAROL (CONT'D)

Done.

CAROL hands the pen and sales slip back to THERESE.

CAROL (CONT'D)

Where'd you learn so much about
train sets, anyway?

THERESE

I - read… Too much, probably.

CAROL

It's refreshing. Thank you. (beat)
And Merry Christmas.

THERESE

Merry Christmas.

CAROL walks away. THERESE watches her, takes her all in -

her manner, her style, her walk. CAROL turns back for a moment, and points to THERESE'S cap.

CAROL

I like your hat.

THERESE watches her go off past the train set and elevators. For a moment she watches as the empty spaces left behind are filled by shoppers and staff. She cranes her neck for one last look but it's no good. She's gone. THERESE sighs. She looks down at the doll desk and sees that CAROL has left her gloves behind.

16. INT.
FRANKENBERG'S. EMPLOYEE LOCKER ROOM.
EVENING.

THERESE stands at her open locker, as the BUZZER indicating that the store is closed blares incessantly. She takes off her Frankenberg's smock and puts on a pair of dark tights that she's just bought, to cover up her bandage. It does the trick. She puts on her coat, scarf, etc. The inside of her locker door is decorated with photographs THERESE has taken, shots of THERESE and RICHARD in Coney Island. As THERESE puts CAROL'S gloves into her handbag, the BUZZING finally stops. She can see RUBY ROBICHEK at her locker across the room, pulling on some winter boots with great difficulty. THERESE quickly dabs on some powder and shuts her locker.

17. INT.
CINEMA PROJECTION ROOM. NIGHT.

THERESE, RICHARD, PHIL and DANNIE McELROY
sit crowded together in the small dark space,
watching a movie through the modest glass panel,
smoking cigarettes. THERESE sits on RICHARD'S lap,
but RICHARD is more content kissing the back
of her neck than watching the film. PHIL McELROY,
the film projectionist and host, sits near the gears while his
brother, DANNIE, sits as close as he can to the movie,
jotting down occasional notes in a small notebook.
The film is *Sunset Boulevard*, and the scene is Norma
Desmond's New Year's Eve party for two when she dances
with Joe Gillis on the marble ballroom floor. THERESE is
fascinated by DANNIE, but PHIL slaps him on the back of his head.

PHIL
Move over. Nobody else can see the screen.

RICHARD
(through his nuzzling of THERESE)
Nobody else is watching.

THERESE
(laughs)
I'm watching.

DANNIE
(to THERESE)
I've seen it six times.
I'm charting the correlation between
what the characters say and how they really feel.

PHIL

My kid brother, the movie jerk.

DANNIE, embarrassed, moves slightly away from the glass.
But he still watches, still jots notes. THERESE watches him.

18. INT.
GREENWICH VILLAGE BAR. NIGHT.

RICHARD and PHIL have been drinking quite a bit.
A row of empty beer bottles is lined up on the table
in front of them. DANNIE sips at a glass of Coca-Cola.
THERESE nurses a glass of wine.

DANNIE

I'm strictly a beer man.
Everything else makes me want to vomit.

THERESE

Wine makes me feel naughty.
In a good way.

PHIL

Is there any other way to feel naughty?

RICHARD

I drink to forget I gotta get up
for work in the morning.

PHIL

That's your problem, Semco.
You really ought to drink because you
remember you have a job.
Employment's a curse.

THERESE

You have a job, Phil.

PHIL

You call that a job? I call it an illusion.

DANNIE

You get paid. Is money an
illusion?

PHIL

My kid brother, the jerk philosopher.

THERESE

(to Dannie)
Where do you work?

RICHARD

(mock respect)
Didn't you know - Dannie works at
the New York Times.

RICHARD and PHIL feign awe.

THERESE

(she's impressed) No kidding.

PHIL

Yeah, 'cept printers don't win Pulitzer Prizes.

DANNIE

(he shrugs)
It's a job. (to THERESE) What I want to do is write.
That's why I watch movies.

PHIL

(rolling his eyes) Everybody's a writer....

DANNIE tries to blend into the woodwork. He catches
THERESE'S eye. She smiles at him. He appreciates it.

PHIL (CONT'D)

Say, Therese - before I get too
drunk to remember....

PHIL digs into a large messenger bag, pulls out a camera,
an old Kodak, and hands it to THERESE.

THERESE

You did it? It's fixed?

PHIL

He said it was a cinch. No sweat.

THERESE

Thank you, Phil! I was missing it!

DANNIE

So, you take pictures?

THERESE

Well.

RICHARD

She's more excited by some chintzy
camera than she is about sailing with me to Europe!

PHIL

Women!

RICHARD

You said it, pal!

RICHARD and PHIL laugh, toast, drink. THERESE isn't amused.

DANNIE clocks this.

19. EXT.
THIRD AVENUE. NIGHT.

THERESE walks with DANNIE. RICHARD and PHIL, now very drunk
and rowdy, walk slightly ahead of them, with RICHARD
guiding his bicycle unsteadily along the pavement.

> PHIL
>
> What you oughta do is hit Spain…
> whatsitcalled - Pamplona. Catch a bullfight!

Up ahead a couple is approaching who everyone knows: JACK
TAFT and his girlfriend, DOROTHY. The men all speak to each
other as DOROTHY speaks to THERESE.

> JACK
>
> Holy smoke, look who's
> coming. Watch out, baby,
> it's a pack of commies!

> PHIL (CONT'D)
>
> I don't believe it! Does the
> House Un-American Activities
> know you're back on the streets?

> DOROTHY
>
> Terry, honey, it's been ages.
> Call me, would you?

> THERESE
>
> Hey Dottie. Hasn't it?
> I will, I promise!

RICHARD turns around as they pass, walking unsteadily
backwards with his bicycle.

RICHARD
That son of a bitch…You still
owe me for that poker game!

THERESE
Richard, watch out, you're-!

But she's too late to save RICHARD from backing into a
lamppost. He falls down, the bicycle topples down on top of
him. PHIL attempts to help but tumbles onto RICHARD, and
they both dissolve into a fit of drunken laughter.

DANNIE
(to THERESE)
Europe. Wow. You're lucky.

THERESE
Am I?

A beat as they watch PHIL and RICHARD make a meal of
getting up.

THERESE (CONT'D)
We should help them.

DANNIE
(after a beat)
You should come to the Times for
dinner some time. I work at night,
so… I've got a good pal who's a
junior photo editor.
He loves to pontificate.
I'll introduce you.

Really?
That - I would - I'd like that.

DANNIE

(pleased)
Yeah? Okay, then.

And they've forgotten all about RICHARD and PHIL.

20. INT.
THERESE'S APARTMENT. LATE NIGHT.

THERESE and RICHARD lie together side by side in bed.
THERESE is fully clothed. RICHARD wears a tank-top
undershirt and boxers. They are engaged in a pretty
passionate embrace.
RICHARD starts to unbutton THERESE'S blouse. She stops him,
gently. He rolls on top of her. Again, she stops him.
RICHARD rolls off THERESE, sits up. He takes her into his
arms, kisses her nose.

RICHARD

Let me touch you.

THERESE

Let me.

RICHARD

You sure?

THERESE nods her head. RICHARD takes THERESE'S hand and

places it on his boxer shorts, over his cock.

RICHARD (CONT'D)
This okay?

She nods. RICHARD moves her hand inside his boxer shorts.
He puts his hand over hers and begins to guide her into a
hand job, slow and steady.

THERESE
Like that?

RICHARD lets go of THERESE'S hand and leans back, closes
his eyes. He lets out a low moan. THERESE watches RICHARD
intently the whole time, as if she's more an observer than
a full participant. RICHARD'S breathing rapidly quickens.

RICHARD
(as he comes)
I love you, Terry.

RICHARD relaxes. THERESE pulls her hand out of RICHARD'S
shorts. She looks down at the semen on her hand. RICHARD
sits up, takes off his vest, switches off the light.

RICHARD (CONT'D)
Jesus, Terry, you shouldn't look at it.

RICHARD laughs, wipes THERESE'S hand with his undershirt

and throws it onto the floor. THERESE laughs, too. RICHARD
leans forward, kisses THERESE deeply, tenderly. THERESE
pulls away suddenly.

Shit, I forgot your aspirin.

THERESE jumps out of bed and runs to the bathroom. RICHARD,
exhausted and happy, falls back onto the bed.

21. INT.
THERESE'S APARTMENT. LATE NIGHT.

RICHARD is asleep. THERESE sits at her small kitchen table.
THERESE holds CAROL'S gloves and the sales slip from
Frankenberg's with CAROL'S name, address and signature
neatly written on it. She considers the slip for a moment
before propping it up against a salt shaker with the gloves.
She draws her knees into her chest and rocks herself to and fro.
She watches RICHARD sleep.

22. EXT.
THERESE'S APARTMENT. LATE NIGHT.

THERESE stands in front of a postbox, wearing a coat over
her night clothes. There's not a soul in sight in the cold
night. She looks at a small package addressed to "Mrs. H. Aird"
for a moment before dropping it into the postbox. She looks up
at her window a moment before being seized by a chill
and running up the stoop to her building.

23. EXT.
SUBURBAN NEW JERSEY STREET. LATE MORNING.

A MAILMAN pulls up to a large stone house with a gabled
roof, along the stately residential street. He grabs a handful of mail,
jumps down and begins walking up the driveway.

24. INT.
CAROL'S HOUSE. ENTRANCE. LATE MORNING.

Mail is dropped through the letter slot, including
THERESE'S package to CAROL. FLORENCE, CAROL'S housekeeper,
glances over to the entry while mopping the floor.

25. INT.
CAROL'S HOUSE. CAROL'S BEDROOM.
LATE MORNING.

CAROL sits with her daughter RINDY, age 4, at CAROL'S
vanity. CAROL is brushing RINDY'S hair, as RINDY counts
along, pretending to powder her face with a powder puff.

RINDY

Fifty-three, fifty-four, fifty- five...
(she looks up at her mother) sixty?

CAROL

(kisses her forehead) Fifty-six.

RINDY

Fifty-six. Fifty-seven...

CAROL hears the sound of her husband's arrival downstairs.

CAROL

That must be your daddy.
We'd better finish up.
Fifty-eight, fifty-nine-

RINDY

Come skating with Daddy and me!

CAROL

Oh, I wish I could, sweet pea.

RINDY

Why not, mommy?
Pretty please!

HARGE, CAROL'S husband, appears in the bedroom doorway.
He carries the pile of mail.

HARGE

(to RINDY)
Hiya, sunshine.

CAROL looks up. She sees HARGE reflected in the vanity mirror.
RINDY turns, sees him, jumps down from her mother's lap
and runs to him.

CAROL

You're early.

HARGE

Mail came.

HARGE waves it vaguely before setting it down on an end-table.

RINDY

Daddy! I want Mommy to come skating too!

She leaps into his arms. He spins her around. CAROL hasn't moved from the vanity.

HARGE

Okeydokey, smokey, one thing at a time.

He puts RINDY down. Catches sight of CAROL staring at him. He puts the mail down onto the vanity.

26. INT.
CAROL'S HOUSE. KITCHEN. LATE MORNING.

CAROL, HARGE and RINDY in the kitchen. RINDY sits on HARGE'S lap. She's using crayons to draw a picture. FLORENCE prepares a hot meal in the background.

HARGE

How 'bout some green for the trees?

CAROL

She loves to color in the sky first.

HARGE

And Cy's wife asked if you were coming-

CAROL

(he does this every time)
-Jeanette.

HARGE

-Jeaneatte. (beat)
I know she'd love to see you.

235

CAROL

Give her my best.
I've always liked Jeanette.

CAROL checks RINDY'S drawing, slides another color over to
her. As she does, HARGE slides a hand over CAROL'S.

HARGE

I'd like you to be there.

CAROL looks at HARGE'S hand on hers. She looks up at him.

CAROL

I'm sorry, Harge. I have plans.

RINDY

Mommy and Aunt Abby are exchanging presents.

HARGE smiles, nods, pats CAROL'S hand, withdraws his hand,
turns his daughter around in his lap to face him.

HARGE

You been seeing a lot of Aunt Abby lately, sunshine?
With mommy?

CAROL shoots HARGE a look. He holds her gaze, not giving
in. CAROL looks away, uncomfortable in FLORENCE'S presence.

CAROL

I'll - try and re-arrange with Abby.

236

HARGE

Thank you.

27. INT.
FRANKENBERG'S DEPARTMENT STORE.
SHIPPING DEPT.

A SHIPPING CLERK sorts through his file of carbon shipping receipts while THERESE stands at the window.

THERESE (CONT'D)

I told the customer it would get
to her by Christmas Eve.
Based on what we've been told.
Three business days from the-

SHIPPING CLERK

(looks up at her)
Should have been delivered this afternoon.

THERESE

Oh. Right. So... It arrived?
She signed for it?

SHIPPING CLERK

(all curt business here)
It arrived.

THERESE

Great. Thanks - thank you.

28. INT.
CAROL'S HOUSE. CAROL'S BEDROOM. NIGHT.

CAROL sits before her dressing table brushing out her hair.

A lit cigarette burns down in an ashtray on the dressing table. A tumbler of scotch on the rocks rests beside the ashtray. CAROL puts down the brush, and glances down at her lap. There she holds the gloves she'd left at Frankenberg's and a note from THERESE. She takes a drag of the cigarette and reads the note again:

> **Salutations from Frankenberg's**
> **Department Store. Employee 645-A.**

She crumples up the letter and tosses it into a small waste basket. She takes another drag on her cigarette, then glances back at the waste basket.

29. INT.
FRANKENBERG'S. DOLL DESK. THE NEXT DAY.
LATE AFTERNOON.

THERESE at her desk is being exhausted by a PICKY FEMALE CUSTOMER. A score of open doll boxes and dolls are sprawled across the desk.

ROBERTA WALLS (O.S.)

Belivet? Miss Belivet?

THERESE looks up. ROBERTA WALLS stands at a desk nearby, crooking a finger at THERESE and holding a telephone receiver up.

ROBERTA WALLS (CONT'D)

Over here please. Now?

She snaps her fingers for another SALES CLERK to take over
from THERESE.

> **THERESE**
> (to CUSTOMER)
> Sorry - I'm - excuse me.

THERESE hurries over to ROBERTA WALLS as the SALES CLERK
takes over the PICKY FEMALE CUSTOMER. ROBERTA WALLS hands
the receiver to THERESE and shoots her a withering look.
THERESE takes the phone.

> **THERESE (CONT'D)**
> Hello?

> **OPERATOR (O.S.)**
> Is this employee 645-A, Tereeza Belivet?

> **THERESE**
> Yes.

> **OPERATOR (O.S.)**
> We're patching you though, ma'am.

30. INT.
CAROL'S HOUSE. KITCHEN. LATE AFTERNOON.

CAROL cooks dinner as she makes her call, which helps her
combat some of her residual shyness. A radio is tuned in to
some BIG BAND MUSIC.

> **CAROL**
> So it was you.

31. INT.
FRANKENBERG'S. DOLL DESK. LATE AFTERNOON.

THERESE on the phone. WALLS, stony-faced and staring.

> **THERESE**
>
> Oh - hello. Mrs. Aird?
> Did you - receive the train set alright?

32. INT.
CAROL'S HOUSE. KITCHEN. LATE AFTERNOON.

> **CAROL**
>
> I did. And the gloves. Thank you so much.
> You're a star for sending them.
> I just called to say - thank you, really.
>
> **THERESE (O.S.)**
>
> of course.

CAROL picks up a saucepan lid but it's too hot and she drops it. It clatters on the floor.

> **CAROL (CONT'D)**
>
> Oh, shit - sorry.
> What I mean to say
> - Do you get a lunch hour there?
> - Let me take you to lunch.
> It's the least I can do.

33. INT.
FRANKENBERG'S. DOLL DESK. LATE AFTERNOON.

THERESE blinks. Hard. She holds a long breath before
replying, mindful of ROBERTA WALLS attuned to her every word.

THERESE

> I - well. Yes, of course.
> But you really don't- (pause)
> Tomorrow? (pause) No, I don't know it.
> Hold on. (sheepishly to ROBERTA) I'm sorry.
> Can I borrow a paper and a pencil?

ROBERTA WALLS isn't happy as she slides a paper and pencil
over to THERESE. THERESE quickly scribbles down an address.

34. INT.
MIDTOWN RESTAURANT. DAY.

THERESE stands at the front of a small midtown restaurant,
with white tablecloths and wooden rafters. She glances up
at the clock which reads 1:12 and checks it against her
wristwatch. She glances out the window. There, through
beveled glass, she spots CAROL hurrying across the street.

35. INT.
MIDTOWN RESTAURANT. DAY. MOMENTS LATER

CAROL and THERESE are seated at a quiet table. CAROL is
removing her hat, glancing at her menu as a WAITER hovers.
THERESE sits transfixed, her eyes quick and alert, taking

in everything about CAROL from the way a delicate gold
bracelet falls against her wrist as she peruses her menu to
the way CAROL'S fingers grip her water glass.

CAROL

I'm so sorry to keep you waiting.
(to the WAITER) I'll have the
creamed spinach over poached eggs.
And a dry martini. With an olive.

CAROL and the WAITER look to THERESE, who realizes she
hasn't even opened her menu. A beat, then:

THERESE

I'll have the same.

WAITER

The meal or the drink?

THERESE

Uhh - All of it. Thank you.

The WAITER nods, starting off, as CAROL clocks THERESE'S
uncertainty. THERESE not wanting to stare at CAROL,
now picks up her menu and thumbs through it.

CAROL

Cigarette?

CAROL offers THERESE a cigarette from her exquisite silver case.
THERESE notices that CAROL'S hands are lovely and smooth,
salon manicured, in contrast to THERESE'S own.

THERESE takes a cigarette from the case. CAROL lights
THERESE'S cigarette and THERESE proceeds to smoke it,
though not without some effort.

CAROL (CONT'D)

So what kind of a name is Belivet?

THERESE

It's Czech. It's changed. Originally-

CAROL

It's very original.

THERESE

(she feels herself blush)
Well.

CAROL

And your first name?

THERESE

Therese.

CAROL

Therese. Not Ter-eeza.

THERESE

No.

CAROL

Therese Belivet. That's lovely.

THERESE

And yours?

CAROL

Carol.

THERESE

Carol.

The WAITER reappears with their drinks and CAROL picks up her glass and toasts.

> CAROL
>
> Cheers.

> THERESE
>
> (clinking glasses)
> Cheers.

CAROL sips at her martini. THERESE watches her for a moment, then samples hers. She tries to hide the surprise of its strength. CAROL smiles.

> THERESE (CONT'D)
>
> (beat) So, you - I'm sure you
> thought it was a man
> who sent back your gloves.

> CAROL
>
> I did. I thought it might be a man
> in the ski department.

> THERESE
>
> I'm sorry.

> CAROL
>
> No, I'm delighted.
> I doubt very much if I'd have gone
> to lunch with him.

THERESE watches as CAROL massages the back of her neck for a moment.

THERESE

Your perfume -

CAROL

Yes?

THERESE

It's nice.

CAROL

Thank you. Harge bought me
a bottle years ago, before we were married.
I've been wearing it ever since.

THERESE

Harge is your husband?

CAROL

Yes. Well. Technically we - We're divorcing.

THERESE

(after a beat)
I'm sorry.

CAROL

(stubs out her cigarette)
Don't be.

THERESE doesn't know what to say. CAROL smiles, changes the
subject.

CAROL (CONT'D)

And do you live alone,
Therese Belivet?

THERESE

I do. (beat) Well, there's
Richard. He wants to live with me.

CAROL looks up at THERESE, raised eyebrow smile.

                    THERESE (CONT'D)
      No, it's nothing like that. It's - he'd like to marry me.
                         CAROL
            I see. Would you like to marry him?

A pause.

                        THERESE
                  (she makes light of it)
         I... barely know what to order for lunch.

CAROL nods, almost looks past THERESE - what is she
thinking about? Suddenly it seems to THERESE that CAROL'S
mood has somehow darkened.
The WAITER appears with their food. He sets their plates down.
CAROL picks up her silverware, the cloud seemingly past.

                         CAROL
                I'm starved. Bon appetit.

CAROL eats and THERESE watches, almost having to force
herself to pick up her fork and knife and join her. But she
does. CAROL looks up at her for a moment:

                    CAROL (CONT'D)
            And what do you do on Sundays?
                        THERESE
         Nothing in particular. What do you do?

CAROL

CAROL

Nothing - lately. If you'd like to
visit me some time, you're welcome
to. At least there's some pretty
country around where I live.
Would you like to come out this Sunday?

CAROL waits for THERESE'S answer.

THERESE

Yes.

CAROL

What a strange girl you are.

THERESE

Why?

CAROL

Flung out of space.

THERESE feels herself blush, and looks away from CAROL.
She tries to attend to her lunch and martini.

36. EXT.
RESTAURANT. DAY.

Through passing CROWDS, THERESE watches from just outside
the restaurant entrance as CAROL climbs into a convertible
across the street. CAROL'S best friend, ABBY, drives. She
and CAROL greet each other with European-style kisses. Then
CAROL turns around and waves to THERESE. THERESE waves back
as the car takes off, disappearing into traffic.

37. INT.
ABBY'S CAR. DAY.

ABBY snakes along Sixth Avenue.

> **CAROL**
> I can just see Harge's mother's face
> when she sees me in this.
> Maybe I should stop home and change.

> **ABBY**
> Don't be a stupe.

> **CAROL**
> Why don't I just not show up?

> **ABBY**
> Because I'll be blamed.
> So you'd better just grin and bear it.
> (beat) You want to tell me about her?

CAROL and ABBY exchange a brief glance.

> **CAROL**
> Therese? (shrugs) She returned my gloves.

> **ABBY**
> And?

> **CAROL**
> And... if you don't get us out of
> this traffic soon, I won't have to
> worry about any damned party.
> (bundling up): Do you ever put the top up?

38. INT.
FRANKENBERG'S. EMPLOYEE LOCKER ROOM. DAY.

THERESE sits opposite her open locker, now wearing her employee smock. She writes inside an appointment diary, on an otherwise empty page, slowly and carefully in fountain pen:

Mrs. Carol Aird. Seventh Avenue entrance. 2:00 PM Sunday.

She considers what she's written, blows on the ink so it dries.

39. EXT.
NEW JERSEY. WEALTHY SUBURBS. EARLY EVENING.

A well-kept road full of wealthy homes, green, sweeping lots, old wealth. ABBY'S car pulls into the circular drive of a large modern home, set back against a cloak of trees - the residence of HARGE'S boss, CY HARRISON. There's clearly a party going on: music, laughter, well-dressed GUESTS arriving, valets opening doors, taking keys, etc.
ABBY shuts off the engine and turns to CAROL, who begins rummaging through her purse in sudden agitation.

CAROL

Where on earth is my compact.
God damn it.

ABBY leans over towards CAROL, touches her arm.

ABBY

You look fine.

CAROL looks at ABBY.

CAROL

Come in with me. Just for a minute.

ABBY

Don't even start. You're the one
who cancelled on us - you nitwit!

CAROL

I know. I know.
I'm sorry - I'm going!

CAROL looks towards the house again, gathering herself.

ABBY

Call me later.

40. INT.
CY HARRISON'S HOUSE.
DEN/LIVING ROOM – EARLY EVENING

A large room for entertaining right off the foyer.
Big, open fireplace. WAITERS circulate with food and drink.
HARGE stands in a group with his parents, JOHN and
JENNIFER, his boss CY and CY'S wife, JEANETTE.

JOHN

(to CY)
I've tried to talk sense to the boy, Cy.
I told him, son, Tri-State Capital's not going to buy
that Murray Hill parcel unless you
improve your golf handicap.

(to his father, slight edge)
I've got a few other things on my mind, Dad.

A reserved silence, as they all know to what he's
referring. HARGE looks off, sees CAROL in the foyer,
handing her coat to a VALET.

HARGE (CONT'D)

Excuse me.

And he makes his way through the GUESTS to join CAROL.

41. INT.
CY HARRISON'S HOUSE.
LIVING ROOM - NIGHT

The party in full-swing. A DANCE BAND plays "Harbor Lights",
and HARGE and CAROL dance a slow fox-trot. CAROL notices
the other women, dressed much more formally than she. HARGE
clocks this and draws her closer to him.

HARGE

You're always the most beautiful woman in any room.

CAROL

Tell your mother that.

They look across the room to see JENNIFER watching them,
and indeed, looking as if she'd just swallowed a clove of garlic.

42. INT.
CY HARRISON'S HOUSE.
BUFFET/DINING ROOM - LATER

Carol and Harge, and Cy and Jennifer are moving through the dinner buffet with their plates.

JENNIFER hovers, tidying the display, and handing stray glasses and napkins to members of the staff.

> #### JENNIFER
> We might hire a local boy to appear
> as Santa for Rindy, Christmas morning.
> If only we could find a way to get him down
> the chimney! (beat; to CAROL)
> How've you arranged it in the past, Carol?
>
> #### CAROL
> What's that?
>
> #### JENNIFER
> Christmas morning. With Rindy.

CAROL exchanges a brief look with HARGE before answering.

> #### CAROL
> Oh, we... usually get up at dawn, Harge and I,
> and we - we wrap Rindy's gifts together.
> Arrange them under the tree and wait for
> Rindy to wake. Which is - she normally-
>
> #### HARGE
> (helps CAROL out)
> Usually, she's down the stairs in

a shot and barely notices us
before she's ripped through all the wrapping.

CAROL

(smiles, grateful to
HARGE)
Yes. That's right.

JENNIFER

But no Santa Claus.

CAROL

No.

JENNIFER

Oh. Well. It is a production - May I serve you?

JEANETTE offers CAROL a commiserating look: oh-brother.

43. EXT.
CY HARRISON'S HOUSE. LATER.

CAROL and JEANETTE in the gardens. The party can be seen
going on through a row of French doors. They smoke cigarettes.
CAROL takes off her shoes, rubs her feet.

JEANETTE

(takes a long deep drag on her cigarette)
Keep an eye out, will you?
Cy'll scream if he catches me with this.

CAROL

(laughs)
What'll he do?
Dock your allowance?

JEANETTE

(very matter of fact)

He doesn't like me to smoke.

CAROL

So? You like it.

But they both know that it's simply the way it is: wives defer to their husband's wishes.

JEANETTE

Carol, I - it's really not my business,
but if you're going to be alone on Christmas,
Cy and I would love to have you.

CAROL

(she's really touched by the offer)
Thank you, Jeanette.

CAROL takes another look inside the party: couples dancing through the tented plastic.

CAROL (CONT'D)

(watching the dancing)
I don't know. I might get away by
myself. At least for a few days.

44. INT.
NEW YORK TIMES. PHOTO DEPT. OFFICE. NIGHT.

DANNIE ushers THERESE into the alluring world of a junior photo editor's office: the contact sheets dangling from

254

light boards, the professional equipment, trays and lenses - but mostly it's the photos themselves that she's in awe of. Candids, crime scenes, sports photos, everything that makes up the visual narrative of a newspaper. DANNIE sits at a desk and sets up dinner, a makeshift array brought from home - wrapped sandwiches, bottles of beer. THERESE breathes it all in, not daring to touch anything.

DANNIE

Don't worry, nothing's gonna break
if you pick it up. You want a sandwich?

THERESE shakes her head, picks up a contact sheet and a magnifier and glances at the pictures. DANNIE watches her.

DANNIE (CONT'D)

What are your pictures like?

THERESE

They're - probably not very good.
I don't know.

DANNIE

I mean, what are they?
What are they of?

THERESE

Trees. Birds. Windows. Anything, really. (beat)
What do you write about?

DANNIE

People.

A pause. THERESE looks through a camera lens at DANNIE.
He looks up at her, she lowers the lens.

> **THERESE**
>
> I feel strange, I think…
> taking pictures of people.
> It feels like - an intrusion or a-

> **DANNIE**
>
> Invasion of privacy?

> **THERESE**
>
> Yes.

DANNIE opens a beer, holds it out to THERESE. She takes it.

> **DANNIE**
>
> Yeah but, all of us, we have,
> you know - affinities for people, right?

THERESE doesn't answer.

> **DANNIE (CONT'D)**
>
> Or certain people.
> There are certain people you like…

> **THERESE**
>
> Sometimes.

> **DANNIE**
>
> And others you don't. And you
> don't really know why you're
> attracted to some people and not
> others, the only thing you know is

- you either are attracted or
you're not. It's like physics -
bouncing off each other like pinballs.

THERESE

(smiles)
So now you're a scientist?

DANNIE

Just trying to explain why I write
about people rather than trees.

THERESE

Sounds more like psychology.

DANNIE

Physics is more comforting.

THERESE grabs a sandwich.

THERESE

Yeah, but... Not everything's as
simple as a bunch of pin balls reacting, or...

DANNIE

Some things don't even react.
But everything's alive.

A beat. DANNIE moves to THERESE, takes the beer bottle away
from her, puts it down. He puts his hand on THERESE'S shoulders.

THERESE

It's late. I should go.

He kisses her, and she lets him, remaining very still.
Then DANNIE steps back and THERESE looks down.

THERESE (CONT'D)
You shouldn't…

DANNIE

Why? Did you mind?

THERESE

No.

DANNIE

Would Richard mind?

THERESE

Probably. (beat) I have to go.

THERESE gathers her things together, goes to the door.

DANNIE

Come back tomorrow? Or Wednesday?

THERESE

Maybe. I don't know.

THERESE leaves.

45. EXT.
CAROL'S HOUSE. LATE NIGHT.

HARGE has brought CAROL home from the party.
They stand together outside the door while CAROL fishes for her keys. HARGE reaches into his pocket and produces his, opens door.

HARGE

Here.

CAROL

Thanks. And thanks for staying
sober and driving me home.
(kissing his cheek)
Goodnight, Harge.

She starts to go inside the house. HARGE stops her gently.

HARGE

Come to my parents for Christmas.
We had a nice time tonight.

CAROL

(not unkindly)
It was one night.

HARGE

I don't like to think of you. Alone.

CAROL

I'm not alone. There's Rindy, there's-

She stops herself. HARGE knows what she was about to say.

HARGE

Abby. There's always Abby.

CAROL

(after a pause)
Abby and I were over long before
you and I were over, Harge. (beat)
I'll have Rindy packed and ready
for you at four on Christmas Eve.

She starts to step inside the house.

It shouldn't be like this.

CAROL

I know.

And she quietly shuts the door on HARGE.

46. INT.
CAROL'S HOUSE. LIVING ROOM. NIGHT.

The living room is dark and quiet. RINDY has fallen asleep on the sofa; FLORENCE, on a chair opposite. CAROL gives FLORENCE a pat on her shoulder and squats down beside RINDY.

FLORENCE

She wanted to wait up for you.

CAROL

Ah, mama's special girl.

CAROL brushes a strand of hair away from her eyes. She gently picks her up and carries her out of the room and up the stairs.

CAROL (CONT'D)

Goodnight, Florence.

47. INT.
CAROL'S HOUSE. LIVING ROOM. LATER

CAROL lifts a holiday blanket from a small platform,

revealing the assembled train set, set up behind a couch.
She switches on the train and watches it begin its slow
route along the tracks. She sips at a nightcap.

48. EXT.
FRANKENBERG'S. SEVENTH AVENUE ENTRANCE.
EARLY SUNDAY AFTERNOON.

THERESE, in coat, scarf and gloves, waits for CAROL'S car
to pull up outside. RICHARD waits with her.

RICHARD

Where's this place in Jersey?

THERESE

The country, I think.
I don't really know.

RICHARD

My uncle Sal lives in Union City
and he claims it's pretty dangerous
out there at night-

THERESE

It's not Union City.

RICHARD

Okay, okay.

CAROL pulls up to the curb.

THERESE

There's my ride.

RICHARD accompanies THERESE to the car. He opens the door
for her, she gets in, shuts the door, rolls down the
window. He leans down to kiss her.

RICHARD
Eight o'clock?

THERESE
Eight o'clock.

RICHARD looks into the car, holds up a hand in greeting to CAROL.

RICHARD
Hi.

CAROL
Hello. Carol Aird.

RICHARD
(leans across THERESE to shake CAROL'S hand)
Richard Semco. Glad to meet you.

CAROL
Likewise.

THERESE
(to RICHARD)
She wanted to meet you.

CAROL
Therese speaks very highly of you.

RICHARD
(pleased to hear it)
Well, that's - swell. So you'll...
get her back safe and sound?

CAROL smiles, salutes her assent. THERESE is slightly embarrassed. RICHARD leans into the car and touches THERESE'S chin lightly.

RICHARD (CONT'D)

Love you.

But THERESE has already rolled up the window, the car has started to go. RICHARD diminishes through the rear window.

49. INT.
CAROL'S CAR. APPROACHING LINCOLN TUNNEL. DAY.

CAROL and THERESE make their way cross town, as a cool winter sun combs through the car windows. CAROL appears at home behind the wheel - relaxed, confident. To THERESE, the world inside CAROL'S car is a revelation, from the tan leather upholstery and mahogany dashboard to the effortless style and elegance of its driver. The sounds of the world - even CAROL'S occasional chatter - have been replaced with the stillest MUSIC, the sound of air and light. The presence of this older, sophisticated woman, who wears silk stockings and expensive perfume, is intoxicating and unnerving in equal measure. Even Carol's purse, which rests beside THERESE on the seat, is quite unlike anything she has seen or examined so closely, full of mystery and makeup and fragrances. From there her eyes wander down to CAROL'S legs, clad in smoky silk stockings. Glancing down at her own legs, wrapped in sensible wool tights, THERESE wonders if she will ever be the kind of woman who owns such a car and wears such clothes.
The MUSIC broods slightly as THERESE looks straight ahead

and the car enters the Lincoln Tunnel. The car plunges into
the semi-darkness as if entering a cocoon, a delirious
descent, which binds them together. She watches CAROL'S
fingers grip the wheel, how CAROL squints slightly when she
concentrates.

THERESE can barely suppress a tiny smile. But glancing
back, CAROL suddenly appears to be miles away. CAROL
switches on the car radio and Jo Stafford's "You Belong to Me"
comes on.

THERESE leans back in her seat as they continue, speeding
through the dark tunnel.

50. INT. / EXT.
CAROL'S CAR. XMAS TREE LOT. NEW JERSEY. DAY.

At a Christmas tree lot, THERESE sits in the car loading
her camera with film. When she's done, she spots CAROL
outside as a TEENAGED BOY ties up their tree, a large Doug
Fir. The TEENAGED BOY has a bad cold and CAROL offers him
tissues. THERESE steps out of the car, aims her camera and
takes a few shots.

51. INT.
CAROL'S CAR. RIDGEWOOD, NEW JERSEY. DAY.

The car makes its way to Carol's house, with the Douglas
Fir laid across the front and back seats between THERESE
and CAROL.

THERESE loves the feeling of the needles against her skin, the way it smells, the way she knows that CAROL is beside her, though she can't see her. The car comes to a halt in front of CAROL'S house. It's a big house, a bigger house than THERESE has ever been inside. CAROL turns off the engine.

> CAROL
>
> You still with me?
>
> THERESE
>
> Yes.

CAROL opens her door, pops out of the car. THERESE is about to get out of the car when she sees the front door of the house open and RINDY come tearing out to greet her mother. FLORENCE stands in the doorway, ready to escort mother and daughter inside.

> RINDY
>
> Mommyyyy!!
>
> CAROL
>
> Hello, my darling! Guess what I
> brought you? I bet you'll never guess…

THERESE watches as mother and daughter proceed inside, chattering away.

52. INT.
CAROL'S HOUSE. KITCHEN. DAY. LATER.

THERESE prepares a tray of tea and cookies. Through the open door we can see CAROL and RINDY in the living room, decorating the tree. Almost finished, CAROL is setting up a ladder beside the tree.

                    CAROL
              Where's the star?

RINDY roots around in the pile of ornaments, finds it.

                    RINDY
              This one, Mommy.
                    CAROL
              That's my girl.

THERESE watches as CAROL ascends the ladder and places the star at the top of the tree.

                CAROL (CONT'D)
              Look how beautiful!

CAROL descends the step ladder and joins Rindy, taking her into her lap.

                CAROL (CONT'D)
          Have you ever seen a more beautiful
          tree? And now... what comes after the star is placed?
                    RINDY
                More stars!

CAROL
(tickling RINDY)
I don't... think... so!

O/S FLORENCE

You find everything you need, miss?

THERESE, startled, turns to see FLORENCE standing at the rear of the kitchen, near a back door.

THERESE

Gosh, you scared me.
How silly.

FLORENCE

(she's not sorry)
I'm sorry, miss. (beat)
I'll take that through for Mrs. Aird.

FLORENCE picks up the tray, walks through to the living room.

53. INT.
CAROL'S HOUSE. LIVING ROOM. NIGHT.

A fire crackles in the fireplace as CAROL, seated under the tree, struggles to wrap the train set. THERESE sits at the piano, improvising, jumping from one bit of a tune to another. A half-empty bottle of white wine and a couple of glasses stand nearby.

CAROL

Were those pictures of me you were taking?
At the tree lot?

THERESE stops playing. A silence.

THERESE

I'm sorry. I should have asked.

CAROL

Don't apologize.

THERESE

I've been trying to… A friend of
mine told me I should be more interested.
In humans.

CAROL

And how's that going?

THERESE

(after a small beat)
Well… actually.

CAROL

I'm glad.

THERESE begins to play "Easy Living." CAROL listens for a
moment, rises, walks over to Therese.

CAROL (CONT'D)

That's beautiful.

She grazes her hand on Therese's shoulder. THERESE freezes,
and CAROL tries to lighten the moment with two quick
strokes to her cheek. THERESE continues to play and CAROL
listens.

CAROL (CONT'D)

Is that what you want to be? A photographer?

THERESE

I think so. If I have any talent for it.

CAROL

Isn't that something other people
let you know you have?
All you can do is - keep working.
Use what feels right. Throw away the rest.

THERESE finishes the song. CAROL starts over to a table by
the couch, opens a cigarette box, takes one out, lights it.

CAROL (CONT'D)

Will you show me your work?
(she sits on the couch)

THERESE

Sure. I mean, I haven't sold
anything. Or even shown a picture
to anyone who could buy one.
I don't even have a decent camera.
But... they're all at my place.
Under the sink, mostly.

CAROL

Invite me round.

From outside, the sound of a car pulling into the driveway.
Car door opens and slams. The moment broken,
CAROL rises quickly, and marches toward the front door.
CAROL comes out of the living room and finds HARGE in the
entry, restringing the mistletoe.

CAROL (CONT'D)
Harge.
What's wrong?
HARGE
Nothing. Does there have to be a problem
for me to visit my wife?

HARGE approaches CAROL, reaching out to greet her, but
stops, spotting THERESE at the piano in the living room.
He looks to CAROL and CAROL looks away. Then HARGE moves
past CAROL down the hall and into the kitchen. THERESE
clocks it all.

54. INT.
CAROL'S HOUSE. LIVING ROOM. LATER.

THERESE browses through a book, alone in the living room,
as she hears CAROL and HARGE conversing in the kitchen.
Through the cracked door she catches glimpses of CAROL
pacing to and fro, anxiously smoking, and hears the sounds
of HARGE repairing a pipe under the kitchen sink. She tries
occupying herself, perusing titles of books from the
bookshelf.

CAROL

… that's not fair, Harge.
We agreed that Rindy would stay with
me until Christmas Eve.

HARGE

What do you suggest I do? - You think
I prefer traipsing off to West Palm Beach for the holiday?

It was all mother's doing-

CAROL

But I'm not - ready - She's not
packed - she's asleep in bed!
What about my Christmas with my daughter-?

HARGE

I'm sorry, Carol, but it can't be helped.
The flight's in the morning
- You think I've packed?…
(the sound of dropped tools)-Goddamnit!

55. INT.
CAROL'S HOUSE. KITCHEN. CONTINUOUS.

HARGE emerges from beneath the sink, having hurt his hand.
CAROL goes to help him up. But as he does he spots THERESE
through the door. He marches over and opens it fully.
THERESE looks caught, startled. A silence.

HARGE

How do you know my wife?

CAROL

Harge, please…

THERESE

I - work at Frankenberg's.
The department store.

CAROL

I ordered a gift from her desk.
I forgot my gloves.
She returned them.
I thanked her.

HARGE

(to CAROL)
That's bold.

HARGE sizes THERESE up for a moment before he turns back
into the kitchen. He walks past CAROL and exits into a
cloakroom at the back of the house where we hear sounds of
his cleaning up. CAROL, exasperated, approaches the living
room doorway.

THERESE

Can I - do-

CAROL

Just… leave it be.

CAROL gently shuts the door. THERESE is left standing
there, shut out.

56. EXT.
CAROL'S HOUSE. NIGHT.

A UNIFORMED CHAUFFEUR sits at the wheel of Harge's car,
alert and silent, as CAROL bundles RINDY into the back
seat. FLORENCE puts her bags in the trunk as HARGE waits
with a cigarette and drink outside the front door.

CAROL

Remember: in bed by seven.
I know how you take advantage of Grandma
Jennifer. (beat) Okay, snow flake.

Gimme a big one.
(she hugs RINDY tightly and kisses her)
You're going to have the most
wonderful Christmas, I promise.

RINDY pulls back from the hug. She has an idea.

RINDY

There's room for you in the car,
Mommy. You can come with us!

CAROL

Oh, darling, I - wish I could...
but sometimes... Mommies and
Daddies decide there isn't enough
room for them both in the same place
at the same time- (unable to go further)
And Mommy has to be here to make sure
Santa's elf doesn't give your presents to
another little girl.
You wouldn't want that, would you?

RINDY gives her a bright smile and CAROL hugs her, and
kisses her eyelids. CAROL clocks the CHAUFFEUR watching her
through the rear view mirror, and quickly looks away.

57. INT.
CAROL'S HOUSE. LIVING ROOM. CONTINUOUS

MUSIC PLAYS softly from the phonograph ("El Americano" by
Xavier Cugat and his Orchestra) as THERESE tidies up,
trying to make herself useful. She can see CAROL through

the bay window, shutting the car door and starting back toward the house, wearing only a thin sweater around her shoulders.

She sees HARGE step off of the front porch, stub out his cigarette, and walk towards CAROL.

58. EXT.
CAROL'S HOUSE. CONTINUOUS.

CAROL heads to the front door, but HARGE pulls her back towards him. A silence, as he takes her hand in one of his.
He can hear the MUSIC from inside the house. He sways a little.

HARGE

You smell good.

CAROL

You're drunk.

He pulls her closer to him, he closes his eyes, tries to dance with her.

CAROL (CONT'D)

Harge, I'm cold.

59. INT.
CAROL'S HOUSE. LIVING ROOM. CONTINUOUS.

Through the open front door THERESE can see HARGE stumble back slightly, away from CAROL and CAROL grabbing his arm to right him.

CAROL

Let me get you some coffee.

HARGE

(a bit drunk)
I'm not drunk.

HARGE takes a step towards CAROL. THERESE ducks back into the living room, not wishing to overhear any more.

HARGE (CONT'D)

You can still come with us.
Go pack a bag.

CAROL

I can't do that.

HARGE

Sure, you can. It's easy.
We can buy you a ticket in the morning.

60. EXT.
CAROL'S HOUSE. CONTINUOUS.

HARGE tries to take her hand, she backs away.

HARGE

What? You're going to spend
Christmas with Abby? Is that it?
Or with your - shop girl?

CAROL

Stop it, Harge.

I put nothing past women like you.

CAROL

You married a woman like me.

61. INT.
CAROL'S HOUSE. LIVING ROOM. CONTINUOUS.

THERESE goes to the phonograph, increases the volume
slightly, so that she can hear only the rising and falling
of the voices outside.

62. EXT.
CAROL'S HOUSE. CONTINUOUS.

HARGE reaches out to grab CAROL, she backs away. He
stumbles, falls onto his knees. A silence, as he catches his breath.

HARGE

Come with me now. If you don't -
if you - let me - open that car
door - if you won't come-

CAROL

(she interrupts him)
Then what? Then it's over?

HARGE is about to respond, but he suddenly realizes he's on
his hands and knees, drunk, before CAROL, who is very still
and very silent.

HARGE

Goddamn you - You were never...
cruel.

CAROL

Harge...

CAROL takes a step towards HARGE. She cannot bear to see
him in this state. But HARGE won't accept her help now.
He rises, and takes a quick look at his waiting car, RINDY in
the back seat. HARGE takes a few deep breaths, smooths his
clothes, wipes his face with the palm of his hand. CAROL
takes another step towards him.

CAROL (CONT'D)

I'm sorry.

HARGE stiffens, recoils, digs his hands deep into his coat
pocket and turns away, striding briskly to his car. CAROL
watches as he piles in and shuts the door. The car drives
off. CAROL hugs herself tight against the cold.

63. INT.
CAROL'S HOUSE. EVENING. CONTINUOUS.

THERESE hears the front door quietly shut, standing at the
phonograph - still, silent. She looks up and CAROL is
there, watching her, but it's almost as if CAROL is looking
through her. Then CAROL goes to switch off the phonograph
and moves off to pour herself a drink. She opens the
cigarette case.

THERESE

I should call a cab.

CAROL

And just when you think it can't
get any worse, you run out of cigarettes.

THERESE

Oh - I - tell me where to go.
I'll buy some for you. Really, I don't mind-

CAROL

(snaps)
You don't have to run out in the
middle of nowhere to buy
cigarettes. Not for me. I'm fine.

A pause. CAROL drinks. THERESE covers her upset.

CAROL (CONT'D)

The next train's at 6.50.
I'll drive you to the station.

64. INT.
CAROL'S CAR. NIGHT.

CAROL drives THERESE to the station. There's no one else on
the road; it's utterly noiseless. At this moment there
couldn't be more distance between them.

65. INT.
TRAIN CAR. NIGHT.

THERESE sits against a window as the train speeds its way

back to Manhattan. A couple of HOLIDAY REVELERS, laughing and tipsy, bump against THERESE'S seat as they make their way through the car. THERESE turns to watch them as they make their way to the end of the car. Their joyfulness is unbearable to THERESE. She makes herself as small as she can against the window. She is crying.

66. INT.
SEMCO APARTMENT. NIGHT.

It's a warm, ramshackle apartment full of overstuffed, mismatched furniture and bowling trophies. In the kitchen, RICHARD washes up a pile of dinner plates while MRS. SEMCO sits at the table with THERESE. She takes a thermometer out of THERESE'S mouth and holds it up to the light to read it.

MRS. SEMCO
(refers to the thermometer)
What is this number?
I can't read it. My eyes!

THERESE reads the thermometer for MRS. SEMCO.

THERESE
Ninety-eight point six.
Perfectly normal. No fever.

RICHARD
You hear that ma, no fever.

MRS. SEMCO
My eyes is no good, not my ears.

You wanna plate of noodles, Terry?
We saved you a big plate.

THERESE

I'm really not that hungry.

MRS. SEMCO

(she's kidding, but she's not)
I thought you was a smart cookie.
You know that's not the way to
a mother-in-law's heart.

RICHARD and THERESE exchange a look. RICHARD'S mother has embarrassed him.

RICHARD

Ma - cut it out.

MRS. SEMCO

What? Cut it out what?

MR. SEMCO appears in the kitchen doorway. He wears a bowling shirt and carries a bowling bag.

MR. SEMCO

(to THERESE)
You showed up. Good. I was tired
of hearing him moan. Do me a favor, Therese.
Settle down with him already.

RICHARD'S even more embarrassed.

RICHARD

Come on, what is this?

The Inquisition?

THERESE

(defusing the situation)
Okay - I'll eat.

MRS SEMCO beams, pinches THERESE'S cheek.

MRS. SEMCO

That's my girl!

She prepares THERESE a plate. RICHARD and THERESE exchange a look. He appreciates her assist.

67. INT.
SEMCO APARTMENT. NIGHT.

RICHARD'S ROOM. THERESE and RICHARD sit on his bed. THERESE holds a wrapped box on her lap.

THERESE

I can't open this now.
It's days before Christmas.

RICHARD

But I want you to. (he shrugs)
I'm impatient.

THERESE unwraps and opens the box. Inside are brochures of France- and two tickets for passage on a ship. The date of departure: March 1, 1953. A pause.

THERESE

Richard… what is this?

RICHARD beams, takes one of the tickets from THERESE.

RICHARD

Well, that one's mine. I thought
it was more romantic to wrap'em up together.

THERESE stares at the ticket in her hand, picks up one of
the brochures full of pictures of Paris landmarks…

RICHARD (CONT'D)

Jeez, Terry, you could cheer up a little.
It's not every day you get
a trip to Europe for Christmas.

THERESE looks up at RICHARD.

THERESE

We're supposed to go in July.

RICHARD

I know, but - look, I was gonna
tell you on Christmas day.
Frankenberg's offered me a promotion.
Assistant manager, beds and bedding.

THERESE just stares at him, unable to say a word.

RICHARD (CONT'D)

It's a big raise. And they're letting me

take a month off in March,
two weeks of it paid.
The summer's a busy time there and-

THERESE

I can't go in March.

RICHARD

Why not? You get laid off next
week. It's not like you have any big plans.

But this stings THERESE, and RICHARD regrets saying it.

RICHARD (CONT'D)

I didn't mean - Terry, you know
I think the world of you and - well,
I thought you wanted to go to France.
With me. And I figured...
what the hell, the sooner the better...

THERESE

I do want to go. I did. (beat)
It's just - soon. March.

A silence. THERESE puts the ticket and brochure back into
the box, puts the lid back on to the box.

68. INT.
THERESE'S APARTMENT BLDG. LATE NIGHT.

THERESE can be seen through a window getting out of a cab,
entering the dark building and wearily climbing the stairs.
As she gets to her apartment door the hall telephone STARTS
TO RING. THERESE turns, sighs, goes to answer it.

                          THERESE

                           Hello?

A door down the hall cracks opens - THERESE'S LANDLADY
peers out towards THERESE.

                          LANDLADY

                  Do you know what time it is,
                        Miss Belivet?

                          THERESE

                   I'm sorry - it just rang...

None too pleased, THE LANDLADY shuts her door.
THERESE returns her attention to the phone.

                      THERESE (CONT'D)

                           Hello?

No one answers.

69. INT.
CAROL'S HOUSE. BEDROOM. CONTINUOUS.

CAROL, on the other line, smokes a cigarette, exhales.

70. INT.
THERESE'S APARTMENT BLDG. CONTINUOUS.

Suddenly, THERESE knows who's on the other end of the line.
She closes her eyes.

Carol.

CAROL (O.S.)

(after a beat)
I was - horrible. Before.
Will you forgive me?

THERESE

Yes… I mean… It's not-

CAROL (O.S.)

Then will you - would you - let me
come see you… tomorrow evening?

THERESE

Yes…Yes. (beat)
I want to - know. I think.
(MORE)

THERESE (CONT'D)

I mean, to ask you… things.
But I'm not sure you want that.

71. INT.
CAROL'S HOUSE. BEDROOM. CONTINUOUS.

CAROL

(after a beat)
Ask me. Things. Please.

72. INT.
THERESE'S APARTMENT BLDG. CONTINUOUS.

THERESE closes her eyes. Silence. Which is suddenly pierced

by A GROUP OF YOUNG PEOPLE entering THERESE'S building, giddy and intoxicated. THERESE is startled, watching them from above, stumbling into the building. By the time she puts the phone back to her ear, she knows CAROL'S hung up.

73. INT. FRANKENBERG'S. EMPLOYEE CAFETERIA. DAY.

The employee Christmas party is in progress, which consists of the same old lunch plus Christmas cookies, holiday music and decorations. THERESE stands next to RUBY ROBICHEK in a long line of staff. When it's RUBY'S turn, the SERVER gives RUBY double of everything in a food box. THERESE notices this, and RUBY sees her notice.

RUBY ROBICHEK

When you live alone, every penny
counts. You economize.
You'll learn.

THERESE

How do you know I live alone?

RUBY ROBICHEK

(very matter of fact)
You got that look.

THERESE and RUBY sit at a table. RUBY digs into her purse, finds a slip of paper and pen, scribbles down her address and telephone number and gives it to THERESE.

RUBY ROBICHEK (CONT'D)

I know everything there is to
know about this place.
I'll fill you in.

THERESE

I'm only here a few more days.

RUBY ROBICHEK

Yeah? Where you going? Macy's?
I knew it! You look like the type
who can go swanky.

This pleases RUBY and she digs into her lunch with gusto.
A silence. THERESE watches her eat. She watches everybody
eat, seemingly in unison. THERESE slides her tray over to RUBY.

THERESE

You take it.
I don't feel like eating.

RUBY ROBICHEK

You sure?
This is good brisket.

THERESE nods. RUBY takes THERESE'S meal and shovels it into
her food box.

RUBY ROBICHEK (CONT'D)

You're a good kid. I can get
through two, three days with this.

THERESE summons a smile in reply, at a loss for words.

74. EXT.
MIDTOWN MANHATTAN. SAME DAY.

From a distance, we see CAROL'S car pull swiftly into a parking space near FRED HAYMES' law offices. CAROL gets out of the car and walks briskly down the busy street into the building.

75. INT.
HAYMES LAW OFFICES. MOMENTS LATER.

FRED HAYMES, CAROL'S lawyer, is just returning to his office when he catches CAROL delivering a small Christmas present to his SECRETARY.

CAROL	SECRETARY
Merry Christmas, Katherine.	Ohhh...

CAROL

It's nothing, I assure you. (looks up)
Well, there he is. Now will you
talk to me?

FRED HAYMES

I didn't want you to come all the
way down here-

CAROL

Just - give it to me, straight,
Fred. What am I not to worry about
until after the holiday?

They settle inside FRED'S office and FRED closes the door.

FRED HAYMES

(after a beat)
Look, Jerry Rix served some papers
this morning. To my complete surprise.
Why don't you sit down?

CAROL

Why is it people think you're
going to take bad news better
if you're sitting down?

An awkward silence. FRED clears his throat.

FRED HAYMES

Harge has sought an injunction
which denies you any access to
Rindy until the custody hearing.
And I'm afraid Harge has changed
his mind about joint custody.
He wants sole custody of Rindy.

CAROL

What?

CAROL is stunned. She sits.

CAROL (CONT'D)

We've already reached an agreement on custody.
What is this all about?

FRED HAYMES

They'll be filing papers
on the twenty-ninth in District Family
Court for the, uh, permanent custody petition.

CAROL

Can he do this? Is it - right?

FRED HAYMES

I don't know if it's right, but it's legal.

CAROL

On what grounds.

FRED HAYMES

(stalling)
Listen. Let's - deal with this
after Christmas. You'll have a chance to-

CAROL

(she interrupts him)
On. What. Grounds.

FRED HAYMES

They're petitioning the judge to
consider a morality clause.

CAROL

A morality - what the hell does
that mean?

FRED HAYMES

(after a moment)
Okay. I won't mince words with you.
Abby Gerhard.

CAROL

Abby is Rindy's godmother. Abby is…
(to herself, really) He's…
If he can't have me, I can't have Rindy - That's…

A silence.

FRED HAYMES

I'm sorry. But they seem serious.

CAROL looks up to FRED, nods.

CAROL

When's the custody hearing?

FRED HAYMES

It's hard to say.
With the holidays and a backlog of cases...

CAROL

Your best guess, Fred.

FRED HAYMES

Not before the middle of March.
Could be April.

A silence.

CAROL

Can I see her?

FRED HAYMES

(not unkindly)
Not - let me put it this way - It would not be
advisable under the-

CAROL

At school? In an office with a-?

FRED HAYNES

The issue is not-

                        CAROL

              Surely a visit supervised by
                  a teacher or a-

                     FRED HAYNES

              Carol, these are serious
              allegations. Forcing contact
              before the hearing you simply
              invite further scrutiny concerning
                  your conduct.

                        CAROL

              My conduct! Jesus Christ.
              I'm her mother for God's sake. (beat)
                  Morality clause. I see.

                     FRED HAYNES

                     Do you.

                        CAROL

              No. There's nothing moral about
                  taking Rindy away from me.

CAROL looks back at him in a state of frozen disbelief.

76. EXT.
FIFTH AVENUE. SAME AFTERNOON.

CAROL reenters the street in a numbing daze. She passes
crowds of Christmas SHOPPERS with places to go and things
to do. She's not one of those people. She finds herself
walking back in the direction of her car through the glare
of winter light. She puts a cigarette to her lips and begins
searching through her purse, struggling to find a light.

Finally glancing up she is struck by the sight of truck backing out of the lot, and collides with a PEDESTRIAN clearing way.

A VOICE

Watchit, lady!

CAROL

Pardon me.

CAROL turns into a shop window where she finally manages to light her cigarette, taking several deep drags. Looking up she focuses a moment on the display. It's a vacation theme: sunglasses on mannequins, cameras slung around their necks, luggage stacked in artful piles. She lets her gaze fall on a large two-tone brown leather suitcase.

77. INT.
RECORD SHOP. EAST 50'S. SAME LATE AFTERNOON.

THERESE waits for a requested title at the front counter of a midtown record store. The STORE CLERK returns with her request: A Billie Holiday album, with "Easy Living" prominently displayed on its cover.

THERESE

Yes, that's it, thank you.

She hands him a five-dollar bill and he begins ringing her up. As she waits for her change, she spots two SHORT-HAIRED WOMEN at the listening station, sharing a single pair of headphones. The more mannish of the two, in horn-rim glasses, leans against the railing dressed in tailored trousers and

jacket over a button-down shirt. The other wears a sleekly
tailored woman's suit, very professional. They are obviously
a couple of some kind: New York lesbians. THERESE observes
them for a moment, until the woman in slacks looks
over - and THERESE quickly looks down.

78. EXT.
RECORD SHOP. EAST 50'S.

RICHARD, waiting outside with his bike, turns to find
THERESE walking briskly out of the record shop.

> **THERESE**
> Let's walk.
> I want to drop this at home.

> **RICHARD**
> Your wish is my command.

They start down the block toward THERESE's apartment.

> **RICHARD (CONT'D)**
> Find what you wanted?

> **THERESE**
> (no big deal)
> Yeah… Something for someone at the store.

> **RICHARD**
> You up for the jazz club later on?

> **THERESE**
> Ohh, I don't know.

RICHARD

S'fine. (beat) But you should stop
by on Christmas sometime.
My Mom's sort of planning on it.

THERESE

Christmas... that's for families.
I'd feel - I don't know...

RICHARD

You are family, Terry.

They turn down a small driveway, cutting through an empty lot.
THERESE tries to change the subject.

THERESE

I'm thinking of putting together a
portfolio, you know, of my pictures.
Start taking portraits, even. Apply for jobs.
Maybe at a newspaper. Maybe at the Times.
Dannie knows someone--

RICHARD

Have you been thinking any more
about Europe? (no answer) Terry?

THERESE stops, brooding, and RICHARD stops and turns to her.

RICHARD (CONT'D)

What?

THERESE

How many times have you been in love?

RICHARD

(laughs, not sure where this came from)
Whoa. Never. Until You.

THERESE

Don't lie. You told me about those
two other girls.

RICHARD

Come on. They were - I had sex with them.
That's not the same thing.

THERESE

Meaning... I'm different because
we haven't...(quietly) gone all the way?

RICHARD

No, no - that's not what I - hey,
what's this all about? I love you.
That's what's different.

THERESE nods. They resume walking.

THERESE

Have you ever been in love with a boy?

RICHARD

(after a long beat)
No.

THERESE

But you've heard of it?

RICHARD

Of course. I mean, have I heard of people like that? Sure.

THERESE

I don't mean people like that.
I mean two people who just...
fall in love. With each other. Say,
a boy and a boy. Out of the blue.

RICHARD

I don't know anyone like that.
But I'll tell you this - there's
always some reason for it.
In the background.

THERESE

So you don't think it could just -
happen to somebody,
just - anybody?

RICHARD

No. I don't. What are you saying?
Are you in love with a girl?

THERESE

No.

They reach THERESE'S building. RICHARD leans his bike
against a railing, takes THERESE'S hands in his.

RICHARD

Don't you know I want to spend my
life with you, Terry? Come to
France with me. Let's get married.

THERESE

Richard, I'm not - ready. For
that. I can't make myself-

RICHARD

What? Tell me.

THERESE

I just... I have to go.

RICHARD

Terry.

THERESE

I'm sorry.

THERESE runs up the stairs to her building's front door, and is in before RICHARD can say another word.

79. INT.
COCKTAIL BAR.
SAME LATE AFTERNOON/EARLY EVENING.

ABBY and CAROL sip martinis in silence at a favorite joint. The brown two-tone suitcase CAROL saw in the shop rests against the table.

CAROL

I found Rindy's hair brush
underneath my pillow this morning.
Full of her hair. She does that,
you know, to let me know she's
been a good girl and brushed
properly. I usually clean it out
but - today, for some reason…

Beat.

ABBY

How could he. How dare he…
A morality what?

CAROL

Clause, he said.

ABBY

Carol - If I'm responsible in any way-

CAROL

Don't you dare - don't you ever.

CAROL downs her drink. She pushes it towards ABBY for a refill. ABBY refills for them both.

ABBY

Hey. You know that tailor's shop
that went bust in Hoboken?

CAROL

Sure. The one with the - the - glass thingy on the-

ABBY

Exactly. The glass thingy.
That one.

CAROL laughs.

CAROL

Bullshit. You have no idea what
I'm talking about.

ABBY

You're right. But it's good to
hear you laugh.

ABBY offers CAROL a cigarette, she takes it, ABBY lights it. CAROL leans back in her chair, relaxes.

ABBY (CONT'D)

Anyway, the landlord offered me a lease.
I was thinking - another furniture shop?
I'll need some help with restorations
every once in a while,
and you're the varnish master, so...

CAROL

You're serious.

ABBY

I'm serious. (beat) Couldn't be
any more of a disaster than the shop we had.

A silence. ABBY looks away from CAROL. CAROL leans in towards her.

CAROL

Hey. We weren't a disaster. It just...

CAROL doesn't have the words.

ABBY

I know. Timing. Never had it.
Anyway, I've got my eye on this
redhead who owns a steak house in Paramus.
I'm talking - serious
Rita Hayworth redhead.

CAROL

Really? You think you have what it
takes to handle a redhead?

They share a naughty smile, thinking about serious
redheads. They toast. ABBY gestures to the suitcase.

> ABBY
>
> You going somewhere?

> CAROL
>
> West, I was thinking… For a few weeks.
> Until the hearing. What else am I going to do?

A silence.

> ABBY
>
> Well I know you don't like driving alone.
> So. (beat; ABBY takes a deep breath, exhales)
> She's young.

CAROL nods her agreement: there's no denying it.

> ABBY (CONT'D)
>
> Tell me you know what you're doing.

> CAROL
>
> I don't. (silence) I never did.

80. INT.
THERESE'S APARTMENT. SAME NIGHT.

Someone is knocking at Therese's door.

THERESE sticks her head out of her bathroom and looks
quickly around the room. She hurries out, still brushing

her hair and fixing her blouse. As she walks to the door
she quickly stashes the Billie Holiday record under a pillow, and
flips on the phonograph ("Smoke Rings," Les Paul & Mary Ford
begins to play). She takes a last look at her freshly tidied
apartment and pulls opens the door.

It's CAROL, the suitcase on the floor beside her.

CAROL

Your landlady let me in.

CAROL lights a cigarette. THERESE can do nothing for a moment
but stare. Then THERESE catches sight of the suitcase, which
CAROL pushes across the threshold with her foot.

CAROL (CONT'D)

Merry Christmas. (beat)
Open it.

THERESE bends down to open the suitcase. Inside is a brand
new camera and plenty of rolls of film.

81. INT.
THERESE'S APARTMENT. LATER.

CAROL looks at THERESE'S photographs. She takes her time,
really examining them. THERESE watches without crowding her
- eager for her good opinion. CAROL comes to the photograph
THERESE took of her at the tree lot, hung on the wall.

She's moved by it, by the primacy of place THERESE has given.

THERESE

It's not that good. I was rushed,
I mean… I can do better.

CAROL

It's perfect.

Leaning against the end-table, CAROL picks up a small photo
in its original cardboard frame: THERESE, aged 5, at a convent
school.

CAROL (CONT'D)

Is this you?

THERESE

Yes.

CAROL puts it down, a bit abruptly, and steps into
THERESE'S kitchen sink/dark room.

CAROL

Do you keep anything in the icebox
besides photo chemicals? I'm feeling-

THERESE

Sure.

THERESE heads to the icebox, where she fishes out a couple
of beers. She turns back to find CAROL another step away,
fighting back tears.

THERESE is frozen for a moment, not knowing exactly what to do. She approaches CAROL but hesitates, looking down at the beers in her hand before setting them down on the counter. She proceeds gingerly, putting a tentative hand on CAROL's shoulder, squeezing it. Very quietly, still turned away, CAROL breaks. She lowers her head as THERESE steps closer.

82. EXT.
THERESE'S ROOF. NIGHT.

Sipping coffee from mugs, CAROL saunters along the perimeter of the roof while THERESE sits on a perch, watching. It's not much of a view, but they can see the tips of the impressive buildings, the lights, the cloudy night sky.

THERESE

Is there any point in,
I don't know… fighting it?

CAROL

The injunction? (beat) No.

THERESE

Three months. I feel - useless.
Like I can't help you or offer anything-

CAROL

It has nothing to do with you.

A pause. The remark stings THERESE, but she tries to conceal it.

CAROL (CONT'D)

I'm going away for a while.

CAROL

THERESE
When? Where?

CAROL
Wherever my car will take me.
West. Soon.

THERESE can't hide her dismay.

CAROL (CONT'D)
And I thought… perhaps you'd
like to come with me.

A beat. CAROL looks directly at THERESE.

CAROL (CONT'D)
Would you?

A long, held moment before THERESE makes a decision.

THERESE
Yes. Yes, I would.

A few flurries of snow have begun to fall.

83. INT.
FRANKENBERG'S. EMPLOYEE LOCKER ROOM.
CHRISTMAS EVE. DAY.

THERESE is removing her personal belongings from her locker
(some stockings, scarves, books) and putting them in her bag.

She separates her Frankenberg's Employee Handbook and her slightly bloody Santa cap and places them in the locker shelf. Down at the other end of the locker room she hears some girls approaching. Beyond them she spots RUBY ROBICHEK seated on a bench, rolling up her calf-length stockings, looking more weary and alone than ever. THERESE carefully shuts her locker.

84. EXT.
FRANKENBERG'S. MOMENTS LATER

Through the Christmas display windows we see THERESE exit the store with her belongings and hail a cab from the street. As the taxi whisks her off we see her glance back one last time.

85. INT.
THERESE'S APARTMENT. CHRISTMAS EVE. DAY.

THERESE and RICHARD at the kitchen table. THERESE'S clothes and suitcase are spread out on the bed.

RICHARD

I don't get it. I don't get it,
Therese. Who is this woman to you?

THERESE

She's a friend.

RICHARD

I'm your friend, Terry.
Phil is your friend - Dannie.
This woman - you don't even know her.

THERESE

(after a pause)
You can forward any mail to
Chicago, General Post, but I just
paid rent through February.
I had a little money saved up for the - for...

RICHARD looks up at her sharply.
THERESE looks away from him.

RICHARD

For our trip. Our trip, Terry.
And now you're - I don't believe this is happening!

THERESE

I can't explain it. I just -

RICHARD

What? You've got one hell of a
crush on this woman is what...
You're like a schoolgirl!

THERESE

I do not - I just like her is all.
I like talking with her.
I'm fond of anybody
I can really talk to.

This stings him, and they exchange a sharp look.

RICHARD

Nice. You know what I think? I
think two weeks from now you'll be
wishing you... She'll get tired of
you and you'll wish you never-

THERESE

-You don't understand-!

RICHARD

I do - I understand completely.
You're in a trance!

THERESE

I'm wide awake. I've never felt
more awake. (beat) Why don't you
leave me alone?

THERESE has surprised herself with her boldness.

RICHARD

Are we over? Is that what this is?

THERESE

I didn't say that. But why should
I want to be with you if all you
do is argue about this?

RICHARD

To say - to say for a minute you
practically want to say goodbye
because of some silly crush!

THERESE

I didn't say that. You said it.

RICHARD grabs his jacket and starts out the front door.

RICHARD

You made me buy boat tickets,
I got a better job for you...

I asked you to marry me, for
Chrissakes...

86. INT.
THERESE'S APARTMENT BUILDING. HALLWAY. DAY.

THERESE

I never made you - I never asked
you for - anything. Maybe that's
the problem.

As he storms down the stairs, the LANDLADY sticks her head
out of her door, observing the row.

RICHARD

I swear to you, two weeks from now
you'll be begging me to forget this ever-!

THERESE

Richard... Richard!

RICHARD

Have a great trip, Terry!

He storms out of the building as THERESE starts back to her
apartment, receiving the LANDLADY's glares.

87. INT.
THERESE'S APARTMENT. LATER.

BRIEF CLOSE-UPS: THERESE places clothes in her new suitcase.
She wraps CAROL's gift. She composes CAROL's gift card.

88. INT.
CAROL'S HOUSE. GUEST ROOM.
EARLY CHRISTMAS MORNING.

THERESE is roused from sleep with the sound of an
approaching car. She opens her eyes, taking in her
surroundings - the comfortable guest room at CAROL'S.
She hears voices from outside and turns to look out her window.

A fresh layer of snow has fallen and ABBY'S car has pulled
up the drive, top-down as usual. CAROL can be seen outside,
with a coat thrown over her robe.

> CAROL
>
> Are you on your way to bed or just
> getting up?

> ABBY
>
> Both.

ABBY tries to stifle a laugh, doesn't quite. CAROL puts a
finger to her lips: "shhh."

> ABBY (CONT'D)
>
> Go for a ride?

> CAROL
>
> You nitwit.

> ABBY
>
> Well, I had to come see you off,
> didn't I?

CAROL

I'm not alone.

ABBY

Uh-oh…

CAROL

(laughs, then)
Come in. There's coffee.

ABBY hops out of the car.

89. INT.
CAROL'S HOUSE. HALLWAY. MOMENTS LATER.

ABBY and CAROL enter the house.

ABBY

This place is gloomy as a coal pit
in the mornings.

They see THERESE sitting at the top of the stairs in her
pajamas.

CAROL

We woke you. Go back to sleep,
it's early…

THERESE

That's okay. Can I - come down?

ABBY stifles a snort. CAROL ribs her, good-naturedly.
THERESE guardedly watches the way the two interact.

Of course.
There's a robe in the closet.

THERESE stands, and ABBY sizes her up.

CAROL (CONT'D)

This is Abby Gerhard.

ABBY

I have no manners.

CAROL

Absolutely none.

ABBY

But it's nice to meet you,
Therese, all the same.

THERESE nods, smiling, then slips back down the hall.

90. INT.
CAROL'S HOUSE. KITCHEN. LATER. DAY

ABBY is finishing preparing sandwiches which THERESE is
wrapping up.

THERESE

Have you known Carol for a long time?

ABBY

Uh-huh.

A pause while they work.

                        THERESE

                 Did you ever take a trip?
                  With Carol, I mean?

                         ABBY

                     Two or three.

THERESE can't quite cover her slight frown. ABBY clocks this.

                     ABBY (CONT'D)

                 We had a furniture shop for
                a couple years, outside Elizabeth.
                So we were always on the prowl for
                   antiques or second-hand stuff.

She grabs a pack of cigarettes from the counter, lights one.
THERESE watches her. ABBY offers her a cigarette and a light.

                     ABBY (CONT'D)

                 You old enough to smoke?

A beat, before ABBY breaks a smile, and THERESE decides to
smile along.

                        THERESE
                         Okay…

A beat, then:

                         ABBY

              You know she's got a lot of worries right now…

You know that, don't you?

THERESE

I know.

ABBY

And she's lonely.

THERESE

Is that why she wants me
to go with her?

ABBY

No...

ABBY looks out a kitchen window, smokes.

ABBY (CONT'D)

Just - don't want to see her
getting hurt. That's it.

THERESE

I'd never hurt Carol.
You think I would?

ABBY

No. (she looks frankly at THERESE) I don't.

THERESE starts putting the food and drinks into a large
picnic basket.

THERESE

What happened to the furniturestore?

ABBY sighs. She suddenly looks a little sad to THERESE.

314

ABBY

It was... (resuming her chores):
Some things don't work out,
no matter how much you want them to.

91. EXT.
CAROL'S HOUSE. LATER. DAY.

THERESE and CAROL finish loading up the trunk and wiping
the last of the snow from the windshield. CAROL slams the
trunk lid shut, strides to the driver's side, opens the door,
gets in. THERESE hurriedly removes the last of the snow
from the back windshield as CAROL starts up the car,
revving the engine. The hot exhaust creates a swirl of
steam as a soft spell of MUSIC rises. THERESE trots up to
the passenger side door, taking a last look around before
jumping into the car.

92. INT.
CAROL'S CAR / EXT ROAD TO PENNSYLVANIA.
LATER. DAY.

MUSIC continues over shots inside the car: THERESE pouring
coffee for CAROL from the thermos - piping hot and precreamed.
THERESE lighting two cigarettes and handing one to CAROL,
as they drive through the black and white of the snowy thruway
towards Philadelphia.

93. INT.
PHILLY DINER. LATER.

CAROL and THERESE eat tomato soup and crackers,

virtually alone in the dreary city diner.
A few dismal strands of tinsel and garland, strewn about
for holiday effect, surround a green and red cardboard
banner which reads: MERY CHTMAS. THERESE puts aside her
meal, gazes out of the window at the largely deserted city streets.

THERESE

I could get used to having a whole city to myself.

THERESE turns to CAROL, who smiles in approval at THERESE'S
plan. THERESE can't wait any longer, reaching under her seat
and producing her nicely wrapped gift for CAROL.

THERESE (CONT'D)

For you. Merry Christmas.

CAROL

No - You shouldn't have.

But CAROL is pleased, and THERESE is pleased that
she's pleased.

THERESE

Open it.

She watches CAROL unwrap the package. It's the Billie Holiday
record with "Easy Living" on it.

THERESE (CONT'D)

I played it for you.
At your house.

316

CAROL

I remember. (beat; she looks up at THERESE)
Thank you.

THERESE picks up her camera, focuses on CAROL, and snaps
a picture. CAROL brings her hands up to her face.

CAROL (CONT'D)

Oh God, I look a fright - don't -

THERESE

You do not, you look…
(she leans over and takes them back down)
wonderful… Just - stay like that.

THERESE realizes she's holding CAROL'S hands in her own.
She quickly looks around the diner, feeling slightly
embarrassed, but no one else is looking. CAROL clocks this,
squeezing THERESE'S hands and gently extricating herself.

CAROL

Do you miss Richard?

THERESE

(she thinks about it)
No. I haven't thought about him all day.
Or of home.

CAROL

Home.

THERESE regrets using the word, watching CAROL's mood
darken, slightly.

94. INT./EXT.
PHILLY DINER. INNER PHILADELPHIA. LATER.

THERESE returns from the ladies room at the rear of the
diner, walking past a WOMAN IN HER THIRTIES gathering her
THREE YOUNG CHILDREN. At first THERESE doesn't see CAROL,
then spots her through the window, at a pay telephone. She
sees her inserting her change and quickly dialing a number.

HEAR THE RINGS: Once. Twice. Three times. CAROL glances
toward the diner window. Through the glass one of the WOMAN's
CHILDREN is making faces through the precipitation.
Just beyond is THERESE, paying the bill at the counter.
CAROL replaces the receiver in its cradle before the call can be
answered. THERESE turns to exit the diner and spots CAROL
smoking a cigarette.

95. INT./EXT.
CAROL'S CAR. NIGHT.

CAROL drives. THERESE is sleeping, huddled up against the
passenger side window. A blanket partly covers her.

RADIO V.O.
…and that concludes our Holiday
Greetings from President-elect and
Mrs. Eisenhower. This is WORPittsburgh
wishing you and yours-

CAROL takes one hand off the steering wheel and pulls up
the blanket so THERESE is covered.

96. EXT.
TWO-LANE HIGHWAY OUTSIDE OF PITTSBURGH. NIGHT

CAROL'S car glides along the empty road, behind it, the eerie glow of the Pittsburgh industrial skyline, ahead of it: pitch darkness.

97. EXT.
ABBY'S HOUSE. NIGHT.

We see HARGE rushing out of the rear door of his car, his CHAUFFEUR idling, and rushing up the walk of a dark, brickfront bungalow.

98. INT.
ABBY'S HOUSE.

Ferocious banging on the front door as ABBY rushes down stairs, tying up a robe as she goes. She opens the door.
It's HARGE, in a state, breathing hard.

HARGE
I have to speak to her.

ABBY
What are you doing? - You're
supposed to be in Florida.

HARGE
(after a beat)
I couldn't do it. I had to - Rindy
- she wanted to see her mother on Christmas.
Not that it's any of your business.

Just go get her. I know she's here.

ABBY

You've got some fucking nerve
ordering me around. And, no. She's not here.

HARGE

That's impossible.
She's not home.
She's not with me.
She must be with you.

ABBY

(after a moment)
Yeah, you know, Harge,
you have a point.
You've spent ten years
making damned sure her only point
of reference is you, her only
focus in life is you, your job,
your friends, your family, your-

HARGE

WHERE IS SHE. (beat; he composes
himself) She's still my wife, Abby.
I'm responsible for her.

ABBY

Well, you know, that's some way of
showing it, Harge - slapping her
with an injunction. I'm closing the door.

ABBY starts to close it but HARGE intercepts.

HARGE

I love her.

ABBY

ABBY quietly shuts the door. But each remains unmoving a moment, in the dark.

99. EXT.
MOTEL. OUTSIDE PITTSBURGH. DAY

THERESE is stepping out of her room with her suitcase, dressed for the day. She walks over to the next room and quietly knocks on the door.

THERESE

Carol?

When there's no answer, she tries the door. It's open.

100. INT.
MOTEL ROOM. OUTSIDE PITTSBURGH. DAY

THERESE peeks her head into the room, to the sound of running water from the bathroom. She sees CAROL's overnight case is open on her bed, her things spread about the room.

CAROL (O.S.)

Therese, is that you?

THERESE

Yes!

CAROL (O.S.)

Would you be a sweetie and fetch my red knit sweater?

It's in the small suitcase.
Upper left hand side.

                    THERESE
                      Okay.

THERESE finds the case, opens it. She takes a moment to
look at CAROL'S clothes in the case before she actually
touches them, feeling the fabrics, the silks and cashmeres,
taking in their powdery smells. Something at the bottom of
the case catches her eye. A glint of metal beneath some
stockings. She removes the stockings, revealing a small,
pearl-handled pistol. She reaches out, tentatively, to
touch it, just as CAROL calls out from the bathroom.

                  O/S CAROL
               Hey, slowpoke…

THERESE quickly withdraws her hand and hurriedly replaces
CAROL'S clothing. She grabs the red sweater.

                   THERESE
                   Found it.

THERESE takes the sweater to the bathroom door and knocks
lightly. The door opens, revealing CAROL standing there
with a towel wrapped around her. Steam filters out of the
bathroom. THERESE hesitates a moment, then hands her the
sweater.

                    CAROL
               Everything all right?

THERESE

Yeah - I'm just - suddenly starving.

CAROL

(closing the door):
I won't be a minute.

101. INT.
CAROL'S CAR. ON THE ROAD. DAY.

CAROL drives, looking out on the increasingly frozen
landscape. THERESE is grabbing a sandwich from a basket on
the back seat. CAROL'S packed suitcase rests beside it.
THERESE settles back into her seat.

THERESE

Do you feel safe?
With me, I mean?

CAROL

(laughs)
You're full of surprises.

THERESE continues thinking, eating her sandwich.

THERESE

But - Do you?

CAROL glances at her. THERESE holds her gaze. CAROL turns
her attention back to the road.

CAROL

It's the wrong question.

THERESE

But you'd tell me. If something
scared you. And I could help.

CAROL shakes her head, smiles.

CAROL

I'm not frightened, Therese.

THERESE considers this, then glances back at CAROL, who peers
out at the open road, the cool winter sun skating across her face.

102. EXT.
MCKINLEY MOTEL. CANTON, OHIO. DUSK.

CAROL'S car pulls into the drive of a small motel with an
elaborate and large painted likeness of William McKinley on
wood billboard.

103. INT.
MCKINLEY MOTEL. CANTON, OHIO. DUSK.

The front desk of the blonde-wood hotel office. A very prim
HOTEL MANAGER assists CAROL, checking in.

HOTEL MANAGER

Our standard rooms come equipped
with stereophonic console radios,

or if you prefer, the Presidential
Suite is available. At a very attractive rate.

CAROL

(thinks a moment, then)
Two standard rooms should be fine.

THERESE

Why not take the Presidential Suite?

CAROL and THERESE exchange a look.

THERESE (CONT'D) (CONT'D)

If the rate's attractive...

104. EXT.
MCKINLEY MOTEL. CANTON, OHIO. NIGHT.

THERESE at the ice dispenser. She's bundled up in scarf,
gloves, overcoat - but wearing bunny slippers.
She struggles to fill an ice bucket, shivering.

YOUNG MAN

Can I - hold that for you?

THERESE looks up. A tall, affable looking young man with
spectacles appears beside her, holding up the lid of the
dispenser while she fills her bucket.

THERESE

Thank you. It's cold.

YOUNG MAN

So cold my glasses've fogged clear over.

THERESE

Thanks again. G'night.

YOUNG MAN

Night.

He tips his hat to her and THERESE heads back to her room.

105. INT.
MCKINLEY MOTEL ROOM. NIGHT.

True to its name, framed photographs of William McKinley
and his wife hang over the twin beds. Also adorning the
suite, a dressing table with a fan-shaped mirror, bedside
cabinets, gold-specked table lamps, striped wall paper.
A record plays on THERESE's portable turntable, ("Easy Living
(1933 version)" by Billie Holiday). THERESE sits beside CAROL
at the dressing table as CAROL carefully applies mascara
to THERESE'S lashes.

CAROL

Don't blink. (beat) Now look at you.

CAROL turns THERESE around to the mirror.

THERESE

I need lipstick.

CAROL chooses a lipstick, gives it to THERESE and watches as THERESE applies it. CAROL hands THERESE a tissue. THERESE blots, hands CAROL the tissue.

THERESE (CONT'D)

Next?

CAROL picks up a perfume bottle, hands it to THERESE.

CAROL

Would mademoiselle be so kind as
to apply at the pulse points only?

THERESE applies perfume to the inside of her wrists, the crook of her arms, and her neck. She turns to CAROL. CAROL holds out her wrists to THERESE.

CAROL (CONT'D)

Me, too.

THERESE applies perfume to the same spots on CAROL. CAROL closes her eyes, arches her neck back slightly.

CAROL (CONT'D)

That's divine. Smell that.

A beat, and THERESE leans forward to smell CAROL'S perfume.

106. INT.
MCKINLEY MOTEL ROOM. LATE NIGHT.

From her neighboring twin bed, THERESE watches CAROL sleep.
Very gently, she slips out of her bed and sits down
silently on the edge of CAROL'S bed, and watches her
breath. She quietly lifts a finger and lightly runs it
along CAROL'S cheek. CAROL turns over in her sleep. THERESE
waits to be sure CAROL won't wake, then returns to her own bed.

107. INT.
MCKINLEY MOTEL OFFICE. MORNING.

THERESE is seated in the improvised breakfast room, made up
of a few mismatched tables and chairs, and a paltry spread
of coffee, juice and rolls. She spots the YOUNG MAN from
the ice dispenser pouring himself a cup of coffee, carrying
a large black case. He spots THERESE and smiles broadly.

YOUNG MAN

Good morning.
Glad to see you
didn't freeze over or nothing.

THERESE

You too.

Before she can even respond he's setting down his cup and
pulling up a chair. THERESE spots CAROL arriving with a roadmap,
making a beeline to the coffee.

THERESE (CONT'D)

Not the best coffee I'm afraid.

YOUNG MAN

Long as it's hot.

THERESE

What's in the case?

YOUNG MAN

Oh. Notions.
I'm a - I sell them. Or try to.

CAROL arrives opposite Therese and plops down.

CAROL

Lousy coffee.

YOUNG MAN

(surprised by her arrival)
Sorry- (he attempts to stand)

CAROL

Excuse me?

THERESE

We were just chatting.

YOUNG MAN

Name's Tucker… Tommy.

THERESE

(extending her hand)
Therese Belivet. Carol Aird.

TOMMY TUCKER

(shaking hands)
Pleased to meet you.

THERESE

Mr. Tucker sells notions.

THERESE makes a gesture to his case, which CAROL regards.

CAROL

I see.

TOMMY TUCKER

(brief silence)
Don't really know what notions are,
exactly. But they do instruct us to
use the word. Says it appeals to
women. So... (beat)
I did sell a shoe-horn yesterday
to a feller in Wheeling.

THERESE

(trying to help him out)
Do you sell lipstick?

TOMMY TUCKER

No. But I have a sewing kit.
(beat) You don't need a sewing
kit. I can tell.

CAROL smiles politely, but returns her attention to the map.

CAROL

(to THERESE)
We should make Chicago by five or
six, if we get an early start.

TOMMY TUCKER

That's where I'm headed.

There's a short cut
across the interstates,
knocks two hours off the drive.

CAROL

Two hours, that's…
That would be great-

THERESE

Can we stop to buy some magazines?

TOMMY TUCKER

(reaching for his case)
I got Field and Stream…
National Geographic?

THERESE

Popular Photography?

TOMMY TUCKER

(a beat as he smiles)
Nope. Course not. I am doomed to
remain without a sale.

THERESE throws a little smile to CAROL, as TOMMY shakes his head. MUSIC picks up, carrying over the following scenes.

108. EXT.
OPEN ROAD. LATER. DAY

The wide open road stretches out before us as CAROL'S car comes gliding by.

109. INT.
CAROL'S CAR. LATER. DAY

Inside, THERESE enjoys the sweet boredom of nothing but time

in CAROL'S company. She scans the radio dial.

110. EXT.
ROADSIDE. LATER. DAY

CAROL and THERESE, bundled in coats and scarves, sit on the
low branch of a tree, just off the road, sharing sandwiches
and thermos coffee.

111. EXT.
DRAKE HOTEL. CHICAGO. NIGHT

The shimmering entrance to Chicago's Drake Hotel is a swarm
of taxis, GUESTS and BELL-HOPS. CAROL and THERESE, bleary
from the road, come to a stop and begin quickly gathering
their things from the car.

112. INT.
DRAKE HOTEL ROOM. LATER.

A BELLBOY carries CAROL and THERESE'S bags into an opulent
room. We hear CAROL tip and thank him as we follow THERESE
into her first encounter with hotel luxury. CAROL collapses
onto one of the beds.

CAROL

Finally. A real bed. Heaven.

THERESE inspects the room like a detective. She bends to
run her hand through the carpet.

                                    THERESE

                    This carpet - it feels like woven
                        silk! Like we shouldn't be
                    stepping on it. And the furniture!

She turns to look at CAROL... fast asleep on the bed.

113. INT.
DRAKE HOTEL. RESTAURANT. LATER.

Carol speaks to the hostess as Therese observes the busy hotel restaurant,
with WAITERS moving briskly and efficiently through the room.

                                    CAROL

                    Table for two, please, for dinner.

                                  HOSTESS

                    Are you staying here at the hotel?

                                    CAROL

                          Yes, it's room...
                      (she searches for her key)

                                  THERESE

                          623. Mrs. Aird.

                                  HOSTESS

                    That'll be just a moment, Mrs.
                              Aird.

                                    CAROL

                          Thank you.

Therese eyes the gifts and souvenirs at the counter:
fancy boxes of candy, souvenir key rings, pens. She lifts a can
of specialty Virginia ham.

Do you think something like this
would appeal to an older woman?

CAROL

I suppose. Depends on the woman.

THERESE

I worked with a woman at Frankenberg's - Ruby.
But she depressed me.

CAROL

Why?

THERESE

She's old. Alone. No money.
It's - silly, I know.

CAROL

I think it's a lovely gesture.
Send it. Here.

CAROL picks up the order form and pencil and hands it to
THERESE.

HOSTESS

Mrs. Aird, your table is ready.

CAROL

Thank you.

Therese takes the form and pencil with her as they are led to
their table.

114. INT.
CENTRAL POST OFFICE. PHONE BOOTH.
CHICAGO. DAY.

CAROL in a phone booth placing a call. She can see THERESE
from the booth, who stands in line to collect general
delivery mail.

115. INT.
CENTRAL POST OFFICE.
CHICAGO. DAY. CONTINUOUS.

THERESE on line to pick up her mail. She looks around for
CAROL, spots her dialing in the phone booth...

116. INT.
HARGE'S OFFICE. NEW YORK. DAY.

His private phone rings. He picks up.

HARGE

Hargess Aird. Hello.

Nothing from the other end.

HARGE (CONT'D) (CONT'D)

All right, Carol. Enough is enough.
Now where are you, goddamnit?... Hello?

117. INT.
CENTRAL POST OFFICE PHONE BOOTH.
CHICAGO. DAY.

CAROL, suddenly unable to respond, leans her head against
the phone box a moment, then quietly hangs up the phone.

118. INT.
CENTRAL POST OFFICE. CHICAGO. DAY.

CAROL joins THERESE at the post desk. THERESE has picked up a few letters.

> CAROL
> (refers to the letters)
> Someone's popular.

> THERESE
> All from Richard.
> (she puts the letters in her bag)
> Aren't you going to check your mail?

> CAROL
> Nobody knows I'm here.

> THERESE
> Were you… making a call?

> CAROL
> What? No - Ladies room.

Carol throws her scarf over her head and starts out.
Therese watches her a moment as she goes, then follows.

119. EXT.
LAKE SHORE DRIVE.
CHICAGO. NEW YEAR'S EVE. DAY.

CAROL and THERESE stand at the side of the frozen road, considering a flat tire. CAROL starts rummaging through her purse when she looks up and hears a car coming.

CAROL

Here's one.

THERESE tries to flag down the approaching motorist for help. A dark-colored '42 Chrysler Sedan slows to a stop and pulls over ahead of them. The driver backs up, revealing it to be TOMMY TUCKER, the notions salesman.

THERESE

Well - what in the world.
(to Carol): Look who just...

TOMMY TUCKER

What do you know?
I thought that might be the two of you.

TOMMY hops out of his car and approaches the women. He inspects the tire.

TOMMY TUCKER (CONT'D)

Yep, that's a flat alright.
Just hope you didn't dent that rim.

CAROL

I felt something pulling,
and then a grinding-

TOMMY TUCKER

Right. Well.
Can I jack her up for you?

THERESE

We - don't think there is one.

TOMMY TUCKER

No jack?

THERESE

(glancing at CAROL)
We think it might have been left at home.

CAROL

Long story.

THERESE

Bigger problem is,
we think it might be flat. The spare.

TOMMY TUCKER

Gotcha. Well… I got a jack. I can
jack her up for you. We just use my spare.

THERESE

But what about you?

TOMMY TUCKER

Me I'm heading home from here - I got
plenty of spares back home.
(inspecting the flat)
Don't think there's rim damage.
Shouldn't take too long I don't expect.

THERESE

There's just… one other thing…

TOMMY TUCKER

What's that, ma'am?

120. INT. / EXT.
TOMMY'S CAR. LAKE SHORE DRIVE. LATER. DAY.

In the front seat, THERESE offers CAROL some coffee from a

thermos. Radio softly plays. Up ahead, TOMMY leans over the hood, his hands black from a lengthy operation.

CAROL

I'm ravenous.

THERESE

So am I.

CAROL

(watching him work)
We're lucky we found him.

THERESE

I'll say.

Silence.

THERESE (CONT'D)

Are you sorry we came?

CAROL

On the trip? No. Are you?

THERESE

No.

They look up to the sound of CAROL's car starting up again. TOMMY climbs out of the drivers seat and approaches, dusting himself off. CAROL and THERESE get out to meet him.

CAROL

Wonderful!

TOMMY TUCKER

Well... It'll get you to your next stop,
but you best get it checked at a garage.
New hose. They'll tell ya the same.

THERESE

Thank you so much.

CAROL

Tommy, what do we owe you.

TOMMY TUCKER

Oh, please - nothing at all, ma'am.

CAROL

Well for the tire at least.

TOMMY TUCKER

No need. Like I said, I've got a
collection. Occupational hazard.

CAROL

Well. Thank you. Again.
For everything.

TOMMY TUCKER

You are surely welcome, ma'am.

CAROL starts off to the car, leaving an uncertain beat
between TOMMY and THERESE.

TOMMY TUCKER (CONT'D)

And Happy New Year.

THERESE

Yes, that's right.
Happy New Year to you.

TOMMY TUCKER

Yep, well, I'm counting on a big night
for sales. Stocking up on hats and
sparklers. I'm hopeful.

THERESE smiles as he back-steps, tips his hat and gets into his car. She glances at CAROL, climbing into the car - and feels a sudden surge of longing.

121. EXT.
WATERLOO, IOWA. EARLY EVENING.

On the road leading into Waterloo, CAROL'S car speeds by a billboard sign with a cartoon of Napoleon being strangled by Nelson. In fancy script below the cartoon is written:

WATERLOO BECKONS. POP. 12,070.

The sky is a deep red.

122. INT.
CABIN. JOSEPHINE MOTOR LODGE. NIGHT.

Twin beds, quilted headboards, the usual. Radio tuned into Guy Lombardo's New Year's Eve broadcast from the Waldorf Astoria. It's almost midnight. A couple of chipped plastic trays carrying the remnants of some ham and cheese sandwiches are set on one of the beds. CAROL sits sipping beer from a Champagne flute, her hair wrapped in a towel. Each dressed in robes, CAROL watches THERESE brush out her hair at a dressing table. The countdown to the New Year begins on the radio. Five. Four. Three. Two. One: HAPPY NEW YEAR! And the familiar Lombardo signature "Auld Lang Syne" begins, but neither woman takes notice. Instead CAROL gets up from the bed, takes the brush from THERESE and begins to brush THERESE'S hair, slowly, carefully. When she's done, she puts the brush down and turns THERESE around to face her.

CAROL

Happy New Year.

THERESE

Happy New Year.

They face each other in silence, listening to the faraway
radio broadcast - a moment when anything could happen.
THERESE, for the first time, reaches out ever so slightly
to brush her fingers against CAROL'S. CAROL looks down at
their fingertips touching.

CAROL

Harge and I never spend New Year's
Eve together. There's always a
business function, always clients to entertain.

THERESE

I've always spent it alone.
In crowds. (beat) I'm not alone this year.

THERESE squeezes CAROL'S hand ever so slightly.
The Guy Lombardo band strikes up a bright New Year's tune.

CAROL unties her robe and lets it fall open, revealing her
nakedness to THERESE. It's so still, it's as if all breath
in the room were suspended. THERESE stands up to join her,
and CAROL takes her face gently in both her hands. She
kisses THERESE'S lips. It's a wondrous kiss for them both,
slow and unhurried. Afterwards, CAROL removes her hands
from THERESE'S face and eases off the towel from her head.

342

CAROL

I'm sorry.

THERESE

For what?

CAROL

For everything that might happen.
Later.

THERESE

(after a moment)
Take me to bed.

CAROL moves towards THERESE, takes her in her arms, leads her to the bed.

CAROL

Lie down.

THERESE does. CAROL lets her own robe drop to the floor then opens THERESE's robe on the bed, taking in her youthful beauty.

CAROL (CONT'D)

I never looked like that.

She climbs onto the bed and straddles THERESE. She strokes her face, her hair. THERESE closes her eyes, but begins to tremble involuntarily.

CAROL (CONT'D)

You're trembling.

CAROL leans down to kiss her lightly on the forehead,
then reaches across the bed to shut off the light. THERESE stops her.

THERESE

Don't. I wan to see you.

CAROL nods, then slides down THERESE'S body and stops just
below THERESE'S navel. She kisses her belly, moves down
THERESE'S body with her mouth. THERESE looks up at the
ceiling, trying to quell her body's shuddering of nerves.
She closes her eyes. CAROL slides up THERESE'S body and
plays with one of THERESE'S nipples with the tip of her tongue.
THERESE moans softly. She pulls CAROL up to her mouth
and they kiss eagerly, passionately. THERESE opens her eyes
and regards CAROL'S face, so close to hers, and smiles.

CAROL

(a whisper)
My angel. Flung out of space.

They begin to make love for the very first time.
FADE TO BLACK

123. INT.
CABIN. JOSEPHINE MOTOR LODGE. DAY

Morning light filters through the drawn curtains as THERESE,
still in bed, watches CAROL packing up for the day ahead.
But suddenly, this day, everything in the world is different.

THERESE

What town are we in?

CAROL

This? Waterloo. Isn't that awful?

124. INT.
OFFICE. JOSEPHINE MOTOR LODGE. LATER.

The deserted office is strewn with empty beer bottles and
cheap New Year's decoration. CAROL looks around for a clerk,
rings the desk bell. An ANCIENT WOMAN shuffles on
out of the back room. She wears a party hat.

ANCIENT WOMAN

You the folks in thirteen?

CAROL

We're checking out.

ANCIENT WOMAN

Telegram come for you last night.

The ANCIENT WOMAN shuffles on out of the room and comes
back with a telegram. She gives it to CAROL. CAROL opens
the telegram. Reads it. It's not good news.

CAROL

When did this arrive?

ANCIENT WOMAN

I ain't a clock, lady. Early.
Seven. Nine.

125. EXT.
JOSEPHINE MOTOR LODGE. MORNING.

CAROL storms out of the office, tearing past the patchy remains of snow, where THERESE is loading the car with their belongings. CAROL pulls open the driver's side door, searching for something she doesn't see, and slams the door shut. She runs up to the cabin they just vacated and tears open the door, almost immediately comes out again, slamming shut the door. She's furious.

> **THERESE**
> Carol! What the hell-

> **CAROL**
> (focusing on THERESE)
> Where's my suitcase?

> **THERESE**
> Carol - wait a minute - what's going on?

> **CAROL**
> (she snaps)
> I want my fucking suitcase.

CAROL storms over to the trunk, brushing past THERESE on the way. She finds her suitcase, flings it open and starts rifling through it. She finds the pistol. THERESE tries to block her way.

> **THERESE**
> What are you doing with that?
> Carol - what happened?!

CAROL pushes past THERESE.

346

126. EXT./INT.
CABIN. JOSEPHINE MOTOR LODGE. MORNING.

CAROL kicks at the door of the cabin next to their's.

CAROL

Open up in there! You hear me?
Right now!

THERESE runs up to the door to join CAROL.

THERESE

Carol, you're scaring me,
you can't-

CAROL

Stand out of the way, Therese.

Carol reaches for the door and finds it unlocked. She kicks
the door open and takes aim. TOMMY TUCKER stands inside
getting dressed, trousers half on, half off. He wears his
hat. He grabs his spectacles off a table and slips them
onto the end of his nose. On the unmade bed before him is
his big black case, opened to reveal an elaborate reel-toreel
tape recorder and sophisticated microphones. THERESE
stares at the equipment, uncomprehending. CAROL cocks her
pistol and assumes the shooting stance, aiming directly at
TOMMY'S head.

CAROL (CONT'D) (CONT'D)

(to TOMMY) Where's the tape, you sonofabitch.

She enters the room, starts pulling apart the case,
the equipment, all the while keeping the pistol aimed at TOMMY.
TOMMY continues to dress himself, rather calmly.

CAROL (CONT'D) (CONT'D)

How much is Harge paying you for this?
I'll give you double, triple.
Anything you want.

TOMMY TUCKER

I wish I could oblige you, ma'am.
But the tape is already on its way
to your husband.

CAROL

That can't be right.

TOMMY TUCKER

(shrugs)
My reputation rests on my
efficiency, Mrs. Aird.

A tense pause. CAROL moves towards TOMMY. He remains
quite calm, still. But he keeps his eye on her all the while.
CAROL advances closer, aiming the pistol at his head.

CAROL

How do I know you're not lying?

TOMMY TUCKER

(a beat) You don't, ma'am.

CAROL tenses up, putting her index finger on the trigger.
All at once she whirls around to the recording equipment,
points the gun to it, and pulls the trigger - but the gun just clicks.

348

She tries again, but the trigger jams. In utter frustration she hurls the gun at the recording equipment.

THERESE, who's been hovering by the door, moves towards CAROL.

THERESE

Carol...

CAROL, exhausted and distraught, gives THERESE the telegram and moves outside of the cabin. She slumps against the railing.

THERESE exchanges a look with TOMMY, who's still cool as a cucumber. THERESE retrieves the gun, joins CAROL outside. CAROL lights a cigarette, looks out towards the highway. THERESE reads the telegram, then looks up through the door to TOMMY, still standing half dressed in his cabin.

THERESE (CONT'D)

(to TOMMY)
How could you.

TOMMY TUCKER

I am a professional, Miss Belivet.
It's nothing personal.

A silence. CAROL smokes, THERESE shakes her head at TOMMY, disgusted, not wanting to believe this is happening. TOMMY tips his hat to THERESE.

CAROL

Let's get out of here.

127. EXT.
ALLEY. WATERLOO. LATER.

THERESE, carrying pistol and telegram, finds some trash
bins in an alley. She lifts the lid on one and tosses the
pistol into it, but it lodges on top. She buries it with
one hand, and does her best to clean it off with the
telegram. She tosses back the lid and hurries back to the
street, rounding the corner. There she finds CAROL at a pay
phone. She steps back instinctively, but overhears the end
of CAROL'S call to ABBY.

CAROL
… earliest flight into LaGuardia
is tomorrow afternoon… Oh Abby,
I don't know how to fix this
- I haven't the strength…

THERESE wishes she could hold CAROL in her arms at this
moment. But she knows she can't.

128. INT.
CAROL'S CAR. EARLY EVENING.

CAROL drives in silence as they approach Chicago. THERESE
smokes a cigarette. You could cut the tension with a knife.

CAROL
You shouldn't smoke. You'll get a cough.
(silence) What are you thinking?…
You know how many times a day
I ask you that?

THERESE

I'm sorry. What am I thinking?
I'm thinking that I am utterly selfish. And I -

CAROL

Don't do this. You had no idea.
How could you have known?

THERESE

I - I should have said no to you.
But I never say no. And it's
selfish because I take - everything.
Because I don't know - anything.
I don't - know what I want.
How could I if I just say
yes to everything?

THERESE begins to cry, softly. CAROL pulls over to the side
of the road, against a frozen bank of snow. She turns THERESE
towards her. She dries her tears. CAROL and THERESE regard
each other, calmly, steadily.

CAROL

I took what you gave willingly.

A pause. CAROL runs a finger along THERESE'S cheek. She turns
back to the wheel. Restarts the car.

CAROL (CONT'D)

It's not your fault, Therese - Alright?

More silence. CAROL, at a loss to make the situation
better, accelerates quickly onto the highway.

129. INT.
DRAKE HOTEL. CHICAGO. NIGHT.

CAROL is finishing a call with ABBY, sitting on one of the twin beds, smoking. THERESE emerges from the bathroom, switching off the light. She stands for a moment in the dark before she climbs into the other bed.

CAROL

> Thank you, pet... Oh, you know.
> Shattered. Sickened... I hope so...
> No... Talk tomorrow... And thank
> you... I will. Night.

She hangs up the phone and looks down a moment. Then she turns to THERESE with a sad tenderness.

CAROL (CONT'D)

> You don't have to sleep over there.

Silence. THERESE gets up, joins CAROL in the other bed. CAROL wraps her arms and legs around THERESE, kissing her gently on the eyes, the lips. THERESE looks at her deeply and then kisses her back, a long, lingering, searching kiss.

130. INT.
DRAKE HOTEL. CHICAGO. MORNING.

A ribbon of daylight over THERESE's face. Eyes still shut, she reaches out for CAROL, but CAROL'S not there. No sound coming from the bathroom. She lifts her head and checks the clock:

8 AM. THERESE sits up in the bed. There, seated in an armchair in the semi-darkness, is ABBY. She smokes a cigarette. And all at once THERESE understands what CAROL'S absence means. Silence.

THERESE

She's gone?

ABBY

Early this morning.

THERESE

Is she coming back?

ABBY

No.

Piercing silence.

THERESE

This is all my fault.

ABBY

Nonsense.

ABBY puts out her cigarette, gets up and pulls open the curtains. Cold, bright sunlight streams into the room.

ABBY (CONT'D)

We should get going.

131. INT.
ROADSIDE DINER OUTSIDE OF CHICAGO. DAY.

THERESE stares out the window; she hasn't touched her meal.

Eat something.
(no response)
Suit yourself.

ABBY slides THERESE'S plate to her side of the table and starts finishing it. THERESE turns to her.

THERESE

Why don't you like me?
I've never done anything to you.

A pause. ABBY starts to say something, thinks better of it. She leans in towards THERESE.

ABBY

You really think I've flown
halfway across the country to
drive you back East because
I hate you and want to see you suffer?

THERESE

It's for Carol.
Not for me.

ABBY

(after a beat)
That's - If you really believe
that then you're not as smart as
I thought you were.

Therese takes this in, then looks up at Abby. Silence.

THERESE

With you and Carol...
what happened?

ABBY

It's completely different - I've known
Carol since I was 10 years old...
(after a long beat)
It was... back when we had the
furniture store. Late one night.
My Ford broke down near my
Mother's house and...
We tried to stay up,
but... curled up together
in my old twin bed.
(MORE)

ABBY (CONT'D)

And that was it...
For a while.
And then it changed. It changes.
Nobody's fault. (beat)
So...

She opens her purse and searches inside.
She produces an envelope.

ABBY (CONT'D)

Here - she...

THERESE

What?

ABBY hands her a letter.

132. EXT.
ROADSIDE DINER. MOMENTS LATER.

In a WIDE lonely frame we see THERESE has stepped outside
the diner to tear open the letter. As she reads, we hear
CAROL'S voice:

> #### CAROL (V.O.)
> Dearest. There are no accidents and
> he would have found us one way or another.
> Everything comes full circle.
> Be grateful it was sooner rather than later.
> You'll think it harsh of me to say so,
> but no explanation I offer will satisfy you.

We see ABBY leave the diner as THERESE continues reading.
She climbs in the car and starts the engine. A soft undertone
of MUSIC has emerged.

133. INT.
ANOTHER MOTEL. NIGHT.

ABBY in the bathroom, washing out some clothes. Through a
crack in the door, she spots THERESE, seated on the bed,
drained by tears, expressionless.

> #### CAROL (V.O.) (CONT'D)
> Please don't be angry when I tell you
> that you seek resolutions and
> explanations because you're young.
> But you will understand this one day.

134. INT./EXT.
COUNTRY ROAD. DAY.

ABBY pulls the car off the road near a small grove of trees
and fading clumps of snow. THERESE jumps out, makes for the
trees and tries to hide herself before she throws up. ABBY lights
a cigarette and remains in the car, watching THERESE
from a distance.

> CAROL (V.O.) (CONT'D)
> And when it happens,
> I want you to imagine me there to greet you
> like the morning sky,
> our lives stretched out ahead of us,
> a perpetual sunrise.

135. INT.
CAROL'S CAR. NIGHT.

ABBY, at the wheel, glances in the rear-view-mirror at
THERESE, stretched out asleep on the back seat of the car.
Distant passing lights comb over her repose.

> CAROL (V.O.) (CONT'D)
> But until then, there must be
> no contact between us.
> I have much to do, and you, my darling,
> even more. Please believe that
> I would do anything to see you happy
> and so I do the only thing I can - I release you.

136. INT.
THERESE'S APARTMENT. NEW YORK. DAY.

THERESE, in her overcoat, suitcase beside her, stands in
the middle of her apartment. It's full of her things, but
it looks like a foreign land. All the photographs on the
wall seem as if they were taken by someone else.

137. INT.
THERESE'S APARTMENT. THAT SAME NIGHT.

THERESE hunches over her sink, bathed in red light.
She takes a quick deep drag of a cigarette, burning in an
ashtray. Rows of negatives hang from hooks underneath the
kitchen cupboards, over the trays of chemicals. She finds
a certain shot on the enlarger, marks it, and focuses. She begins
the process of developing the print.

Finally, she watches the photo in its bath slowly appear -
a shadow here and there, a shape forming - and it's CAROL,
asleep on her back, her body akimbo in a tumble of sheets,
one hand resting delicately.

138. INT.
THERESE'S APARTMENT BUILDING. HALLWAY.
LATE NIGHT.

THERESE is creeping down the half-lit stairway. She picks
up the phone without making a sound and stares at the dial.
She hangs up. Then in one continuous gesture she picks it up

again and dials the number. She stands frozen. One long ring. Silence. Another long ring. Then someone picks up the line. But there's silence on the other end.

Nothing. THERESE is frozen.

THERESE

> Hello? (beat) Carol?

The silence that follows is like an answer. THERESE holds the receiver close: a precious thing.

139. INT.
CAROL'S HOUSE. KITCHEN. NIGHT.

CAROL in the dark, on the other end, still. She makes a movement as if to say something, but doesn't. We see her finger softly graze the receiver button before pressing it down.

140. INT.
THERESE'S APARTMENT BUILDING.
HALLWAY PHONE. NIGHT.

Extremely CLOSE on THERESE hearing CAROL disconnect, but holding on in the void.

THERESE

> (prayerful)
> I miss you. I miss you.

141. INT.
HARGE'S PARENTS HOUSE. NEW JERSEY. DAY.

HARGE, CAROL, JENNIFER and JOHN are seated together for a weekday lunch, with everything distinctly in its place. Eisenhower's inauguration proceedings can be heard and glimpsed on the living room television set.

JENNIFER

More mashed potatoes, Carol?

CAROL

Yes - Thanks. They're delicious.

CAROL reaches over to take the bowl of mashed potatoes, but HARGE gets to it first, spoons some out for CAROL. The atmosphere is polite, but far from relaxed.

CAROL (CONT'D) (CONT'D)

Thank you. (beat) I thought...
perhaps... Chester and Marge would
be here by now. With Rindy...

JENNIFER

Marge said to go ahead,
not to wait.

HARGE

(to CAROL)
I'm sure they'll be here soon.

CAROL appreciates HARGE'S small kindness.

JOHN

Harge tells us you've been getting
along quite well with your doctor, Carol.

JENNIFER

And why shouldn't she be getting
on well. He's a very expensive doctor.

CAROL

He's actually not a doctor
but a psychotherapist.

JENNIFER

Well he comes very well regarded.

JOHN

(to HARGE)
A Yale man, like your uncle.

CAROL

(ever so slightly edgy)
But that doesn't make him a doctor.

HARGE throws her a little look.

CAROL (CONT'D) (CONT'D)

I do like him. Very much.
He's been a great help.

JENNIFER and JOHN continue eating in silence.

142. INT.
HARGE'S PARENTS HOUSE. LATER.

CAROL sits alone near the living room window, caught in a stare.

She's jolted out of it by the sound of JENNIFER,
approaching with a cup of tea. CAROL turns.

> **CAROL**
>
> Thank you Jennifer,
> but I'm fine, really-

> **JENNIFER**
>
> It'll calm your nerves.

JENNIFER sets it down on a small end table, and places a hand
on CAROL's shoulder. Just then we hear the sound of a car
coming up the drive.

> **CAROL**
>
> They're here.

CAROL rises, gives her hair a quick pat and starts off toward
the door.

> **JENNIFER**
>
> Just a moment, dear.

CAROL stops, turns. JENNIFER walks over to where CAROL stands
her and adjusts her collar. CAROL manages to maintain composure,
then turn from JENNIFER and continues on to the door.

143. EXT.
HARGE'S PARENTS HOUSE. LATE AFTERNOON
EARLY EVENING1. CONTINUOUS.

CAROL runs to greet RINDY, who walks hand-in-hand with a

MIDDLE AGED COUPLE, RINDY'S AUNT AND UNCLE.
When she sees her Mother, RINDY lets go of their hands
and runs towards CAROL. They meet. CAROL kneels
down and sweeps RINDY into her arms. She hugs her tightly,
holding on for dear life.

CAROL

Oh baby… my baby girl…

144. INT.
THERESE'S APARTMENT. AFTERNOON.

DANNIE is over, helping THERESE repaint her apartment.
THERESE is on a ladder, painting some molding near the
ceiling and DANNIE is below. As the RADIO plays ("Lullaby
of Birdland" by Georges Shearing), DANNIE spots THERESE
wiping sweat from her brow. They've clearly been at it a while.

DANNIE

I think it's break time.
Let me fetch some brews.

THERESE

Sounds good.

DANNIE goes to the kitchen to grab some beers and an opener.
THERESE has been developing more photos - almost all of them
pictures of CAROL from their trip. DANNIE can't help but
take a look.

He hears something behind him and turns. It's THERESE.

DANNIE

These are seriously good. I mean,
they really capture - whoever this is.

THERESE

They're just practice.

THERESE crosses the room and begins picking up the pictures,
tidying the area.

DANNIE

You really should put together a portfolio.
Say the word, I'll introduce you
to my pal at the Times.
There's always a clerk job going.

THERESE shakes her head, takes the pictures into the other room
and pulls open a drawer to stash them in.

DANNIE (CONT'D)

You went away with her, right?

THERESE

Yes.

DANNIE

So what happened?

THERESE

Ohh. Nothing. It's - hard to...

DANNIE

(after a beat)
Is it because I tried to kiss you that day?
Because if it is, don't even think about that,
I mean, don't be afraid of-

THERESE

I'm not afraid.

THERESE is stopped a moment by her own words, reminding her
of another time and place. She looks back at him.

THERESE (CONT'D)

Let's finish while we still have light,
okay?

DANNIE shrugs and they get back to work.

DANNIE

I still think you should put
together that portfolio.

145. INT.
THERESE'S APARTMENT. LATE NIGHT.

THERESE sits on her kitchen floor sorting photographs,
a cigarette burning in an ashtray beside her. She's busy
placing them into neat piles.
We see her older work - LANDSCAPES, STILL LIFE'S,
ARCHITECTURAL DETAILS - and all her newer work - PHOTOS OF
KIDS PLAYING IN THE STREET, OLD WOMEN DRAGGING SHOPPING
CARTS, CITY FACES - virtually all of them depicting people.
At the bottom of one pile she discovers the picture of
CAROL BUYING THE XMAS TREE. She considers it a moment
before pulling it out of the stack.

146. EXT.
CENTRAL PARK. A FEW DAYS LATER. AFTERNOON.

It's a gray, rainy day at the park. Walkers with umbrellas.
RICHARD has brought THERESE a box of her belongings.

> **RICHARD**
>
> Everything's there. (beat) My mother
> washed and ironed your blouses.

> **THERESE**
>
> Thank her for me?

> **RICHARD**
>
> You can thank her yourself.

> **THERESE**
>
> Richard…

> **RICHARD**
>
> What do you expect me to say?
> I mean… You never even wrote-

THERESE looks away.

> **THERESE**
>
> I tried, I just…
> I couldn't find the words.

She tries to touch his shoulder, he moves away from her.

> **RICHARD**
>
> Please don't touch me. (he shakes his head).
> After what we had - after what you did… Throwing it all away.

THERESE

What did we have?

RICHARD

Thanks, that's…

THERESE

No - tell me!

RICHARD

You tell me, Terry. Did you - did you
love me even a little?

They hold a look, but THERESE can't hurt him like this.
She turns away.

THERESE

Please, please don't hate me.
I'm still… me. Still the same person
I always was.

RICHARD

No. You're not, alright?
You're someone else now. And I can't.
I can't forgive you. (beat) So long, Terry.

A beat, before RICHARD leaves. THERESE doesn't move.

147. INT.
CAROL'S HOUSE. DUSK.

CAROL sits in the lantern seat off her stairway, looking out
at the night. From down below she hears the RADIO REPORT
blaring on, announcing the death of Stalin.

The radio is lowered and CAROL looks down. She sees Abby starting up the stairs with two cups of coffee. CAROL starts down to meet her.

ABBY

Stay. Stay.

CAROL

Don't be silly.

She takes her cup from ABBY and starts back up to her seat. CAROL returns to where she was sitting and ABBY sits on the stairs below her. ABBY can read CAROL's despondency from a mile away.

CAROL (CONT'D)

I don't know if I can do it, Abby.
What more can I do? How many more -
tomato aspic lunches...
just to come home every night without her.
To this!

ABBY

And... Therese?

CAROL

What about her?

ABBY

Have you - heard anything?

CAROL

Oh no. No. It's been over a month
since she tried to call.
Nothing since then. I wish I...

(but she stops, then):
Have you? Heard anything?

ABBY

From Therese? No. (beat) She must
have started her job at the Times, though.
That's something.

CAROL

I should have said: Therese. Wait.

ABBY reaches out, puts a hand on CAROL'S foot. All at once
a pair of headlights swing by, lighting up the windows, and
they are jolted. CAROL turns and ABBY stands, startled.
A look between them: is someone here? Is this trouble? And then
the headlights disappear.

CAROL (CONT'D)

Who the hell is turning around in my drive?

ABBY

I should go.

CAROL

You don't have to-

ABBY

-I do.

ABBY squeezes CAROL'S hand - courage. And they start down the
stairs together.

148. EXT.
HUDSON RIVER PIER. NEW YORK. NIGHT.

DANNIE and THERESE sit together on the pier, looking across

the river to New Jersey.

> **DANNIE**
>
> I'm glad you called…
> I never see you no more!
> Now that you've got the fancy job
> with the smooth hours.
> You punch out, I punch in.

> **THERESE**
>
> It doesn't feel fancy, hauling
> gallon jugs of developer all day.
> But I kind of love it, you know?

> **DANNIE**
>
> Sure. (beat) Hey - guess what
> happened to me?
> No? Can't think of it?

THERESE smiles, shakes her head.

> **DANNIE (CONT'D)**
>
> I met a girl. Louise. She's got green eyes,
> she's a movie encyclopedia,
> and the most amazing thing?
> She thinks I'm boss.

> **THERESE**
>
> (she's pleased for DANNIE)
> Go figure.

> **DANNIE**
>
> (he's pleased she's pleased)
> Yeah. (beat) If you want,
> we can all hang out some night.
> Go to a movie.

That sounds swell.

I'd love to meet her. (pause)

Did, uh - Have you seen Richard?

DANNIE

I seen him. (beat) Think he wanted

to talk, maybe. But I, uh...

I don't know. I feel bad for him.

But I don't wanna get-

He stops, glancing up at THERESE, then looking away.
THERESE's thoughts seem to harden and a brief darkness
falls over her.

THERESE

Use what feels right.

Throw away the rest.

DANNIE

(laughs)

Where'd that come from?

THERESE

Something Carol once said to me.

DANNIE

(a beat, then:)

Did she... do that? To you?

THERESE struggles for this...

THERESE

I can't - go. Back. To that place.

Where you keep it all locked up…
the sadness, shame…You let people down.
You let yourself - down.
So you cry and you… hide and think - things,
constantly, crazy things, like…
if you stare at the phone long enough or
- take a train and just… lurk…
it could all… return. (silence)
And then one day the phone is just a phone.
A train going to Jersey is just a train to Jersey.
You stop - crying and hiding.
And you know you're able to
use things and throw them away.

The river looks like a swath of black cellophane.

149. EXT.
41ST STREET & BROADWAY. MORNING.

Through passing cars and car windows we suddenly see
THERESE, dressed for work in a smart dark suit, hurrying
through the morning commuter CROWD towards the New York
Times building. Her style of hair and dress has taken on a
sophistication and maturity we can't help but associate
with CAROL.

150. INT.
TAXI. TIMES SQUARE. MORNING.

CAROL, in the cab on her way to FRED HAYMES'S office,
is looking distantly out the window when she suddenly spots her.
The light changes and the taxi starts to move -

THERESE flickers from view. CAROL looks back over her shoulder through reflections.

151. INT.
ELEVATOR / JERRY RIX LAW OFFICES. DAY.

CAROL, turned away, inside the elevator. The doors open.
She turns to look a moment before heading out the door and down the hall.
Gathered inside, HARGE, RIX, FRED HAYMES and a STENOGRAPHER all turn and note her arrival.

152. INT.
JERRY RIX LAW OFFICES. DAY. MOMENTS LATER

Everyone is gathered around the conference table.

JERRY RIX

Well-(coughs)- we feel,
given the seriousness of the charges and the
incontestability of the evidence,
my client has every reason to
expect a compliant and favorable outcome.

FRED HAYMES

Not so fast, Jerry. My client's
psychotherapist is perfectly
satisfied with her recovery
from… the events of the winter,
asserting she's more than capable
of caring for her child. She's had
no further contact with Therese
Belivet. And we have sworn

depositions from two Saddlebrook
Institute psychiatrists clearly
stating that, in their opinions,
a series of events, precipitated by
my client's husband, drove her to
suffer an emotional break,
which resulted in this- described behavior.

HARGE

(looks to his lawyer for help)
That's absurd! - Are they serious-?

JERRY RIX

Alright, Fred - okay,
if this is how you're going to play this-

FRED HAYMES

Furthermore,
given the manner in
which these tapes were obtained and recorded,
we're confident in their inadmissibility-

JERRY RIX

Okay, okay.
First off, I'd like to see
these depositions. And second-

CAROL

(interrupts him)
Fred - please. Don't - May I speak?

A silence, as everybody in the room looks to CAROL.

CAROL (CONT'D)

I won't deny the truth of what's
contained in those tapes.

FRED HAYMES

(signals to the STENOGRAPHER)
This is off the record, honey.

CAROL

Might as well be on the record.

A pause as JERRY nods to the STENOGRAPHER to continue and
CAROL pours herself a glass of water.

CAROL (CONT'D) (CONT'D)

I wanted - I did want - to talk
about… duty… sacrifice.
That was what I-(beat)… But now that
I'm here I don't… I don't know
what I believe… Or what I even know…
except that… I know I want to see my daughter
- to hear her voice… Always.
To be there when she's-

She stops, holding back tears, which she refuses to allow.
Gathering herself, she levels her eyes directly to Harge, and
makes her case directly to him.

CAROL (CONT'D)

Harge, I want you to be… happy.
I didn't give you that - I failed you
- we both could have… given.
More. (beat) But we gave each other Rindy,
and that's - the most - breathtaking, the most…
generous… of gifts. (beat)
So why are we spending so much time…
coming up with ways to

keep her from each other. (beat)
What happened with Therese...
I wanted. I won't deny it or-

HARGE looks down.

> CAROL (CONT'D)
>
> ... But I do regret, I - grieve...
> the mess we're about to make...
> of our child's life. We, Harge...
> we are both... responsible. Let's...
> set it right. (beat) I want Harge
> to have... permanent custody-

Amidst the sudden chaos HARGE's eyes take hold of her
and don't let up.

FRED HAYMES	JERRY RIX
Let's take a break, folks and resume when I've had a moment to confer with my-	Fred - no, I think your client has made it perfectly clear given her statement-

> CAROL
>
> No, Fred. Let me have my say.
> Because - if you stop me...
> I won't... be able... to cope...

CAROL stands, stepping away from the table, to regain her
composure. Silence returns before she continues.

> CAROL (CONT'D) (CONT'D)
>
> I'm no martyr. I have no clue...

what's best for me.
But I do know…
I feel, I feel it in my bones…
what's best for my daughter.

She starts to turn and walk again, addressing HARGE.

CAROL (CONT'D)

(beat) I want visits with her,
Harge. I don't care if they're supervised.
But they need to be regular.
(beat) There was a time…
I would have locked myself away
- done most anything…
just to keep Rindy with me. But…
what use am I to her… to us…
living against… my own grain?
Rindy deserves - joy. How do I give her
that not knowing what it means… myself.

She pours herself another glass of water.

CAROL (CONT'D)

That's the deal. Take it or leave it.
I can't - I won't negotiate.
If you… leave it, we go to court and it gets ugly.
We're not ugly people, Harge.

Feeling suddenly shaky she turns and starts out of the room.
HARGE stands, staring at her as she goes, as FRED leaps
to his feet and hurries after her, calling her name.

153. EXT.
COFFEE SHOP. SEVENTH AVENUE. DAY.

Through reflections we see CAROL seated at a table,
writing a note. Beside her a pot of coffee and cigarette burning in
an ashtray. She signs it. Seals it inside an envelope, and
begins gathering her things.

154. INT.
NEW YORK TIMES. PHOTO DEPARTMENT. DAY.

THERESE organizes black and white prints during a meeting
of photo editors, gathered around a large table. Smoke in
the air. Through the glass a MESSENGER is seen speaking to
a CLERK. The CLERK spots THERESE inside the room and brings
her the envelope.

CLERK

Belivet.

THERESE, looks up, and hurries over to the CLERK by the
door. He hands her the envelope.

CLERK (CONT'D)

Hand delivered. Swank.

THERESE takes the envelope and returns to the table.
Glancing down, she recognizes CAROL'S handwriting.

155. INT.
NEW YORK TIMES. PHOTO DEPARTMENT. LATER.

THERESE types labels at her cubicle. The open note sits beside her on her desk. She stops typing and looks over at the note. She picks it up and holds it for a moment before crumpling it up and tossing it into a desk drawer. She returns to typing.

156. INT.
RITZ TOWER HOTEL. NIGHT.

CAROL is entering the hotel from the street entrance, removing her scarf and adjusting her hair. She makes her way to the pay telephones and slips inside an empty booth. There we see her dial a number and make a quick call. She hangs up, takes out her compact and powders her nose. She steps out of the booth and stops.

157. INT.
RITZ TOWER HOTEL. BAR / LOUNGE. NIGHT.

There, across the room, is THERESE being shown to a corner table, THERESE looking more grown-up and put together, THERESE thanking the MAITRE D', THERESE sitting down... CAROL takes a breath, then makes her way across the room.

THERESE looks up and sees her.

CAROL

I wasn't sure you'd come.
It's nice of you to see me.

Don't say that.

CAROL settles in opposite THERESE, moving her coat aside.

CAROL

Do you hate me, Therese?

THERESE

No. How could I hate you?

CAROL

I suppose you could.
Didn't you?
For a while?

THERESE looks down. She pours herself some tea.

CAROL (CONT'D)

Abby tells me you're thriving.
You've no idea how pleased I am
for you. (beat) You look very fine,
you know. As if you've suddenly blossomed.
Is that what comes of getting away from me?

THERESE

(answers quickly)
No.

She frowns, regretting answering so quickly, and looking down. When she looks up again, CAROL is staring at her, quite intently.

THERESE (CONT'D)

What?

CAROL

Nothing. I was just thinking about
that day. In the doll department.

THERESE

I always wondered…
Why did you come over to me?

CAROL

Because you were the only girl not
busy as hell. (beat) Disappointed?

THERESE shakes her head no. CAROL smiles at the memory and
lights a cigarette.

CAROL (CONT'D)

Harge and I are selling the house.
I've taken an apartment.
On Madison Avenue. And a job, believe
it or not. I'm going to work for a furniture house
on Fourth Avenue as a buyer.
Some of my ancestors
must have been carpenters.

THERESE gives CAROL a little smile - a bit of thaw.

THERESE

Have you seen Rindy?

CAROL

(after a beat) Once or twice. At the lawyer's office.

She sat on my lap and we...
(holding THERESE'S gaze):
She's going to live with Harge.
For now. It's... the right thing.

CAROL can't quite cover the pain of this, but she tries.

CAROL (CONT'D)

Anyway, the apartment's a nice big one
- big enough for two. I was hoping you
might like to come and live with me,
but I guess you won't. (beat) Would you?

A held breath.

THERESE

No. I don't think so.

CAROL

That's... your decision.

THERESE

Yes.

A silence.

CAROL

I'm meeting some people from
the furniture house at the Oak Room at nine.
If you want to have dinner...
if you change your mind... I think-- you'd like them.
(beat) Well. That's that.

CAROL puts out her cigarette, stares at her cigarette lighter
on the table.

CAROL (CONT'D)
I love you.

A silence. THERESE wants to say something, but can't.

O/S JACK TAFT
Therese? Is that you?

And the moment is gone. THERESE looks up, turns towards
the source of the greeting.

It's a smiling JACK TAFT, halfway across the room, near the bar.

JACK
What do you know! (starts over) I'm
saying to myself, I know that girl.

THERESE watches JACK make his way over to her. She gives
CAROL a quick look - CAROL, staring down at the table, not
knowing what to do, vulnerable... THERESE rises to greet JACK.

THERESE
Jack.

JACK
Gee but it's great to see you.
It's been, well, months.

THERESE
Months.

CAROL lights a cigarette. THERESE glances at her, and they

hold a look for a moment before THERESE speaks.

                    THERESE (CONT'D)
                 Jack, this is Carol Aird.

JACK holds out his hand. CAROL shakes it.

                         JACK
                 Pleased to meet you.
                        CAROL
                      Likewise.

CAROL retreats back to her own thoughts, smokes.

                         JACK
            Hey, Ted Gray's meeting me here
            and a bunch of us are heading down
                    to Phil's party.
               You're going aren't you?
                       THERESE
              Well - yes. I just planned to get
            there a little...(looking to Carol)
                        CAROL
                You should go ahead.
                         JACK
                 You coming along?
                        CAROL
            No, no. (to THERESE) I should make
            a few calls before dinner, anyway.
                I should really run.

384

THERESE

You sure?

CAROL

Of course.

THERESE

(to JACK)

Well… it would be great to catch a ride.

CAROL takes a step towards THERESE, but no more.

CAROL

You two have a wonderful night.
Nice meeting you, Jack.

JACK

Nice meeting you.

And she's gone. THERESE doesn't move, doesn't turn around to watch CAROL leave.

JACK (CONT'D)

Alright, well let me go make sure
the loaf is on his way. Back in a flash.

And JACK'S off to the phone booth. A beat, before THERESE turns around. She scans the bar and beyond for CAROL, but she's not there. THERESE walks to the lobby entrance - she scans the lobby - but CAROL is well and truly gone - and it only now hits THERESE that she let CAROL walk away. THERESE turns and makes her way to the LADIES ROOM in a bit of a daze.

158. INT.
RITZ TOWER HOTEL. LADIES ROOM. NIGHT.

THERESE stands at the sink, water running. She can barely
bring herself to look into the mirror. She splashes cold
water on her face.

159. INT./EXT.
TAXI. NEW YORK CITY. NIGHT.

THERESE stares out the window, still wrapped up in thoughts.
Up front, JACK is pointing out the West Village apartment
building ("Here-here-here!") and the taxi screeches
to a halt. Everyone tumbles out as JACK pays the driver.
Before she knows it, THERESE is climbing the stairs
to PHIL McELROY'S building. A window is thrown open above them
and PHIL McELROY, with typically unkempt hair, leans out.

PHIL
It's about time, Belivet.
Say hello at least - It hasn't been that long!

THERESE
Hello - Phil - sorry, I was…

DANNIE, PHIL'S brother, leans out of the window next to PHIL.

DANNIE
There she is! Get up here!
(picking up on her state): What?

THERESE

Nothing! There better be beer.
Or wine.

OTHERS

Or beer!

Someone rings THERESE and the others in. It makes an
annoying sound - a buzzing sound that makes THERESE frown,
and she moves up the stairs and into the building.

160. INT.
PHIL'S APARTMENT. NIGHT.

"You Belong To Me" also plays as several COUPLES DANCE,
among them RICHARD and a PRETTY YOUNG WOMAN who
he clutches tightly. THERESE, drinking a beer, watches them from a
hallway just outside the living room.

RICHARD catches sight of THERESE, tensing slightly, before
spinning his partner up and away from THERESE'S view.
THERESE looks down, pulling out a cigarette from her purse
and lighting it. She spots an attractive dark-haired woman
on the opposite side of the living room whose eyes are
clearly on her. THERESE holds her gaze for a few seconds,
but she can feel herself blush, and she looks down. When
she looks back up, the WOMAN has disappeared. THERESE
saunters a bit, glancing into the next room where she spots
DANNIE and his girlfriend LOUISE slow-dancing. They barely
move, holding on to each other the way people do when
they're newly in love.

161. INT.
PHIL'S APARTMENT. NIGHT.

The party is in full swing - more of a crowd, more LAUGHTER, boozing. THERESE stands at a window near a SMALL GROUP OF PEOPLE, including GENEVIEVE CANTRELL, the woman she spotted earlier. THERESE tries to watch GENEVIEVE without being seen as a MALE PARTY GUEST dominates.

> **MALE PARTY GUEST**
> I don't know, man. You can have her.
> She's one of these real
> Greenwich Village phonies,
> if you ask me. (to someone else):
> Where you goin' Dave?
> Stick around a minute.

> **GENEVIEVE**
> You're Phil's friend, aren't you?

> **THERESE**
> I am, yes. And Dannie's.

> **GENEVIEVE**
> Aren't you going to ask me how I knew that?

> **THERESE**
> Aren't most people here Phil's friends?

GENEVIEVE smiles - touche. THERESE smiles, too, loosening up, enjoying the flirting.

> **GENEVIEVE**
> I can see why Phil speaks so highly of you.

THERESE

Can you?

GENEVIEVE

Oh, definitely. I can see a lot.

THERESE

Really? What do you see?

GENEVIEVE

(gives her a good long look)
Great - potential.

GENEVIEVE hands THERESE a beer, and they clink in a toast. THERESE smiles, she enjoys GENEVIEVE'S attention, but she can't hold GENEVIEVE'S gaze, something about its boldness draws her away from the moment, from the party...

162. INT.
PHIL'S APARTMENT. NIGHT.

THERESE sits on the edge of the bathtub next to the open window, taking in the air. She can hear the party in progress, people having a great time, but she's not ready to rejoin them. A couple of RAPID KNOCKS on the door.

THERESE

Sorry. Just a second.

THERESE gathers herself, gets up, opens the door. It's GENEVIEVE. She wears her coat and scarf.

THERESE (CONT'D)

Oh. You're leaving.

GENEVIEVE

Just about. Will you miss me?

THERESE doesn't look away from GENEVIEVE this time.
GENEVIEVE moves closer to THERESE, whispers in her ear.

GENEVIEVE (CONT'D)

Listen, Therese.
There's an intime gathering,
quite exclusive you understand, later on. At my place.
(beat) Quick. Show me your hand.

THERESE

You a fortune teller?

GENEVIEVE

I'm a fortune giver.

GENEVIEVE takes THERESE'S hand, writes her address in ink
onto THERESE'S palm.

GENEVIEVE(CONT'D)

So you don't forget.

And GENEVIEVE'S off. THERESE watches her wind her way to
the door.

163. INT.
PHIL'S APARTMENT. NIGHT.

THERESE threads her way through PHIL'S GUESTS on her way
to the front door - it's no easy task navigating, especially since

no one seems to notice THERESE, or anything other
than their own good time. When she finally reaches the door,
THERESE takes a look back into the living room to see
if she's missed out on any good-byes. She spots DANNIE
and LOUISE on the floor, knees-up to PHIL'S small black and
white TV set, intently watching a film, oblivious to the noise around
them. DANNIE jots notes every once in a while in his little notebook.
All seems right here - for others at least.
THERESE slips out the door.

164. EXT.
GREENWICH VILLAGE STREET. NIGHT.

THERESE walks down a quaint, cobbled street. It's a lovely
night and there are various PEDESTRIANS out strolling.
It seems to THERESE that she's the only person who isn't
smiling, isn't engaged with someone who's actually beside
her on such a lovely evening. She looks at the palm of her
hand, checks the address, keeps walking. As she approaches
the address, THERESE spots an ELDERLY COUPLE arm in arm,
supporting each other, walking down the street towards her.
They look like they've been together for ever: the ELDERLY
WOMAN leaning in to her husband as they pass, the ELDERLY
MAN tipping his hat to THERESE.

We HEAR SHARP LAUGHTER from a nearby apartment and THERESE
turns to see GENEVIEVE CANTRELL lean backwards out of
a window. She holds a bottle of champagne which spills down
into the street below. GENEVIEVE gestures to someone inside,
and ANOTHER WOMAN joins GENEVIEVE at the window -

the two begin to make out. THERESE watches their embrace
for a moment; it's tremendously sexy. GENEVIEVE pulls the
WOMAN back into the apartment, and the window's slammed
shut behind them. The night is suddenly very quiet.
THERESE looks off in the direction the ELDERLY COUPLE took.
She starts walking, away from GENEVIEVE, toward something else.
She begins to walk more quickly, and more quickly still,
brushing past the world of strangers.

165. INT.
THE OAK ROOM. PLAZA HOTEL. NIGHT.

THERESE, winded, enters the restaurant. A WAITER stops her.

WAITER

Do you have a reservation?

THERESE

I'm looking for someone.

WAITER

I'm sorry ma'am,
I can't seat you without-

She moves away from the WAITER and scans the crowded room.
Nothing. Then, out of the corner of her eye, almost imperceptible
at first, at a table towards the rear of the room,
she sees a woman's blonde head thrown back in laughter;
the woman seems to be encapsulated in or protected by a haze of
light and smoke.

It's CAROL, CAROL as THERESE has always seen her and as she will

see her evermore: in SLOW MOTION, like in a dream or a single, defining memory, substantial yet elusive.
She moves towards her. CAROL raises a wine glass to her lips and as she does, she turns slightly and spots THERESE.
She is not startled. We see her face softening.

THERESE continues to approach. CAROL watches with a smile burning in her eyes. THERESE has nearly arrived.

THE END

UNIT PRODUCTION MANAGER	GWEN BIALIC	CARD 1
FIRST ASSISTANT DIRECTOR	JESSE NYE	
SECOND ASSISTANT DIRECTOR	KYLE LEMIRE	
HAIR DEPARTMENT HEAD	JERRY DECARLO	CARD 2
MAKE-UP DEPARTMENT HEAD	PATRICIA REGAN	
PERSONAL HAIR TO MS. BLANCHETT	KAY GEORGIOU	
PERSONAL MAKE-UP TO MS. BLANCHETT	MORAG ROSS	
UNIT PRODUCTION MANAGER	KARRI O'REILLY	
ART DIRECTOR	JESSE ROSENTHAL	
SET DECORATOR	HEATHER LOEFFLER	
PROPERTY MASTER	JOEL WEAVER	
CONSTRUCTION COORDINATOR	PAUL PEABODY	
COSTUME SUPERVISOR	DAVID DAVENPORT	
KEY SET COSTUMER	MARTHA SMITH	
GAFFER	JOHN DEBLAU	CARD 3
KEY GRIP	JAMES MCMILLAN	
A CAMERA OPERATOR	CRAIG HAAGENSEN	
STILLS PHOTOGRAPHER	WILSON WEBB	
PRODUCTION SOUND MIXER	GEOFF MAXWELL	
LOCATION MANAGER	DEIRDRE COSTA	
CO-LOCATION MANAGER	ALAN FORBES	
SCRIPT SUPERVISOR	BELLE FRANCISCO	
PRODUCTION ACCOUNTANT	SHELLIE GILLESPIE	
ASSISTANT TO TODD HAYNES	TANYA SMITH	
LOCATION CASTING	D. LYNN MEYERS	
EXTRAS CASTING	CHENNEY CHEN	
POST PRODUCTION SUPERVISOR	GRETCHEN MCGOWAN	CARD 4
ASSISTANT EDITOR	PERRI PIVOVAR	
VISUAL EFFECTS PRODUCER	CHRIS HANEY	
COLORIST	JOHN J. DOWDELL III	
TITLE DESIGN AND CONCEPT	MARLENE MCCARTY	
TITLE ANIMATOR	NAT JENCKS	

SOUND DESIGNER/MIXER	LESLIE SHATZ
SUPERVISING DIALOGUE/ADR EDITOR	ELIZA PALEY
SUPERVISING FX EDITOR	JAMES REDDING
MUSIC EDITOR	TODD KASOW

CARD 5

CAST

CAROL AIRD	CATE BLANCHETT
THERESE BELIVET	ROONEY MARA
HARGE AIRD	KYLE CHANDLER
RICHARD SEMCO	JAKE LACY
ABBY GERHARD	SARAH PAULSON
DANNIE MCELROY	JOHN MAGARO
TOMMY TUCKER	CORY MICHAEL SMITH
FRED HAYMES	KEVIN CROWLEY
PHIL MCELROY	NIK PAJIC
GENEVIEVE CANTRELL	CARRIE BROWNSTEIN

CARD 6

JACK TAFT	TRENT ROWLAND
RINDY AIRD	SADIE HEIM
	KENNEDY HEIM
JENNIFER AIRD	AMY WARNER
JOHN AIRD	MICHAEL HANEY
JEANETTE HARRISON	WENDY LARDIN
ROBERTA WALLS	PAMELA HAYNES
JERRY RIX	GREG VIOLAND
SHIPPING CLERK	MICHAEL WARD
MCKINLEY MOTEL MANAGER	KAY GEIGER
LANDLADY	CHRISTINE DYE
MOTEL CLERK	DEB G. GIRDLER
MALE PARTY GUEST	DOUGLAS SCOTT SORENSON

CARD 7

RITZ BARTENDER	KEN STRUNK
FRANKENBERG SECURITY GUARD	MIKE DENNIS
FLORENCE	ANN RESKIN
EMBARRASSED MOM	ANNIE KALAHURKA
DRAKE HOSTESS	LINNEA BOND
NEW YORK TIMES CLERK	STEVE ANDREWS
FRED HAYMES' SECRETARY	TANYA SMITH
NYC WAITER	RYAN GILREATH
OAK ROOM WAITER	CHUCK GILLESPIE
DOROTHY	JEREMY PARKER
PARTY GIRL #1	GIEDRE BOND
PARTY GIRL #2	TAYLOR MARIE FREY

CREW

LEADMAN	ROBERT SMITH
GANG BOSS	SCOTT LAWSON
SET DRESSERS	AMY CLUXTON
	HAL CARLTON FORD
	JON GRIFFITH
	LEYNA HALLER
	THOMAS HUNT
	TIMOTHY JOHNSON
	VANESSA O'KELLEY
	CHRIS PAPPAS
	GREG PUCHALSKI
BUYER	SARAH YOUNG
ON-SET DRESSER	KELLEIGH MILLER
CAMERA SCENIC	JEFF CROWE
ART DEPARTMENT COORDINATOR	DEBORAH STRATUS
SET DEC PRODUCTION ASSISTANT	NATALIE BLAKE
ART PRODUCTION ASSISTANTS	ALIX BELLEVILLE
	ALEX LINDE
	ANA WEISS
FOOD STYLIST	MARY SEQUIN
RESEARCH	JIM WARREN
PROPERTY MASTER	DANIEL FISHER
1ST ASSISTANT PROPS	LAURA DENNINGS
2ND ASSISTANT PROPS	AMY BRADFORD
CONSTRUCTION FOREMAN	BOYSIE LINK
PROP MAKERS	CHRIS BARBIEA
	ART BERKLEY
	TIM CARL
	DANIEL DIGNAN-CUMMINS
	KEVIN EVISTON
	BRAD KIDNEY
	DARRYL KIDNEY
	JOHN MYERS
	LUKE NYE
	JOHN STELIVER
	CHRIS WALTERS
	JASON WARNDORF
SHOP CRAFTSMAN	JIM BUTLER
CONSTRUCTION PRODUCTION ASSISTANT	LYDIA MACKENZIE

SCENIC CHARGE	PAT SPROTT
SCENIC FOREMAN	BLAIR GIBEAU

SCENICS

JEN BRINKER	BEN MILLER
SUSAN BROOK	TERRY MYERS
ALEX CARDOSI	JENIFER RICHESON
JACK GARNDER JR.	DAVID SCAULAN
KIRSTEN LEE HOUCK	BRENT WACTHER
TIFFANY LAUFER	

A CAMERA FIRST ASSISTANTS	RICK CRUMRINE
	TOM CHERRY
A CAMERA SECOND ASSISTANTS	CHRIS RATLEDGE
STEADICAM	KIRK GARDNER
	ADAM WHITE
B CAMERA OPERATOR	JEFF BARKLAGE, S.O.C.
B CAMERA FIRST ASSISTANTS	AMY FAUST
	ALEX ESBER
B CAMERA SECOND/LOADER	COLLEEN MLEZICA
CAMERA PRODUCTION ASSISTANT /ADDITIONAL LOADER	TRAVIS GEIGER

VIDEO ASSIST	BOB ROCKLIN

BOOM OPERATOR	NIGEL MAXWELL
ADDITIONAL BOOM OPERATOR	DINO DISTEFANO
SOUND UTILITY	BRIEN MASTER

BEST BOY ELECTRIC	RUSS FAUST
RIGGING GAFFER	SCOTT LIPEZ
RIGGING BEST BOY	CHANCE MADISON
SET LIGHTING TECHNICIANS	KEVIN HINES
	JAKE HOSSFELD
	DONNIE SCHNEIDER
RIGGING ELECTRIC	CLIFTON RADFORD

BEST BOY GRIP	MICHAEL STOECKER
RIGGING KEY GRIP	MIKE DICKMAN
RIGGING BEST BOY GRIP	JEFF FISHER
GRIPS	MIKE DITTIACUR
	DAVE JARRED
	KEVIN MARTT
	AARON SMITH

B CAMERA DOLLY GRIP	CHRIS SALAMONE
TECHNOCRANE OPERATORS	STUART ALLEN
	CRAIG STRIANO
SPECIAL EFFECTS CONSULTANT	DEITER STURM
SPECIAL EFFECTS COORDINATOR	KENNETH COULMAN JR.
SPECIAL EFFECTS FOREMAN	KELLY LAUFENBERG
SPECIAL EFFECTS TECHNICIAN	MATTHEW STRATTON
ASSISTANT COSTUME DESIGNERS	MEGHAN COREA
	CHRISTOPHER PETERSON
SET COSTUMER	GINA NALLI
COSTUMERS	KIMBERLEE ANDREWS
	JOY GALBRAITH
	MARY MURPHY
BACKGROUND COSTUMERS	CARLA SHIVENER
	KAREN YOUNG
SEAMSTRESSES	CHRISTINE LEE
	MEGAN MCGILVERY
COSTUME COORDINATOR	JENN MCLAREN
COSTUMES PRODUCTION ASSISTANTS	BROCK KOMON
	JACLYN LARAVIE
2ND MAKE-UP ARTIST	ASHLEY FLANNERY
MAKE-UP ARTISTS	JENI DINKEL
	ANNE TAYLOR
KEY HAIR STYLIST	JOHN "JACK" CURTAIN
ADDITIONAL HAIR	TONYA JOHNSON
	DEBORAH LILY
	SCOTT REEDER
LOCATION LIAISON	CHRIS PETRO
LOCATION PRODUCTION ASSISTANTS	ERIC RISHER
	AMANDA ROBINSON
	PAUL ROSE
	CASEY SHELTON
	JANE STREETER
1ST ASSISTANT ACCOUNTANT	ADAM TAYLOR
2ND ASSSITANT ACCOUNTANT	LISA KURK

PAYROLL ACCOUNTANT	JACKIE ROBERTS
ACCOUNTING CLERK	SELENA BURKS-RENTSCHLER
	KAY WOLFLEY
PRODUCTION COORDINATOR	MEREDITH NUNNIKHOVEN
PRODUCTION SECRETARIES	JOHNATHAN BOWLING
	ERIN FORBES
KEY OFFICE PRODUCTION ASSISTANT	PAULINE STORMS
OFFICE PRODUCTION ASSISTANTS	ASHLEY BRANDON
	ALEXANDER MAXWELL
ASSISTANT TO ELIZABETH KARLSEN	BILLY BOWRING
ASSISTANT TO STEPHEN WOOLLEY	KATIE JACKSON
PICTURE CAR RESEARCHER	BETSY HODGES
ON SET PICTURE CARS	KEN DUTTON
	ED HOLDER
BACKGROUND CAR WRANGLER	RICK FREUDIGER
SECOND SECOND ASSISTANT DIRECTOR	DEREK RIMELSPACH
KEY SET PRODUCTION ASSISTANT	DEVAN LINFORTH
BASECAMP PRODUCTION ASSISTANT	ASHLEY GWEN PATRICK
SET PRODUCTION ASSISTANTS	GREG BRITTAIN
	SHAYNE FARRELL
	MIA LA MONICA
	SARAH SEMENAS
ADDITIONAL SET PRODUCTION ASSISTANTS	NICHOLAS ROLLINS
	JOHN SAYLOR
	BRENDEN SMITH
DIALECT COACH TO MS. BLANCHETT	CARLA MEYER
PERSONAL ASSISTANT TO MS. BLANCHETT	GEORGINA PYM
ASSISTANT TO MS. BLANCHETT	JAYNA SCHIMBERG
ASSISTANT TO MS. MARA	REBECCA ORSAK
ASSISTANT TO MR. CHANDLER	STEVE HAVIRA
ASSISTANT TO MS. PAULSON	EMILY RIEDY
DIALECT COACH	KATE WILSON
PIANO TEACHER	JOHN FISHER
PHOTOGRAPHY CONSULTANTS	BRIAN BLAUSER
	MICHAEL WILSON
DANCE CONSULTANTS	DREW LACHEY
	LEAH LACHEY

RESEARCHER	BRYAN O'KEEFE
CLEARANCE RESEARCHER	LAUREN ITO
CATERING	BASECAMP GOURMET
CHEF	MICHAEL GIANNINI
1ST ASSISTANT CHEF	NICK FIRKINS
CHEF ASSISTANT	BENITO VILLANUEVA
KEY CRAFT SERVICE	PAM FORD
CRAFT SERVICE ASSISTANTS	LARRY FORD
	JESSICA LEWIS
TRANSPORTATION COORDINATOR	JOHNNY GOODWILL
TRANSPORTATION CAPTAIN	BILLY BAXTER, JR.

DRIVERS

TOM BROWN	MIKE CARPENTER
TYLER CHILDS	CRAIG EASTEP
BOBBY GALLIHER	RICHARD GROENDYKE
BRIAN HINKLE	GREG HINKLE
JOHN HOLT JR.	JOHN HOLT SR.
BILLY LYONS	TOM MAWYER
DENNIS SISSLE	CRAIG METZGER
DAVE MILLER	WADE NAPIER
DENNIS NEAUBAUER	DREW PERKINS
LLOYD "RED" MCMULLEN	

PRODUCTION INTERNS

STEPHANIE ADAMS	NATHAN HIPPENMEYER
CYRUS ADELI	LEW HOLDER
ASHLEY ALF	HANNAH HOLTHAUS
KEYAUNA BEACH	DIJON C. KINNEY
KASEY BEGGS	ALEX KUNTZ
ELIZABETH BLAIR	JENNIFER MCADOW
SHIERA LINDSEY BOYD	RANDY MILLER
ANNA BROWN	SAM PENNYBACKER
DAN CUOMO	DANTE PILKINGTON
ANDREW LEE DAVIDSON JR.	SHERI RILEY
JILLIAN GOINS	TORI ROLOSON
TAYLOR HARRIS	KATIE STREIT

CASTING ASSOCIATES (NEW YORK)	JODI ANGSTREICH
	MARIBETH FOX

CASTING ASSISTANT (NEW YORK)	KIM OSTROY
LOCATION CASTING ASSISTANT	DORI BRANCH
EXTRAS WRANGLER	DAVID GETZ
STAND-INS	ALISON GINGERICH
	MIA VERA
SECOND DIALOGUE/ADR EDITOR	TONY MARTINEZ
FOLEY EDITOR	LIDIA TAMPLENIZZA
ADR MIXER	KRISSOPHER CHEVANNES
ADR VOICE CASTING	DANN FINK & BRUCE WINANT
FOLEY MIXER	JULIEN PIRRIE
POST SOUND INTERN	MARI MATSUO
FOLEY ARTISTS	GARETH RHYS JONES
SOUND MIX TECHNICIAN	ROBERT TROELLER
	RABB WHITEHEAD
SOUND STRATEGIST	JIM GARDNER
DOLBY SOUND CONSULTANT	STEVE F. B. SMITH
POST PRODUCTION SOUND FACILITY	GOLDCREST POST PRODUCTIONS NEW YORK
FILM SCANNING/DAILIES PROVIDED BY	GOLDCREST DIGITAL LABORATORY - NY
ARRISCAN/DIGITAL DAILIES TECHNICIANS	BOON SHIN NG
DAILIES COLORIST	SCOT OLIVE
PICTURE FINISHING SERVICES	GOLDCREST POST - NY
FINISHING ARTISTS	BOON SHIN NG
	MICHELLE AMBRUZ
DI PRODUCER	MARGARET LEWIS
DI EXECUTIVE PRODUCER	TIM SPITZER
POST PRODUCTION ASSISTANT	JAIME SUKONNIK
POST PRODUCTION ASSISTANT TO TODD HAYNES	SINEAD KEIRANS
TITLES ANIMATOR	SARAH LASLEY

VFX FROM GOLDCREST   VFX FROM THE MILL

VFX TECHNICAL SUPERVISOR	JASON GANDHI	COMPOSITORS	TOMAS WALL
VFX ON SET SUPERVISOR	ED CHAPMAN		JIYOUNG LEE
ASSISTANT VFX SUPERVISOR	DAVID TANG		KYLE CODY
COMPOSITORS	MARKUS WHITE		NICK TANNER
	CECILIA CALLES		DAE YOON KANG
	JOSHUA BOLIVER		ROB MEADE
	LESLIE CHUNG		RONALD BOWMAN
	MARIKA COOPER		

DYNAMIC EFFECTS TRACKER	ZACK DETOX JUDSON JARROD AVALOS	3D ARTIST	ANDRES EGUIGUREN
		VFX PRODUCTION SUPERVISOR	BOO WONG
LOLA VFX SUPERVISOR	EDSON WILLIAMS	VFX PRODUCTION	JONATHAN ROBINSON
LOLA PRODUCTION SUPERVISOR	ALLISON PAUL	VFX PRODUCTION	DIANA CHANG
MATTE PAINTER	ROB OLSSON		
COMPOSITORS	DEMITRE GARZA DREW HUNTLEY		
VFX TECHNICAL SUPERVISOR	JASON GANDHI		

FOR NUMBER 9 FILMS

FOR GOLDCREST FILMS

HEAD OF PRODUCTION	JOANNA LAURIE	HEAD OF PRODUCTION	GRETCHEN MCGOWAN
HEAD OF DEVELOPMENT	KATE LAWRENCE	HEAD OF BUSINESS AFFAIRS	CLAIRE WARNES
BUSINESS AND LEGAL AFFAIRS	KATE WILSON		
ACCOUNTANT	JOHN MORGAN		
PRODUCTION LEGAL SERVICES	SHERIDANS ROBIN HILTON		

FOR KILLER FILMS

	JAMES KAY	PRODUCTION EXECUTIVE	BRAD BECKER-PARTON
	NICK MAHARA	PRODUCTION EXECUTIVE	DAVID HINOJOSA

FOR FILM4

FOR STUDIO CANAL

HEAD OF FILM FINANCE	HARRY DIXON	HEAD OF UK DEVELOPMENT	DAN MCRAE
HEAD OF PRODUCTION	TRACEY JOSEPHS	HEAD OF UK LEGAL AND BUSINESS AFFAIRS	STEPHEN MURPHY
HEAD OF EDITORIAL	ROSE GARNETT		
SENIOR DEVELOPMENT EDITOR	EVA YATES		
HEAD OF COMMERCIAL AND BRAND STRATEGY	SUE BRUCE-SMITH		

FOR INGENIOUS

BRAND AND MARKETING EXECUTIVE	HANNAH SAUNDERS	ELEANOR WINDO	CHARLES AUTY
		LESLEY WISE	TED CAWREY

WORLDWIDE SALES BY HANWAY FILMS

FOR TWC

	PETER WATSON	CHIARA GELARDIN	PRESIDENT, PRODUCTION, ACQUISITIONS AND TV, EUROPE	ROBERT WALAK
	JAN SPIELHOFF	MATTHEW BAKER	VP, PRODUCTION & DEVELOPMENT	JULIE OH
	JONATHAN LYNCH-STAUNTON	CLAIRE TAYLOR	EXECUTIVE VP, ACQUISITIONS & BUSINESS AFFAIRS	MICHAL PODELL STEINBERG

PRODUCTION LEGAL COUNSEL	GABRIELLA LUDLOW HAMISH BERRY
US PRODUCTION LEGAL	READER & FEIG LLP GLENN D. FEIG, ESQ.

LEGAL REPRESENTATION FOR INGENIOUS	WIGGIN LLP
	DAVID QULI
	DANIEL WHYBREW
PRODUCTION INSURANCE PROVIDED BY	HISCOX INSURANCE COMPANY
E&O INSURANCE PROVIDED BY	AXIS PRO INSURANCE
COMPLETION GUARANTEE PROVIDED BY	FILM FINANCES INC
	MAUREEN DUFFY
	KATRINA STAGNER
COLLECTION AGENT SERVICES PROVIDED BY	FREEWAY
PAYROLL SERVICES PROVIDED BY	INDIEPAY, L.L.C.
CFO	DAVID REYNOLDS
SENIOR VP, OPERATIONS	MICHAEL LEIBA
SENIOR PAYMASTER	JAMES LOVAGLIO
POST ACCOUNTING SERVICES PROVIDED BY	JFA, INC.
POST ACCOUNTANT	PETE HAYES
POST ACCOUNTANT	ANTHONY PUTVINSKI
EXTRAS PAYROLL SERVICES PROVIDED BY	CAPS
SCRIPT CLEARANCE RESEARCH PROVIDED BY	CLEARANCE DOMAIN
SUPER 16MM FILM STOCK PROVIDED BY	KODAK
SUPER 16MM PROCESSING PROVIDED BY	TECHNICOLOR NEW YORK
FILMED ON THE	ARRI 416
CAMERA EQUIPMENT PROVIDED BY	ARRI CSC
CAMERA SUPPORT PROVIDED BY	THE CAMERA DEPARTMENT
ELECTRIC EQUIPMENT PROVIDED BY	MIDWEST GRIP AND LIGHTING
GRIP EQUIPMENT PROVIDED BY	EYES OF MOHR
TECHNOCRANE PROVIDED BY	PANAVISION NEW YORK
CAMERA CAR PROVIDED BY	MIDWEST CAMERA CAR
TRANSPORTATION EQUIPMENT PROVIDED BY	HADDADS
	STARWAGGONS
AVID/EDITORIAL EQUIPMENT PROVIDED BY	GOLDCREST POST NEW YORK
COMMUNICATION EQUIPMENT PROVIDED BY	ROCKBOTTOM RENTALS

HOUSING PROVIDED BY

21C MUSEUM HOTEL	CJ LECKY, SALES AND MARKETING
THE HILTON NETHERLAND PLAZA	ERIC LAFFERTY, EXPRESS ACCOUNT EXECUTIVE SALES
THE WESTIN	CINCINNATI, OHIO

VEHICLE RENTALS

ENTERPRISE	HERTZ
KAREN LANKFER, RENTAL EXECUTIVE	CATHERINE KAMENSKI AND ROBIN G. WHYTE
TRAVEL SERVICES	PROVIDENT TRAVEL
	WAFA LANGENBRUNNER, SENIOR TRAVEL CONSULTANT
HEALTH LIASON	DOUG HARRIS, TRIHEALTH/GOOD SAMARITAN HOSPITAL
MUSIC SUPERVISOR	RANDALL POSTER
MUSIC CLEARANCE AND LICENSING EXECUTIVE	MATT BIFFA
MUSIC PRODUCTION COORDINATOR	MEGHAN CURRIER
ASSISTANT TO MATT BIFFA	EMILY APPLETON HOLLEY
MUSIC SERVICES PROVIDED BY	CUTTING EDGE
ORCHESTRATED AND CONDUCTED BY	CARTER BURWELL
MUSIC SCORING MIXER	MICHAEL FARROW
MUSIC CONTRACTOR	DAVID SABEE
MUSIC LIBRARIAN	ROBERT PUFF
COMPOSER'S ASSISTANT	DEAN PARKER
RECORDED AT	STUDIO X
MIXED AT	THE BODY, NEW YORK CITY

MUSIC

"WILLOW WEEP FOR ME"
PERFORMED BY VINCE GIORDANO & THE NIGHTHAWKS
WORDS AND MUSIC BY ANN RONELL
ⓒCOPYRIGHT BY BOURNE CO.
COPYRIGHT RENEWED
RIGHTS FOR THE WORLD OUTSIDE THE U.S.A. CONTROLLED BY BOURNE CO.
ALL RIGHTS FOR THE UNITED KINGDOM CONTROLLED BY BOURNE MUSIC LTD.
ALL RIGHTS RESERVED INTERNATIONAL COPYRIGHT SECURED
ⓒ COPYRIGHT 1932. ANN RONELL MUSIC/ASCAP.
ALL RIGHTS RESERVED. USED BY PERMISSION.
MASTER RECORDING LICENSED COURTESY OF STARR SCORE HOLDINGS, LLC

"FARMERS MARKET"
PERFORMED BY ANNIE ROSS
WRITTEN BY FARMER/ROSS
PUBLISHED BY UNIVERSAL MUSIC PUBLISHING LTD
COURTESY OF CONCORD MUSIC GROUP, INC.

"LOOK FOR THE SILVER LINING"
PERFORMED BY VINCE GIORDANO & THE NIGHTHAWKS
ARRANGED BY VINCE GIORDANO
PUBLISHED BY STARR SCORE HOLDINGS, LLC
MASTER RECORDING LICENSED COURTESY OF STARR SCORE HOLDINGS, LLC

THANKS

ALEX DIGERLANDO   MARK FRIEDBERG   RICHARD GLATZER
J. SCOTT GRANT   TOM KALIN   CAMDEN MORSE   CYNTHIA SCHNEIDER
STORM THARPE   WASH WESTMORELAND   PATRICIA WHITE

BOB SIGNOM AND THE CITIZENS MOTOR CAR COMPANY
THE PACKARD MUSEUM - DAYTON, OHIO
DANA KACKNEY, BRIAN HACKNEY, JASON HACKNEY, AMY HEEKIN
MERCEDES-BENZ OF CINCINNATI, OHIO

MERCEDES-BENZ OF WEST CHESTER, OHIO
FILMDAYTON, MEGAN COOPER, EXECUTIVE DIRECTOR
THE CINCINNATI MUSIC HALL, THE CINCINNATI OPERA
THE HILTON NETHERLAND PLAZA, CINCINNATI, OHIO
ARNOLD'S BAR AND GRILL (SINCE 1861)
CINCINNATI TRANSIT HISTORICAL ASSOCIATION
NINA, MELISSA AND TERRY AT SPITZFADEN OFFICE SUPPLIES
PAT, CHEVIN, RAY AND RANDY AT THE CAREW TOWER
RYAN LEVIN

THE CITY OF CINCINNATI, OHIO, THE CITY OF HAMILTON, OHIO
THE CITY OF LEBANON, OHIO, NYS POST
VICTORIA FOX, FOX SOUND STUDIOS

CINCINNATI POLICE SPECIAL EVENTS UNIT
SERGEANT GREG LEWTON, POLICE COORDINATOR
SPECIALIST SCOTT KRAUSER, POLICE COORDINATOR
DEPARTMENT OF TRANSPORTATION & ENGINEERING, CITY OF CINCINNATI
JON CHILDRESS, GREG LONG

COOPER BURKETT   CAROLINE CAHILL   KYAI CAHILL   PATRICE CAHILL
CLAIRE ENTRUP   JONATHAN FU   FRANK KAMMERER   MICHAEL LISICKY
HANA MATSUO   REN MATSUO   LAWRENCE O'NEIL
CHARLOTTE RITCHIE-SHATZ   ROXY SWEENEY

DENNY CLAREMONT   SIMON BROAD   DAVE PULTZ

SPECIAL THANKS
*Special thanks header and actual names in larger font per Todd

JIM DOUGHERTY   ROBYN GARDINER   CRAIG GERING
JAYNE HOUDYSHELL   MEL KENYON   PAM KOFFLER
ERIC KRANZLER   BRENT MORLEY   BRYAN O'KEEFE
MARYANN PLUNKETT   HYLDA QUEALLY   NICK QUESTED
JOHN QUESTED   KELLY REICHARDT   AND ROTH
KRISTEN ERWIN SCHLOTMAN

NEW YORK STATE GOVERNOR'S OFFICE FOR
MOTION PICTURE & TELEVISION DEVELOPMENT

THE GREATER CINCINNATI
AND NORTHERN KENTUCKY FILM COMMISSION

IN ASSOCIATION WITH COMPTON INVESTMENTS
(NOTE - MUST BE LARGER FONT, CONTRACTUALLY)

DEVELOPED WITH THE ASSISTANCE OF GOOD MACHINE

DEVELOPED WITH THE SUPPORT OF THE BFI FILM FUND

MUSIC SERVICES PROVIDED BY CUTTING EDGE

SAG·AFTRA.

DEVELOPED WITH THE ASSISTANCE OF GOOD MACHINE

PRODUCED BY LARKHARK FILMS LIMITED

THIS PRODUCTION PARTICIPATED IN THE OHIO MOTION PICTURE TAX INCENTIVE PROGRAM

THIS PRODUCTION PARTICIPATED IN THE NEW YORK STATE GOVERNOR'S OFFICE
FOR MOTION PICTURE & TELEVISION DEVELOPMENT'S
POST PRODUCTION CREDIT PROGRAM

서신:
캐롤과 15년을 동행해 온 필리스 나지는
기적을 믿게 되었다.

90년대 후반에 『소금의 값』을 각색할 기회가 왔을 때, 나는 패트리샤 하이스미스가 1952년에 펴낸 이 급진적인 소설을 각색하는 과정이 얼마나 어려울지 겁낼 줄도 모를 만큼 어리고 어리석었다. 사실 나는 하이스미스가 작고하기 전 10년 가량을 그와 꽤 잘 알고 지냈다. 90년대 초에 『소금의 값』을 『캐롤』이라는 제목으로 재출간한 후에 이 책에 대해 수다를 떨기도 했다. 쉬울 거라고 생각했다. 원작 소설은 쉬이 얇아 보이는 두께로 하루이틀 저녁이면 다 읽을 수 있다. 플롯은 복잡하지 않고, 어린 주인공(테레즈 벨리벳)의 거의 주술적인 독백을 동력으로 한다. 문체는 실용적이고 성겨서 테레즈와 그녀가 욕망하는 대상인 캐롤 에어드 사이의 열정적이지만 억눌린 끌림과 훌륭한 대조를 이룬다.

그때나 지금이나 각본을 쓰면서 가장 좋았던 건, 하이스미스가 등장인물들의 성 정체성에 대해 고리타분한 정신분석을 늘어놓지 않는다는 점이었다. 테레즈도 캐롤도 자신이 내린 성적인 결정을 후회하지 않는다. 이들에게 자기 정체성은 숨 쉬듯 편안하다. 누구도 자살하려 하지 않는다. 캐롤의 친구 애비 게르하르트라는 세 번째 인물을 포함해서, 이 소설에 나오는 모든 레즈비언들은 불안정한 헤테로섹슈얼 캐릭터들보다도 자연스럽고 편안하다.

이런 책은 본 적이 없고, 이 소설의 진보적인 성격은 지금 봐도 시대를 앞선 것 같다. 섬세한 톤, 문화적 규범에 대한 놀랍지만 납득할 수 있는 전복성은 내가 가장 소중히 여긴 특징들이고, 집필

단계에서 살리기 위해 분투했던 것들이다. 하지만 소설을 아주 뛰어나게 만드는 특징들 가운데 각본에서 절대 구현할 수 없는 것들도 있다. 가장 대표적으로, 원작에서 캐롤은 마치 유령 같은 존재다. 그녀 삶의 희미한 디테일들이 테레즈의 눈을 통해 독자들에게 파편화되어 전달될 뿐이다. 소설에서는 이것이 아름답게 표현되어 있고, 따라서 독자들이 각자의 캐롤을 상상할 수 있다. 하지만 영화를 위해서는 캐롤의 삶에도 내러티브가 필요했고, 소설의 일인칭 시점을 유지하는 대신 두 연인 사이에서 힘의 균형이 역동적으로 변화하게 만들어야 했다.

11년이 지나고, 네 가지 버전의 원고가 나왔다. 그 사이에 왔다가 떠난 감독들과 투자자들을 위해 약간씩 수정한 것들을 합치면 그 수는 두 배가 된다. 이 각본을 같이 발전시키며 붙들고 있던 테사 로스와 Film4가 이따금 우리가 믿음을 잃지 않게 이끌어줬다. 나는 다른 일을 받았고, HBO를 위해 〈해리스 부인〉이라는 영화를 쓰고 연출했다. (이 영화를 제작한 리즈 칼슨과 그리스딘 바숑이 후에 〈캐롤〉을 제작했다) 하지만 내 심장과 가장 가까이 품고 있던 프로젝트는 〈캐롤〉이었다.

그리고 소설에 대한 판권 계약이 만료됐다. 나는 〈캐롤〉이 죽었다고 생각했다. 죽음 자체는 받아들였지만 마음은 부서졌다. 그리고 그래도 괜찮았다. 나는 어떤 연인보다도 더 오랜 시간 동안 캐롤과 함께 살았다. 글을 써서 돈을 받은 첫 번째 각본이었다. 영화 각본을 쓸 때 알아야할 모든 것과 몰랐으면 더 좋았을 것들을 〈캐롤〉을 통해 배웠다. 빠르게 결정하는 법을 배웠고, 내가 좋아했던 글을 위해 싸우는 것과 남길 가치가 있는 글을 위해 싸우는 게 다르다는 걸 알게 됐다. 나는 이 융통성 없는 산업에서 수완을 갖는 법을 알게 됐다.

이런 것들은 대부분의 작가가 어떤 프로젝트에서도 얻을 수 없는 경험이라는 것을 받아들이고, 나는 앞으로 나아갔다. 1년이 지나고, 리즈 칼슨에게 전화가 왔다. 하이스미스 유산 상속인을 마법처럼 설득해 〈캐롤〉의 판권을 따낸 것이다. 내 각본을 바탕으로 영화를 만들고 싶어 했고, 언제나 그렇듯 테사 로스가 우리의 뒤를 든든히 지켜주고 있었다. 함께 해야 할까? 일말의 망설임도 필요치 않았다.

나는 싫다고 했다.

할 만큼 했다. 거짓으로 시작해 실망으로 끝나는 일을 너무 많이 겪었다. 나는 더 이상 순진하게 이 소설의 어두운 심장을 건드리던 그 작가가 아니었다. 10년이 지난 후, 지금의 나라는 작가가 원래 괜찮았던 부분들을 모조리 망쳐버릴까 두려웠다.

리즈가 이제 드디어 이 영화를 만들 수 있다고 나를 설득하는 데 꼬박 1년이 걸렸다. 마침내 믿고 나아갔고, 마치 캐롤과 테레즈처럼, 뒤를 돌아보지 않았다. 쉽지는 않았지만, 뭔가 그보다 훨씬 더 좋은 것이었다. 기적적이었다.

2015. 11.
필리스 나지
로스앤젤레스타임즈 기고문

The Envelope:
Walking with 'Carol' for a decade and a half taught Phyllis Nagy to believe in miracles

When the opportunity to adapt "The Price of Salt" came to me in the late 1990s, I was young and foolish enough to have no fear of the challenges inherent in adapting Patricia Highsmith's radical 1952 novel. After all, I'd known Highsmith pretty well over the last decade of her life. We'd even chatted about the book after she republished and re-christened it "Carol" in the early '90s. I thought it would be easy. It's a deceptively slim volume, easily read in an evening or two. Light on plot and motored by the almost incantatory interior monologue of its young protagonist (Therese Belivet), the prose is functional and spare, in brilliant contrast to the passionate attachment — however restrained — between Therese and the object of her desire, Carol Aird.

What most excited me about tackling a script then, and still, was Highsmith's refusal to engage in banal psychologizing about her characters' sexual identities. Neither Therese nor Carol regrets the sexual choices each makes. Their identities are as natural to them as breathing. Neither attempts suicide. In fact, all of the novel's lesbians — there is a third, Carol's friend, Abby Gerhard — are more comfortable in their own skins than are the novel's heterosexual, less settled characters.

I'd never read another novel like it, and its forward-thinking qualities still seem ahead of the times. Its delicate tone, its startling but understated subversion of cultural norms — these are the qualities I most cherished and fought to preserve through the writing process. But some of the same qualities that make the novel work so well are exactly the qualities that don't work in screenplays: most notably, that Carol herself is a ghostly character, the scant details of her life relayed to the reader in shards, through Therese's eyes — beautifully apt in the novel, so that the reader can visualize his or her own Carol. For film, a narrative life had to be created for Carol and a dynamic, shifting balance of power between the lovers substituted for the single point of view in the novel.

Eleven years later, we'd been through four drafts and double that in small revisions for directors and potential financiers who came and went. Every once in a while, Tessa Ross and Film4 — the other constants over the script's development — guided us to keep the faith. I took other jobs, wrote and directed the film "Mrs. Harris" for HBO that was produced by Liz Karlsen and Christine Vachon (both producers of "Carol"). Yet "Carol" was the project I held closest to my heart.

And then the rights to the novel lapsed. I thought "Carol" had died. I resigned myself to its demise, however heartbroken I was. And I was fine with that. I'd lived with "Carol" longer than I'd lived with any lover; it was the first script I was paid to write. It taught me all I'd need to know — and some things I wish I never had to learn — about the craft of screenwriting. It taught me how to think on my feet and to tell the difference between how to fight for writing worth keeping rather than for writing I loved. I learned to be a diplomat in a decidedly undiplomatic industry.

I figured this was a great deal more than most writers are gifted with on any project and moved on. A year later, the call came from Liz Karlsen. She worked magic in persuading the Highsmith estate to grant her the option on the novel. She wanted to use my screenplay as the basis for the film; Tessa Ross, as ever, had our backs. Would I join them? I didn't hesitate for a moment.

I said "no."

418

I'd had enough, been through far too many false starts ending in disappointment. I was no longer the same writer who naively tackled the dark heart of the novel — I feared that, a decade gone, the writer I'd become would screw up everything that was fine about the script in the first place.

It took Liz a year to convince me to believe we could finally make this film. I took the leap and, much like Carol and Therese, we've never looked back. It was never easy, but it's been something much better — it's been miraculous.

NOV. 2015
PHYLLIS NAGY
LOS ANGELES TIMES

"테레즈 벨리벳, 예쁜 이름이네요"

글: 이다혜 (작가/씨네21 기자)

아카데미 시상식의 장편영화 시나리오에 주어지는 상은 각본상과 각색상 두 가지가 있다. 각본상은 창작 시나리오에, 각색상은 원작이 있는 시나리오에 주어진다. 〈캐롤〉이 6개 부문 후보에 오르고 무관에 그친 2016년 아카데미 시상식의 각색상은 〈빅쇼트〉의 아담 맥케이가 받았다. 각본을 쓴 필리스 나지를 비롯해 아무도 오스카 트로피 없이 귀가한 〈캐롤〉을 떠올리면 드는 실망감이야 영화를 아낀 사람들의 자연스러운 감정이라고 생각하지만 분명 이상한 일은 더 있다. 캐롤을 연기한 케이트 블란쳇은 여우주연상 후보에, 테레즈를 연기한 루니 마라는 여우조연상 후보에 올랐다는 사실이다. 두 사람이 사랑에 빠지는 내용을 담은 영화에서 주연과 조연을 나눈 기준은 무엇인가? 이들이 모두 여성이기 때문에 생긴 일은 아닌가.

2016년에 영국영화협회(British Film Institute)는 영화평론가, 영화제작자, 영화연구가, 그리고 영화제 프로그래머 등 100명이 넘는 전문가를 대상으로 한 설문을 통해 〈캐롤〉을 영화 역사상 최고의 LGBT 영화로 선정했다. 무엇이 이 작품을 특별하게 만드는가. 패트리샤 하이스미스의 소설 『캐롤』을 경유해 필리스 나지의 영화 시나리오 〈캐롤〉을 거쳐 토드 헤인즈의 영화 〈캐롤〉에 이르는 변신 과정에서 무엇이 더해지고 빠졌을까를 중심으로 살펴본다.

〈캐롤〉의 시나리오를 쓴 필리스 나지는 연극과 영화 연출가인 동시에 영화 시나리오와 희곡을 모두 쓰는 극작가다. 뉴욕에서 태어난 필리스 나지는 1992년 런던으로 이주해 극작가로 활동을 시작했다. 당시 로열 코트 시어터의 상임작가였던 스티븐 달드리의 지도를 받기도 했다. 드라마 〈해리스 부인〉의 각본과 연출로 에미상 후보에 오른 것을 비롯해 지금까지 24개 상의 후보에 올랐고 뉴욕비평가상의 최고 시나리오상 등 13개 상을 수상했다.

필리스 나지는 런던에서 활동하기 전에 소설가 패트리샤 하이스미스에게 브루클린의 그린우드 공동묘지에 대해 무언가를 써보지 않겠느냐는 제안을 한 일이 있었는데, 당시 필리스 나지는 시니컬하기로 악명 높던 하이스미스와 공동묘지에 함께 방문하기도 했다. 그들의 우정이 그렇게 시작되었는데, 필리스 나지가 런던으로 이주한 뒤 성공한 극작가가 되는 동안 하이스미스는 유럽에서 생의 마지막 날들을 보냈다. 하이스미스의 레즈비언 러브 스토리 『캐롤』의 각색은 하이스미스의 사망 이후 시작되었다.

필리스 나지는 〈배너티 페어〉 〈가디언〉 등 여러 매체와의 인터뷰에서 영화 〈캐롤〉의 시나리오화에 대해 밝힌 적이 있었다. "팻이 죽은 뒤 몇 년이 지나도록 나는 그녀가 살아있고 우리가 친구였던 시간에 여전히 가깝게 있다고 느끼고 있었다. 나는 팻의 소설 『소금의 값』(『캐롤』이 처음 출간되었던 때의 제목)을 그녀가 죽은 직후에야 읽었고, 영화 제작자가 내게 작업을 제안했던 때, '그래, 때가 되었어'라고 생각했다. 나는 영화 시나리오를 쓰고 싶었다.

나는 각색을 하고 싶을 뿐이지... 연출은 아니었다. 모든 게 알맞은 자리에 있는 듯 보였다. 초안은 1997년 정도에 완성되었던 것으로 기억한다." 그 시기는 여성 배우 두 사람이 주인공인 영화들이 많이 만들어지지 않던 때이기도 했다. "케이트 블란쳇도 지금의 케이트 블란쳇이 아니었다." 다른 많은 영화들처럼 〈캐롤〉의 시나리오는 잠깐 관심을 얻다가 몇 년씩 아무 진척 없이 묵혀있는 일을 반복했다.

필리스 나지는『캐롤』영화화가 2013년경 토드 헤인즈와 루니 마라가 관심을 가지면서 본격적으로 속도를 얻기 시작했다고 한다. 토드 헤인즈가 원작에서 높게 샀고 필리스 나지에게 더 깊게 파고들라고 한 방향은 캐롤과 테레즈의 로맨스가 어떻게 대사 외의 방식으로(subtextually) 진행되게 할 수 있겠느냐는 것이었다. "흥미로운 점은, 〈캐롤〉이 대사로 가득한 작품이며, 패트리샤 하이스미스의 소설과는 아주, 아주 다르다는 것이다- 하지만 아무도 그것을 알아차리지 못했다!"

패트리샤 하이스미스의 소설과 완성된 토드 헤인즈의 영화를 비교하면, 소설『캐롤』쪽은 테레즈의 심리를 밀착해 묘사하며 젊고 커리어가 불안정한 여성이 겪는 불안증을 보여주는데 영화 〈캐롤〉보다 더 많은 분량을 할애한다는 차이가 있다. 젊은 여성이 나 자신보다 나이 든 여성들을 보며 경험하는 불안 - 저렇게 되면 어떡하지? 저렇게 되면? 아니면 저렇게? 즉, 시야에 들어오는 나이 든 여성 태반이 자신이 되고 싶지 않은 무언가일 때 경험하는 불안, '나는 저렇게 되고 싶지 않아' 그와 동시에 헤아릴 수 없는 연민과 죄책감이 함께 있다-을 소설 속 테레즈는 패트리샤 하이스미스의 문장을 통해 드러낸다.

두 사람이 맨 처음 만나는 백화점 상황을 예로 들어보자. 시나리오
와 영화에서 캐롤은 테레즈 앞 진열대 위에 가죽장갑을 툭 놓으며
말을 건다. 캐롤의 딸을 위한 크리스마스 선물용 인형과 기차에
대한 이야기를 나눈 뒤 구입이 완료되고 캐롤이 자리를 떠난다. 그
런데 가죽장갑을 두고 간 채다. 소설 『캐롤』에는 이 부분이 없다.
하지만 영화에서는 이 말없는 장갑이 진열장 위에 놓이고, 주인
없이 남겨지고, 그것을 누군가가 발견하는 순간이 관심 혹은 관계
의 시작을 암시하게 된다. 필리스 나지의 말을 빌면 "가죽 장갑은
하이스미스의 책에는 없어요! 하지만 모두 그 장면이 있다고 생
각해요. 그래도 괜찮아요."

시나리오가 소설과 다른 가장 큰 부분이 있다면, 시나리오를 완성
하는 사람은 작가도 감독도 아닌 배우의 육화 된 연기라는 데 있
다. 어느 정도는 연기자를 믿고 남겨두는 것이다. 시나리오 〈캐롤〉
은 그 자체로도 굉장히 아름다운데, 더 놀라운 것은 영화와 함께
감상할 때다. 이미 완성되어 있는 작품이 다른 방식으로 완성되
는 모습을 보게 되기 때문이다. 필리스 나지는 케이트 블란쳇, 루
니 마라, 사라 폴슨, 카일 챈들러까지 영화 〈캐롤〉의 배우들이 서
로 다르지만 상호보완적 관계에 놓인데 대해 높게 평가했는데, 그
들이 연극 무대 경험이 있다는 것이 이유라는 분석을 내놓기도
했다. "(연극은 영화와는 다른 방식으로) 텍스트와 연기의 관계
가 존재하는 곳이기 때문이다." 또한 소설 『캐롤』이 일정 부분 패
트리샤 하이스미스의 자전적 이야기의 성격을 지녔으며 특히 테
레즈 캐릭터와의 유사성이 있다는 점을 감안하면 필리스 나지의
이 말은 배우 루니 마라에 대한 큰 상찬이다. "영화화가 이루어지
리라는 가능성이 가시화된 순간부터 루니 마라는 언제나 내가 생
각한 테레즈였다. 루니 마라는 언제나 그런 분위기를 갖고 있었

다. - 순전히 우연이겠지만 - 팻의 무언가를 갖고 있었다는 말이다. 아주 이상한 일이었다." 영화 속 루니 마라가 보여준 특정한 움직임, 멈춤, 고양이 같은 면들은 젊은 하이스미스가 갖고 있던 무엇이라고. 게다가 테레즈의 대사는 순전한 팻의 그것과 유사하다는 것이다. 『캐롤』의 영화화에 15년이 넘는 시간이 걸린 이유는 레즈비언 두 사람이 영화의 주인공이기 때문일까를 묻는 〈가디언〉의 질문에 대한 필리스 나지의 답변은 이렇다. 오랜 시간 동안 아주 많은 사람들과 이야기를 나누며 영화로 만들어보고자 했던 기억을 돌이켜보면 "레즈비언인 것보다는 여자들 이야기라는 게 더 문제로 받아들여졌던 것 같다. 영화 투자의 문제에서 여성들이 나오는 영화라는 사실은 굉장히 일을 까다롭게 만든다. 이런 말을 하는 게 굉장히 슬프지만 하지 않을 수 없다. 심지어 〈텔마와 루이스〉가 한 세대 전이다." 레즈비언과 영화에 집중해 말하면, "동성애자 이야기가 영화화된다면 그것은 주로 남자들의 경우다." 필리스 나지는 〈캐롤〉이 성공한다면(성공했다) 유사한 영화들이 몇 편 더 만들어질 것이라면서 극장가의 레즈비어니즘이 "정상성"(state of normality)의 세계에서 무한한 다양성과 풍부함으로 다루어지기를 원한다고 밝혔다.

시나리오 〈캐롤〉은 영화의 최종 편집에서 삭제된 장면들까지 볼수 있게 한다. 시나리오와 영화의 가장 큰 차이는 캐롤과 테레즈의 관계를 중심으로 영화를 압축하면서 시나리오상에는 보다 풍부한 맥락으로 존재하는 두 여성의 분량을 영화가 크게 줄였다는 것이다. 첫 번째는 테레즈가 프랑켄베르크 백화점에서 본 50대 여직원들, 그중에서 특히 로비첵 부인의 이야기다. 사진을 찍고 싶지만 생업으로 백화점 일을 하는 테레즈는 자신이 백화점에서 벗어나지 못할까봐 두려워한다. 저런 삶을 살기는 싫어. 그런 두

427

려움을 한데 뭉쳐놓은 인물이 바로 로비첵 부인이다. 로비첵 부인은 한때 손바느질을 해서 제법 괜찮은 옷을 만들곤 했지만 시력이 나빠져 이젠 한쪽 눈이 거의 보이지도 않는다. "테레즈가 두려운 건 바로 절망감이었다. 백화점에서 일하는 로비첵 부인의 지친 몸이 뿜어내는 절망감."(소설 『캐롤』 중에서) 필리스 나지는 로비첵을 크리스마스 유령과 같다고 표현했는데, 소설의 로비첵은 프랑켄베르크에서 4년 일한 사람으로 나오지만, 영화의 로비첵은 백화점에서 18년을 일한 사람으로 나온다.

테레즈
저는 연휴 동안만 임시로 일하는 거예요.

루비 로비첵
(어깨를 으쓱하며)
나도 그렇게 말했었지.

이런 대목도 있다. 캐롤과 여행을 하면서 테레즈는 로비첵을 위해 기념품을 산다.

테레즈
나이 든 여자분이 이거 좋아할까요?

캐롤
아마도요. 누구냐에 따라 다르겠지만.

테레즈
프랑켄베르크에서 같이 일하던 루비라는 분이 있는데…
보면 좀 우울했어요.

캐롤
왜요?

테레즈
늙고, 혼자고, 돈도 없고. 바보 같은 생각이죠, 알아요.

캐롤
다정한 것 같은데요. 보내요. 여기.

또한 캐롤의 친구(이자 전 애인)인 애비가 캐롤과 혹은 캐롤에 대해 나누는 대화도 많은 부분 삭제되었다. 캐롤의 심리를 보다 잘 알 수 있는 대목들이지만, 결과적으로 이 부분들이 빠짐으로써 영화는 (전지적이기보다는) 테레즈의 입장에서 캐롤을 동경하는 마음으로 더 바라보게 되었다. 예를 들면 이런 대목이다.

애비
나 진지해. (잠깐 침묵)
우리가 했던 가게보다 재앙일 순 없겠지.

침묵. 애비는 다른 곳을 본다.
캐롤이 그녀에게 몸을 기울인다.

캐롤
우리가 재앙은 아니었어. 그냥...

캐롤은 단어를 찾을 수 없다.

애비
알아. 타이밍. 늘 안 좋았지. 아무튼,
요새 꽂힌 빨강 머리가 있는데,
퍼래머스 외곽에 있는 스테이크집 사장이야.
리타 헤이워드는 저리 가랄 정도야.

여행중인 캐롤과 테레즈를 뒤쫓으며 캐롤의 양육권 소송에 불리한 증거를 수집하는 사립탐정이 하는 하등 쓸모없는 이야기들도 거의 다 삭제되었다. 테레즈의 전 남자친구인 리처드와 관련된 부분(예를 들어 테레즈가 손을 이용해 그를 사정하게 하는 대목 전체)도 삭제되었다.

〈캐롤〉 각본집은 한국어와 영어 대사가 함께 수록되었는데, 한국어 부분은 의미를 통하게 한다는 장점이 있겠지만, 영어 대사와 지문은 배우의 연기와 더 밀착된 글을 읽는다는 느낌을 받게 될 것이다. 한국어로 대사 하는 영화 시나리오를 영어로 읽고 한국어로 읽는다고 생각하면 이해가 쉬울 것이다. 대사는 글인 동시에 말이다. 시나리오는 배우의 연기가 덧입혀지기 전의 몸짓을 담고 있는데, 영화와 함께 시나리오를 보면 글과 말이 어떻게 입체적으로 살아나는지 볼 수 있다. 말이 생명을 얻는 느낌으로 읽을 수 있다. 영어 대사의 경우는 더 흥미로운 지점이 있는데, 한국어 자막은 의미 중심으로 되어있지만(또한 당연하게도 가능한 글자 수를 줄여야 한다), 영어 자막은 의미와 음성을 모두 염두에 둔 결과물로 보인다.

하지만 〈캐롤〉 각본집에서 가장 좋은 부분, 영화와 비교할 것도 없이 그 자체로 모든 것이 완성되는 부분은 〈캐롤〉의 지문이다. 이 대목들은 배우들의 연기를 덧입고 완성되어 잊을 수 없는 장면들로 남았지만, 설령 오로지 글로만 남았다 해도 머릿속에서 쉽게 떠나지 않는 이미지를 만들어낸다. 예를 들면 처음 테레즈와 캐롤이 만나는 순간, 테레즈의 눈으로 본 캐롤은 이렇게 묘사된다. "이 여자는 거기 유일하게 존재하는 단 한 명의 손님처럼 보인다." 뒤에 "캐롤 에어드다."라는 문장이 붙는다.

녹색 실크 스카프를 머리와 목에 느슨하게 두른 여자가 테레즈의 시선을 끈다. 이 여자는 거기 유일하게 존재하는 단 한 명의 손님처럼 보인다. 캐롤 에어드다. 캐롤은 기차 세트를 살피기 위해 몸을 굽히고 무심코 전원을 껐다 켰다 한다. 기차가 멈춘다. 캐롤이 일어나, 인형 코너를 향해 돌아선다. 마치 도움을 청하듯, 미소를 지으며. 테레즈는 묘한 찰나의 순간 동안 캐롤과 눈이 마주친다. 당황한 엄마와 소리를 질러대는 아기가 다른 무엇도 보이지 않게 테레즈의 시야를 가로막기 전까지.

테레즈가 자신이 원하는 직업의 일부를 엿보는 장면에도 인상적인 지문이 등장한다. 대니라는 이름의 남자 친구가 자신이 일하는 〈뉴욕타임스〉 사무실 안을 보여주는 대목이다. 대니가 테레즈에게 키스한다는 점을 상기하면 그는 자신의 일터를 여성을 유혹하는 수단의 하나로 사용하는 정도의 인물이지만, 테레즈는 그곳에서 자신이 원하는 자신의 미래를 본다. "테레즈는 감히 아무것도 만지지 못한다"는 문장은 영화에서 지문만이 할 수 있는 심리묘사일 것이다.

대니가 사진 편집자의 매혹적인 세계로 테레즈를 안내한다. 라이트 보드에 매달린 인화지들, 전문 장비, 쟁반과 렌즈들. 하지만 그녀가 가장 경탄하는 건 사진들 그 자체다. 몰래 찍은 사진, 범죄 현장, 스포츠 사진, 신문의 시각적 내러티브를 만드는 모든 것들이 있다. 대니는 책상에 앉아 집에서 가져온 부실한 저녁을 준비한다. 포장한 샌드위치와 맥주 몇 병이다. 이 공간의 모든 것을 흡수하고 있는 테레즈는 감히 아무것도 만지지 못한다.

테레즈가 캐롤과 함께 여행 중인 자동차 안, 테레즈는 이렇게 느끼고 있다. "테레즈에게 캐롤의 차 안이라는 세계는 그녀에 대한 하나의 폭로와도 같다. 이 세계의 소리, 심지어 이따금 캐롤이 재잘대는 소리까지도 모두 가장 고요한 '음악'인 빛과 공기의 소리로 대체된다." 특히 지문의 아름다움으로 말이 멎는(대사가 필요 없고 실제로도 없다) 마지막 장면은, 이 책을 직접 읽기를 권한다.

"Therese Belivet. That's lovely."

Lee Da-Hyeh (Writer / Cine21 Reporter)

At the Academy Awards, screenplays are eligible for two award categories – 'best adapted screenplay' and 'best original screenplay'. At the 2016 Awards, where *Carol* was nominated for 6 awards and walked away with none, the best adapted screenplay went to Adam McKay's work on *The Big Short*. While the fact that *Carol* won no Oscar trophies, including for screenwriter Phyllis Nagy, might have been an understandable disappointment for fans of the film, the peculiarities surely did not end there. For one, there is the fact that Cate Blanchett (Carol) was nominated for 'best actress' while Rooney Mara (Therese) was nominated for 'best supporting actress'. In a film about two people who fall in love, where is the dividing line that determines the lead and the support? Might this not owe to the fact that both protagonists were women?

In 2016, the British Film Institute ran a poll on more than a hundred industry experts including film critics, film makers, film researchers, and film festival programmers, which led to *Carol* being named the best LBGT film of all time. So what made this film special? This article will look at the transformation process – from *Carol* as a novel by Patricia Highsmith, to *Carol* as a screenplay by Phyllis Nagy, and finally *Carol* the film by Todd Haynes, with a focus on what has been added and what has been taken out.

The screenplay for *Carol* was written by Phyllis Nagy, who is a theatre and film director as well as screenwriter and playwright. Born in New York, Nagy relocated to London in 1992 to begin her career as a playwright. She received artistic direction from Steven Daldry, who was the writer-in-residence at the Royal Court Theatre. She has been nominated for 24 awards, including an Emmy for her writing /

direction of the drama *Mrs. Harris*, and has won 13 awards including the New York Film Critics Circle award for best screenplay.

Prior to her time in London, Nagy once proposed to Highsmith about writing up a piece about the Green-Wood Cemetery in Brooklyn, going so far as accompanying the notoriously difficult novelist on a visit to the cemetery. This led to a friendship between the two writers. While Nagy relocated to London and was achieving success as a playwright, Highsmith was spending the end of her days in Europe. The adaptation of Highsmith's lesbian romance story, *Carol*, began after her death.

In interviews with various outlets including Vanity Fair and the Guardian, Phyllis Nagy described how the screenplay for *Carol* came to be - "It was actually a couple years after Pat had died, and I was still fairly close to that period when I knew her and we were friends. I had read the book only shortly after she'd died, and when this producer came to me, I thought, O.K., it's time. I want to write film. I only want to write adaptations... I don't direct. Everything seemed right, so I took it on. It was probably mid- to late 1997 when the first draft was delivered." This was at a time when few films were being made with two female leads, not to mention the fact that "Cate Blanchett wasn't even Cate Blanchett yet." As was the case with so many other films, the screenplay for *Carol* would occasionally be visited with interest, only to languish in production limbo for years at a time.

According to Nagy, things began to pick up speed around 2013, when Todd Haynes and Rooney Mara expressed interest. The angle that Haynes particularly appreciated about the work, and encouraged Nagy to explore further, was how the romance developed in a subtextual manner. On this, Nagy remarks, "What's interesting, is it's full of dialogue and it's very, very different from Patricia Highsmith's novel—but no one's noticed that!"

436

Comparing the novel by Highsmith and the finished film by Haynes, it is noticeable that the former describes Therese's psychological state more intimately with a greater focus on the anxiety experienced by a young woman in a precarious career. This is an anxiety that arises from her observing so many aged women that she might end up becoming in the future. This intense feeling of 'not wanting to end up like them', which is accompanied by an unfathomable pity and sense of guilt, is apparent in Therese as she is portrayed in Highsmith's novel.

One particularly striking instance of this can be found in Carol and Therese's first sit-down, that famous scene where Carol first pronounces the name "Therese Belivet":

"What kind of a name is Belivet?" she asked.
"It's Czech. It's changed," Therese explained awkwardly. "Originally –"
"It's very original."
"What's your name?" Therese asked. "Your first name?"
"My name? Carol. Please don't ever call me Carole."
"Please don't ever call me Thereese," Therese said, pronouncing the th.
"How do you like it pronounced? Therese?"
"Yes. The way you do," she answered. Carol pronounced her name the French way, Terez. She was used to a dozen variations, and sometimes she herself pronounced it differently. She liked the way Carol pronounced it, and she liked her lips saying it. An indefinite longing, that she had been only vaguely conscious of at times before, became now a recognizable wish. It was so absurd, so embarrassing a desire, that Therese thrust it from her mind.
                                        - From *Carol* by Patricia Highsmith

That moment at which one falls in love, or becomes seduced by someone, cannot be described without mentioning the rush of emotion felt when merely hearing one's name being said by that person feels transformative, so that one's name (or very being) becomes different from what it once was. In the film, the whole of this dialogue and psychological description is replaced by Carol's line, "Therese Belivet. That's lovely." These words, delivered in Blanchett's characteristically deep and smooth voice, gives not only Therese but also the audience the uncanny sensation that one's name has been caressed with a velvety touch. Thus, the audience also partake in the experience of falling in love. This evocative feel is apparent in both the screenplay and the film – another notable scene is where the two women first meet in the department store. In the screenplay and the film, Carol sets down her gloves before addressing Therese. She discusses dolls, or a train set, as gifts for her daughter. A purchase is made and Carol leaves, leaving her gloves behind. This part is not in the novel. However, in the film, the gloves that are left behind and later discovered create a moment that foreshadows the beginning of an attraction, or a relationship. Commenting on the leather gloves, Nagy mentions that they "are not in Highsmith's book! But everyone remembers that they are, which is fine."

The most important difference between a screenplay and a novel would be the fact that it is the physical performance of the actor – not the author or director – that completes a screenplay. Thus, there is a certain part that is left and entrusted for the actor to complete. The screenplay for *Carol*, which is superbly beautiful in and of itself, is even more striking when seen along with the film. This is because one can appreciate how an already-finished work can be completed anew in a different manner. Nagy has voiced approval for how the actors and actresses in *Carol* - Cate Blanchett, Rooney Mara, Sarah Paulson, and Kyle Chandler, with their differences, came together in a mutually complementary manner. She attributed this to their background in theatre where, unlike film, "there's a different relation to text." Furthermore, considering the partly autobiographical nature of the novel and the similarities between Therese and Highsmith, Nagy's words represent high praise for Rooney Mara as an actress:

"From the moment the movie became a real possibility, she was always the person I thought should do it. And she had that about her on set— it was completely accidental—she had something of Pat, it was very peculiar.", which she describes as "a certain way of moving: a certain stillness. A certain cat-like thing." Describing Therese's dialogue as 'sheer Pat', Nagy remarks that she thought about how "[Pat] might speak" when writing Therese's dialogue.

Also, no matter how harshly disapproving Highsmith might have been of the film adaptation of *Carol* had she been alive (of all the writers in the world, none might be as notorious as Highsmith for misanthropy – reading her novels, one seldom finds any hint of affection for her characters. In that regard, *Carol* is an exception), Nagy gathers that Highsmith would have at least loved the casting decision, her imagined reaction being, "Cate Blanchett. Yeah! That's my Carol!!".

When asked by the Guardian whether it was the presence of two gay female leads that accounted for the 15 years it took for *Carol* to finally be adapted, Nagy replies, "My feeling, having talked to and tried to put it together with so many people over the years, is not so much it being gay women; it's about it being women. In film-financing terms, that's very tricky. It's very sad that I have to say this. But even *Thelma & Louise* was a generation ago. (...) If we're talking specifically about gay women, about who they're allowed to be, who gets to make the movies, it's generally men." Nagy comments that were *Carol* to do well (which it has), she would hope for more and more similar films to be made in "a world in which the 'state of normality' of lesbianism sells at the cinema in infinite variety and richness." The Guardian interview article with Nagy closes with the following remark: "To change the world a little bit, it just needs to make money."

Through the screenplay of *Carol*, one can also look at the scenes that didn't make the final cut. The major point of departure between the film and the screenplay is that, in the process of compressing the film around the relationship between Carol and Therese, much of screenplay's richer context within which the two women exist has been left out of the film. Firstly, there are the middle-aged women Therese observes in the department store – Mrs. Robichek in particular. Despite aspiring to become a photographer, Therese must make ends meet by working at the department store and is terrified of becoming trapped in that job. Mrs. Robichek is the very personification of all that Therese fears she might end up becoming in the future - Mrs. Robichek, who was once handy enough with needlework to make nice dresses for herself, and who was now losing her sight in one eye. "[It] was the hopelessness that terrified her and nothing else. It was the hopelessness of Mrs. Robichek's ailing body and her job at the store..." (from the novel *Carol*). Nagy once compared Mrs. Robichek to the Ghost of Christmas Future – while in the novel she is into her fourth year working at Frankenberg's, in the film she has been there for 18 years.

THERESE

I'm just a temporary. For the holiday.

RUBY ROBICHEK

(shrugs) I said that once.

There's even an exchange like the following. During her trip with Carol, Therese buys souvenirs for Mrs. Robichek.

THERESE

Do you think something like this would appeal to an older woman?

CAROL

I suppose. Depends on the woman.

THERESE

I worked with a woman at Frankenberg's - Ruby.
But she depressed me.

CAROL

Why?

THERESE

She's old. Alone. No money.
It's - silly, I know.

CAROL

I think it's a lovely gesture.
Send it. Here.

Also, much of the dialogue by Carol's friend (and former lover) Abby, both with and about Carol, have been left out of the film. Although these scenes help form a better understand of Carol's mind, their removal ultimately leads the film away from omniscience, instead following Therese's viewpoint in her admiration for Carol. Take, for instance, the following exchange:

ABBY

I'm serious.
(beat) Couldn't be any more of a disaster
than the shop we had.

A silence. ABBY looks away from CAROL. CAROL leans in towards her.

CAROL

Hey. We weren't a disaster.
It just…

CAROL doesn't have the words.

I know. Timing. Never had it.
Anyway, I've got my eye on this redhead
who owns a steak house in Paramus.
I'm talking serious Rita Hayworth redhead.

Additionally, almost all of the inconsequential tidbits about the private detective, trailing the couple as he collects evidence to be used against Carol in the custody suit, have been left out. Also gone are the parts about Therese's ex-boyfriend Richard (including, for instance, the entire scene where she gives him a hand job).

This edition of the *Carol* screenplay includes both the English and Korean dialogues. While the Korean text allows for meaning to be conveyed, the English dialogue and scene direction give the reader a feeling of greater intimacy with the actors' performances. This might be more readily understood if one imagines what it would like be to read the Korean and English screenplays for a Korean-language film. Dialogue is written text, but also spoken word. The screenplay presents actions as they are before a further layer is applied via the actors' performances. Viewing the film together with the screenplay, one can appreciate how text and speech come to life in a rich manner, in which the words can be read as if they have been infused with life. It is also interesting to read the English dialogue. While the Korean subtitles are focused on conveying meaning (not to mention the obvious need to be as brief as possible), the English subtitles appear to have taken account of both meaning and sound.

However, the most delightful parts of the screenplay are the scene directions, which are self-contained in a way that bears no comparison to the film. Even though these directions have been realised by actors' performances to create unforgettable scenes, the text itself is enough to conjure up images that are truly haunting. There is, for instance, the moment when Therese first meets Carol. In Therese's eyes, Carol is described thus: "This WOMAN appears to be the only customer surrounded by no one else.", followed by "This is CAROL AIRD".

...a woman whose green silk scarf tied loosely around her neck and head catches THERESE'S attention. This WOMAN appears to be the only customer surrounded by no one else. This is CAROL AIRD. CAROL bends down to examine the train set, and inadvertently toggles the on/off switch - the train shuts down. CAROL stands up, turns around towards the doll department, smiling, as if asking for help.

THERESE meets CAROL'S eyes for a strange split second - until the EMBARRASSED MOM and the screaming TODDLER appear in front of THERESE, blocking her view of anything else.

Another notable bit of scene direction occurs in the scene where Therese catches a glimpse of the career she hopes to pursue when a male friend, Dannie, invites her to his New York Times office. The fact that Dannie moves in to kiss her suggests that he is merely a character who uses his job as a means of seducing women. For Therese, on the other hand, the occasion gives her a look into the future she wishes for herself. The text which ends with "...not daring to touch anything." is a piece of psychological portrayal that can only be achieved through scene direction.

DANNIE ushers THERESE into the alluring world of a junior photo editor's office: the contact sheets dangling from light boards, the professional equipment, trays and lenses - but mostly it's the photos themselves that she's in awe of. Candids, crime scenes, sports photos, everything that makesup the visual narrative of a newspaper. DANNIE sits at a

desk and sets up dinner, a makeshift array brought from home - wrapped sandwiches, bottles of beer. THERESE breathes it all in, not daring to touch anything.

Travelling with Carol in her car, this is how Therese feels: "To THERESE, the world inside CAROL'S car is a revelation (...) The sounds of the world - even CAROL'S occasional chatter - have been replaced with the stillest MUSIC, the sound of air and light." And then, most notably, there is the breathtakingly beautiful scene direction of the final scene, in which dialogue is unnecessary (and is in fact absent) – it is most definitely worth reading for oneself.

CAROL

FILM 4 PRESENTS IN ASSOCIATION WITH STUDIOCANAL HANWAY GOLDCREST DIRTY FILMS AND INFILM PRODUCTIONS

AN ELIZABETH KARLSEN STEPHEN WOOLLEY NUMBER 9 FILMS KILLER FILMS PRODUCTION

IN ASSOCIATION WITH LARKHARK FILMS LIMITED A FILM BY TODD HAYNES

CATE BLANCHETT ROONEY MARA "CAROL" SARAH PAULSON JAKE LACY AND KYLE CHANDLER

CASTING BY LAURA ROSENTHAL COSTUME DESIGNER SANDY POWELL MUSIC SUPERVISION RANDALL POSTER

MUSIC BY CARTER BURWELL EDITOR AFFONSO GONCALVES PRODUCTION DESIGNER JUDY BECKER DIRECTOR OF PHOTOGRAPHY ED LACHMAN BSC

CO-PRODUCER GWEN BIALIC EXECUTIVE PRODUCERS TESSA ROSS DOROTHY BERWIN THORSTEN SCHUMACHER

BOB WEINSTEIN HARVEY WEINSTEIN DANNY PERKINS AND CATE BLANCHETT ANDREW UPTON ROBERT JOLLIFFE

PRODUCED BY ELIZABETH KARLSEN STEPHEN WOOLLEY CHRISTINE VACHON

BASED ON THE NOVEL THE PRICE OF SALT BY PATRICIA HIGHSMITH SCREENPLAY PHYLLIS NAGY DIRECTED BY TODD HAYNES

SOUNDTRACK AVAILABLE ON VARÈSE SARABANDE

캐롤 각본집

Copyright © Number 9 Films Ltd 2015

초판	1쇄 발행 2019년 11월 15일
2판	1쇄 발행 2020년 2월 17일
지은이	필리스 나지
번역	박예하
펴낸이	백준오
편집	임유청
관리	이보람
디자인, 장갑 일러스트	이유희 (PYGMALION)
앞표지 일러스트	최숙경
해외 커뮤니케이션	장현후
해설	이다혜
한영 번역	배기준, 장현후
도움주신 분	엘리자베스 칼슨, 맨디 신 (Number 9 Films)
	소피 돌란, 트레이시 하이드, 조디 쉴즈 (Casarotto Ramsay & Associates)
	토드 헤인즈
펴낸곳	플레인아카이브
출판등록	2017년 3월 30일 제406-2017-000039호
주소	경기도 파주시 회동길 337-16, 302호 (10881)

www.plainarchive.co.kr
cs@plainarchive.com
instagram.com/plainarchive

25,000원
ISBN 979-11-960760-8-5 (03680)

이 도서의 국립중앙도서관 출판예정도서목록(CIP)은
서지정보유통지원시스템 홈페이지(http://seoji.nl.go.kr)와
국가자료공동목록시스템(http://www.nl.go.kr/kolisnet)에서 이용하실 수 있습니다.

CIP제어번호: CIP2019043856

First released theatrically in the USA on 20th November 2015 and released in the UK on 27 November 2015.